SPATIAL FRAGMENTATION OF POLITICAL BEHAVIOUR IN INDIA

Spatial Fragmentation of Political Behaviour in India

A Geographical Perspective on Parliamentary Elections

SHEEL C. NUNA

CONCEPT PUBLISHING COMPANY
NEW DELHI-110059

The Indian Council of Social Science Research gave the financial support towards the publication of this work. However, the responsibility for the contents of the book — facts, opinions, conclusions, etc. - is entirely that of the author and not of the ICSSR.

ISBN 81-7022-285-0
First Published 1989

Sheel Chand **Nuna** (**b.**1955-

Published by
Ashok Kumar Mittal
Concept Publishing Company
A/15-16, Commercial Block, Mohan Garden
NEW DELHI-110059

Lasertypeset by
Microtech Advance Printing Systems (P) Ltd.
H-13 Bali Nagar,
NEW DELHI-110015

Printed in India at
D.B. Offset Works
B-218, Naraina Ind. Area
NEW DELHI -110028

To

My Mentor

Professor Aijazuddin Ahmad

PREFACE

Elections have an important place in democratic politics. They often act as an instrument of peaceful political change by bringing about a redistribution in the power structure. In developing countries, where vast sections of the population are still inadequately literate or in the preliterate state and generally lack political awareness, elections provide the only opportunity to the masses to have a direct interaction with the political system. In fact, in exercising their right of franchise they participate in the crucial act of electing their government. Conversely, the political parties also get an opportunity to redefine their position, *vis-a-vis* the major policy issues facing the polity and thus come to terms with the political realities at the grass-root level. In the Indian context such a reciprocal relationship acquires extraordinary significance. Paradoxically, in India, the political parties neither act as catalysts of change nor exercise a modernising influence on the electorate, particularly on its rural segment. This is evident from the fact that even the major political parties align themselves on caste or ethnic lines and thus help in keeping alive an obscurantist social system based on the inequality of man. The multiplicity of political parties and a large number of the so-called independent candidates in the electoral fray confuse the main issues. In such an electoral setting, party programmes hardly matter.

Voting behaviour in a developing society such as India's is evidently governed by a complex set of socio-economic factors. Political forces get polarized within the framework of major social and ethnic formations. Most of the voting behaviour studies have noted the significant role played by socio-economic conditions in determining the voting behaviour of the masses. This point acquires great significance in the Indian context where the polity is characterized by a high degree of socio-cultural diversity. Thus the voting patterns tend to reflect the inherent contradictions subsumed under socio-cultural diversity. It is interesting to note that the socio-cultural diversity in India has a specific geographical patterning. This partly explains the fragmented naturc of Indian polity.

This book, the outcome of my Ph.D thesis accepted by the Jawaharlal Nehru University, New Delhi, deals with the political phenomenon which has acquired new meaning in recent years. The primary concern of the work has been to identify the process of spatial fragmentation in the political behaviour of the Indian people as evident in the Lok Sabha elections of 1971, 1977 and 1980. It analyses the phenomenon through the spatial patterns observed in party victories, their relative strength from constituency to constituency and from time to time, swings in the votes polled by the parties and consistency in party following. An attempt has been made herein to identify the geographic patterning of party domains and to analyse the implications of the emergent pattern of voting behaviour. It also analyses the phenomenon of the operation of centrifugal forces in the Indian polity and develops an index to measure these tendencies in quantitative terms.

In the course of this work the researcher has developed an insight into the genetic relationship between the political behaviour and the plurality of the Indian polity. While reference has been made to the various facets of this relationship at different places in the text, the problem is worthy of a far more comprehensive and rigorous probe. It has also been noted that the geographical studies of the electoral process in India continue to be retarded. The present exercise in the identification of the pattern of spatial fragmentation embodies an unable attempt to remove this deficiency to a certain extent.

I owe a debt of gratitude to Prof. Aijazuddin Ahmad, not only for supervising my doctoral work, but also for his paternal care. I am also indebted to Prof. Moonis Raza for suggesting the new ideas during the course of this work and for giving continual guidance. Thanks are also due to Prof. Satya Bhushan who has been a constant source of inspiration.

I am also thankful to Shri V. Murali Dhar for his help in data processing. Thanks are also due to Indian Council of Social Science Research for granting me the doctoral fellowship and for providing publication grant for this book. I also thank Shri Chander Prakash for his help in word-processing.

October 19, 1988

SHEEL C. NUNA

CONTENTS

LIST OF MAPS AND DIAGRAMS

LIST OF TABLES

LIST OF APPENDICES

ABBREVIATIONS

ADMK	All India Anna Dravida Munnetra Kazhagam
APHLC	All Party Hill Leaders Conference
BC	Bangla Congress
BCM	Backward Class Mahasabha
BJS	Bhartiya Jana Sangh
BKD	Bhartiya Kranti Dal
BRP	Chotanagpur Bhumi Rakshak Party
BSP	Bhartiya Socialist Party
CONG	Congress/Congress (I)
CONG (O)	Congress Party (Organization)
CONG (U)	Congress Party (Urs)
CPI	Communist Party of India
CPI (M)	Communist Party of India (Marxist)
DMK	Dravida Munnetra Kazhagam
FBL	All India Forward Bloc
HMS	Akhil Bhartiya Hindu Mahasabha
IGL	All India Gorkha League
ILP	All India Labour Party
IND	Independent
ISP	Indian Socialist Party
IUML	Indian Union Muslim League
JC	Jana Congress
JKD	Jharkhand Party
JKP	Akhil Bhartiya Jharkhand Party
JKN	Jammu and Kashmir National Conference
JMD	All India Shiromani Baba Jiwan Singh Mazahabi Dal
JNP	Janata Party
JNP (S)	Janata Party (Secular)
KCJ	Kerala Congress (Joseph)
KCP	Kerala Congress (Pillai)
KEC	Kerala Congress

KMP	Uttar Pradesh Kisan Mazdoor Party
LRP	Lok Raj Party of Himachal Party
MAG	Maharashtrawadi Gomantak Party
MFB	Marxist Forward Bloc
MLO	Muslim League (Opposition)
MLP	Minorities Labour Party
MRP	Manipur Peoples' Party
MUL	Muslim League
MUM	Muslim Majlis of Uttar Pradesh
NNO	Nagaland Nationalist Organization
PHJ	Bihar Prant Hill Jharkhand
PPA	Peoples' Party of Arunachal Pradesh
PPC	Peoples Conference
PROUT	Proutist Bloc of India
PSP	Praja Socialist Party
PWP	Peasants' and Workers' Party
RCPI	Revolutionary Communist Party of India
RPA	Republican Party of India (Ambedkar)
RPG	Republican Party of India (Gaekwad)
RPI	Republican Party of India
RPK	Republican Party of India (Khobragade)
RSP	Revolutionary Socialist Party
RRP	Akhil Bhartiya Ram Rajya Parishad
RSP (ML)	Revolutionary Socialist Party (Marxist-Leninist)
SAD	Shiromani Akali Dal
SCR	Sikkim Congress (Ruling)
SJP	Sikkim Janata Parishad
SPC	Sikkim Prajatantra Congress
SSD	Soshit Samaj Dal
SSN	Shiv Sena
SSP	Samyukta Socialist Party
SUCI	Socialist Unity Centre of India
SWT	Swatantra Party
TC	Telangana Congress
TPS	Telangana Praja Samiti
TUS	Tripura Upjati Juja Samiti
UC	Utkal Congress
UDF	United Democratic Front
UGS	United Goans
UFN	United Front of Nagaland

ONE

INTRODUCTION

This book is an attempt at evaluating the on going process of spatial fragmentation in political behaviour as evident in the results of the General Elections to the Indian Parliament held in 1971, 1977 and 1980. The process of spatial fragmentation is seen here as a phenomenon having great social and political implications. Explicit as it is in the electoral history of the last fifteen years or so, the process of fragmentation has brought the Indian polity to a highly critical phase in our national democratic evolution. It analyses the phenomenon with the help of observed spatial patterns in party victories, their relative strength from constituency and from time to time, swings in the votes polled by the parties and consistency in party following. An attempt has been made to identify the geographic patterning of party domains and analyses the implications of emergent pattern of voting behaviour. It also analyses the phenomenon of the operation of the centrifugal forces in the peripheral regions of the country and develops an index to measure these tendencies in quantitative terms.

The recent electoral history reveals that there exists a high degree of political fragmentation in the country. The phenomenon of fragmentation is seen in the multiplicity of political parties as well as in the changing allegiance of the people to different political parties. It implies that no single political party commands an abiding hold on the public opinion represented over large areas in the country or for a reasonable period of time.

The explanation foaar the process of fragmentation lies in the evolution of Indian polity and existing socio-cultural and ethnic diversity in the country. Scholars have described India as a deep net into which various races and people of Asia have drifted and are caught.[1] These people of various races settled in different parts of the country and in the process India was recognized as a socially heterogeneous entity. Its socially diverse units developed their own identity as the interaction between them was greatly limited due to physical and other social barriers. The magnitude of the physical barriers may be seen in the Vindhyan complex which stands as a formidable barrier between the northern plain and the southern plateau. Its dividing effect is obvious in Aryan North and Dravidian South. (However, Maharashtra and Gujarat, lying at the south-western extremity of India, are enclaves of Indo-Aryan speech family). Between these two lies a transitional zone, characterized by a rugged terrain and thick forests, which has been homelands of tribes. The north and south themselves are not homogeneous at the

meso level and are further divided into various linguistic units of a lower order. In the north lack of significant barriers throughout the plain have given rise to a homogeneous cultural complex, from the sandy waste of Rajasthan and the banks of Sutlej in the west to the Rajmahal hills in the east. This is recognized as the Hindi-Hindustani region. The Lower Ganga Plain, though culturally akin to the rest of the plain, constitutes Bengal. On the southern flank of the Gangetic Basin lies the Vindhyan plateau complex. The Brahmputra valley which has its own linguistic identity is separated from Bengal by the Shillong plateau. In the south, the upper basin of the Krishna and Godavari, south of the Vindhyas is the land of Marathas which roughly corresponds with the Deccan Trap. Lower basin of these two rivers is the homeland of Telugus. The rocky triangle formed by the western and eastern Ghats and the Mysore plateau is Karnataka. From constriction of Nagari hills and Pulicat lake running along the east coast is the land of Tamils. The narrow coastal plain - north and south of the Palghat gap in the Western Ghat - constitute Kerala. The Mahanadi valley surrounded by hills and plateau corresponds with Orissa, and the peninsula of Saurastra and the northern part of the west coast constitute Gujarat.

Despite the presence of social diversity of such a magnitude, these people have lived in conditions of comparable stability.

However, it is this social diversity which has forced centripetal and centrifugal forces to operate simultaneously.[2] While the former always tried to impose a fundamental unity based on common social heritage, the latter counteracts the forces of unification. The operation of these two opposite forces may be seen throughout the history of India.

It is this pattern of social diversity which has introduced the element of fragmentation in the Indian polity. The lack of emotional fusion of the various groups has further accentuated this process. Although, attempts have been made to make the masses politically conscious in order to break social rigidities, success has been unimpressive and the masses continue to be guided by group affinities.

SIGNIFICANCE OF THE STUDY

India attained Independence on August 15, 1947 and the Constitution was adopted two years later in 1949. It was a charter for the kind of government, indeed the kind of society, the leaders of the national struggle for Independence desired and envisioned to build. Its preamble stated:

> We the people of India, having solemnly resolved to constitute India into a Sovereign Democratic Republic and to secure to all its citizens: **Justice,** social, economic and political; **liberty** of thought, expression, belief, faith and worship; **Equality** of status and opportunity; and to promote among them all **Fraternity** assuring the dignity of the individual and the unity of the nation; in our Constituent Assembly this twenty-sixth of November 1949, do hereby adopt, enact and give to ourselves this Constitution.

The experience since 1947 reveals that although, the Constitution provides a democratic political system the country has yet to develop the basic infrastructure for the success of the democracy even after the three decades of planned development. The basic conditions for the viable working of the democracy are a high level of economic development,[3] a high degree of educational status,[4] a sense of identification,[5] a relatively small nation and a gradual historical change.[6] But most of these conditions have no practical meaning in

Indian situation where the society continues to be shaped along ethnicity, religion, caste and language. The concept of "civic culture" as developed by Almond and Verba[7] postulated that in a modern democracy the forces of unity dominate over the forces of conflict which are in a rudimentary form. Even the questions of national importance fail to evolve a consensus[8] due to a high degree of social heterogeneity and multitude of apparently irreconciable interests.[9] Although, modernization has sown the seeds of change in social structure, these changes, not always for the better, often accelerate inter-group and inter-regional tensions.

In democratic societies elections provide the only opportunity to the masses to have a direct interaction with the political system.[10] Voting behaviour in such societies, such as India, is evidently governed by a complex set of socio-economic factors. Political forces get polarized within the framework of main social and ethnic formations. In such a situation the democratic process leads to the emergence of a large number of pressure groups which mobilise themselves at the political front in order to attain diverse goals. It may be assumed that the political forces having a wider appeal would naturally become rather liberal than sectarian or parochial. The voting behaviour in such an enviornment tends to reflects the inherent social diversity. In the final analysis it also reveals the capability of the major political parties to come to terms with this overall socio-cultural diversity. The socio-cultural diversity in India has a geographical expression and that partially explains the fragmented nature of the Indian polity. This view is supported by Krehbiel's study which noted that "geographical or natural factors...contributed materially in creating the conditions which determine political predictions."[11] It is in this context that election statistics have some value for political or social geographers.[12] The primary problem of political geography (is) the analysis of the degree to which the diverse regions of the state constitute a unity.[13]

It is in this perspective that the present study has been attempted with a view to identifying the spatial parameters of voting behaviour[14] as evident in the results of the three Parliamentary elections held in 1971, 1977 and 1980 (a summary of past electoral trends is presented in Appendix I). It analyses the regional diversities in the voting behaviour of the Indian masses and measures the relative importance of the different political parties in different constituencies of the country with the help of a number of related variables.

So far electoral studies have been largely the concern of political scientists and sociologists. The geographers' concern in this area have been only marginal. Although, the seeds of the electoral geography were sown in the beginning of this century,[15] the quantum of research in this field has rather been negligible. The studies which were conducted earlier were isolated in nature and limited in scope. The interest of geographers in the field is a recent phenomenon. In the initial stages the field developed with a traditional concern with the maps[16] but with the growing knowledge of quantitative techniques and richness of the work in other disciplines, the geographers' horizons have widened considerably.[17]

The importance of geography of elections may be illustrated by the changing definition of human geography. There is an increasing consensus that human geography deals with spatial organization of society.[18] This organization consists of two basic elements. The first is *de facto* organization which reflects the natural geographical distribution of society and the second is *de jure* organization which is explicitly for the administrative purposes.[19] The elections represent both types of organization. For example, the voters are registered on the basis of their place or locality, which is governed by a number of factors such as access to financial resources, race and religious consideration. It is not surprising that the local environment should affect the pattern of voting. In other words the voting pattern will reflect the spatial organization of social and economic forces. This implies that there is a geography of voting. The environment of the neighbourhood may have an effect on voting patterns. Social contacts may play a significant role. Further, the political parties may not pay equal attention to all the areas. All these enhance the role of spatial factors in explaining electoral patterns. Finaly, the act of voting takes place in a set organizational framework-constituencies, which are defined by the agency responsible for conducting elections. The location of the boundaries of these constituencies is a significant factor in determining the outcome of elections. Therefore, there are three elements of geography in the elections: geography of elections, geographical influences on the elections and geographical influences on the electoral representation. While the first two are examples of *de facto* organization, the latter is an example of *de jure* organization.

In this perspective the significance of this study lies in that it provides a new dimension to the study of voting behaviour in India. It lays a great emphasis on the spatial location, distribution and spatial interrelationship. The very nature of the approach distinguishes this study from the on going research on voting behaviour in other disciplines.

AN OVERVIEW OF RESEARCH

Electoral studies have attracted scholors from various disciplines. But the main contribution to the field, as mentioned erlier, has come from political scientists and political sociologists. Although, geographers have contributed very little to the field of electoral studies, the first geographical work on elections dates back to 1913 when Siegfried introduced the field in France.[20] This work was followed by Krehbiel who categorically emphasised that "Geographical or natural factors... contributed materially in creating the conditions which determine political predictions" in Britain.[21] After these two pioneering works in the field of electoral geography, there was a gap of nearly two decades which was broken by Paullin[22] and Wright[23] in 1932 who attempted an electoral geography of the U.S.A. After these initial attempts the research in the field was highly scattered. The significant contributors were Dean,[24] Crisler[25] and Smith and Hart.[26]

All these studies were attempted within the framework of traditional approach which had a great concern for the maps depicting man-land relationship. However, with the advancement of knowledge of quantitative techniques, the geographer's horizons have widened considerably. This is significant to note that although, other branches of geography adopted quantification much earlier, the new approach in electoral geography was introduced at a later stage because of the late arrival of quantitative revolution in political geography.[27]

It was only in the early sixties, that electoral geography became a theme of research investigation on a wider scale and by the middle of the seventies the scholars considered it as "one of the branches of the subject most relevent to current social, economic and political issues."[28] The increasing interest in electoral geography with a great concern for new methodologies may be seen in the works of Burghardt,[29] Lewis,[30] Reynolds and Archer,[31] Cox,[32] McPhail[33] and Taylor and Johnston.[34] The basic factor which contributed to the growing interest in the field of electoral geography is its "conceptual and methodological emphasis on the new mainstream of contemporary geographic research."[35] One student of the subject has gone to the extent of saying that:

> If political geography is to be integrated into geography as a science with an emphasis upon rigor in drawing hypothesis testing, and theory construction, then it is likely that studies of areal variations in the level of different political activities will play an important role in this integration. Data collected by bounded areal units referring to such areal phenomena as voting for different parties or issues are among the most available data for the political geographer to apply to political geography cannons of scientific methods used in other branches of the field.[36]

Despite the richness of the field, the geographical research on voting behaviour in india is an incipient phenomenon. There have been a few isolated attempts to analyse the voting behaviour in a space context. Amani attempted a study of Haryana elections with an emphasis on spatial pattern. He pointed out that the personality of the candidates and caste play the significant role in determining the choice of the candidates. He further emphasised that the policies and programmes of the political parties matter very little.[37] In another study of 1967 and 1971 Parliamentary elections in Uttar Pradesh he emphasised that "in two elections the constituencies have changed hands in a highway indicating that the people have discarded one party in favour of the other. At the same time the voting pattern in the two elections does not provide any measure of the regional following, except in a few cases, of a single party."[38] Amani, in an another contribution explained the spatial patterns of seats won by political parties in 1971 Parliamentary elections.[39] He pointed out that the Congress Party has failed in those areas where a strong regional party existed.

However, scholars from other disciplines have taken keen interest in analysing the various aspects of voting behaviour in india. A great emphasis has been laid on analysing the role of caste in Indian elections. A significant contribution to the field has been made by Weiner and Osgood Field.[40] Their work spreading over 4 volumes, throws much light on Indian elections. The first volume is devoted to the analysis of Communist Party in West Bengal; the second volume focusses attention on three disadvantaged sectors, *viz.*, Scheduled Tribes, Princely States and Women; the third volume is devoted to the impact of modernization and the last volume deals with party cleavages. Dasgupta and Morris-Jones attempted a quantitative analysis of first 4 Parliamentary elections.[41] Their main emphasis has been to apply rigrous statistical techniques on Indian electoral data to discern major electoral trends. The hypotheses tested in the work cover wide aspects like participation, competition, institutionalization and party performance. His study reveals that the areal support of the parties is not uniform. The parties with parochial tendencies show a greater uniformity. Significantly, the study pointed out that the Swatantra Party has wider enclaves of following.

Broadly speaking, studies on voting behaviour in India can be grouped into two categories. The first category consists of those studies which describe the process. The second category consists of those studies which try to understand voting behaviour. In the studies of the first category the major emphasis has been to describe the emergent pattern of voting behaviour. Significant contribution to this aspect of research has been made by Rajni Kothari,[42] Morris-Jones[43] and Gopal Krishna.[44] These studies have characterized the Indian political system as that of 'One Party Dominance.'

The studies of second category cover a significant part of research in the field of voting behaviour. They are conducted either in an Assembly or Parliamentary constituency. These studies have considered the support to a political party as a dependent phenomenon and have tried to explain this with the help of a number of socio-economic variables. Although, a large number of variables have been used, caste and religious affinities have received the larger attention. Although, scholars have derived conflicting conclusions, there is a general agreement that caste is the dominant variable affecting voting preferences. However, it has been pointed out that caste or religion seems to be significant only in those groups which have not been assimilated into society at large and therefore, lack a feeling of security.[45] Similarly there seems to be no direct relationship between class and party affilliation.[46] In fact the Indian Institute of Public Opinion Survey reveals that Indian parties"... appeal to and secure support from all major sections."[47] But there is certain evidence to show that all sections of society are not equally active in politics. For instance, in rural areas the middle class peasantry, whose fate depends upon government policies are more active than rich peasants or agricultural labourers.[48]

Another significant observation which emerges from some of the studies is that the public issues matter little in determining the voting preferences. It has been pointed out that the masses desire to get certain things done either for themselves or for the constituency. In this background they are influenced not by the candidates ideology but by his capacity to do good for the constituency.[49] Several studies have supported this phenomenon by showing that personality rather than ideology of the candidates play significant role in determining the choice of the candidate.[50]

These are not all but a few studies pertaining to the field of voting behaviour. But even all the findings are put together the fact remains that quite a few aspects of voting behaviour remain to be explored and even those which have received significant attention have to be thoroughly investigated in order to derive scientific generalization. It is noted that intensive studies of geographical nature are conspicuous by their absence. The geographers, equipped with their tools of spatial analysis, can provide a meaningful interpretation of voting behaviour.

DATA BASE

The study is based on secondary sources of data. The electoral data for 1971 and 1977 Parliamentary elections have been collected from the Reports on the Fifth and Sixth General Elections to the House of the People in India published by Election Commission of India, New Delhi. However, the data for 1980 Parliamentary elections have been taken from the 'Provisional Report on the Seventh General Elections to the House of the People in India.' The information for each Parliamentary constituency is given under the following heads; Size of electorate; total votes polled, votes rejected; valid votes polled, and the division of votes among different political parties and independents.

The analysis of party programmes and policies is based on their election manifestos and the personal interviews of some of their leaders in the selected parts of the country. Interviews were conducted in the months of November-December, 1979 at the following places:

Calcutta and Diamond Harbour (West Bengal); Chaibasa and Jamshedpur (Bihar); Madras (Tamil Nadu) and Bombay (Maharashtra).

Persons who were identified for interview included contestants, party functionaries and voters. Contestants were interviewed to assess the nature of issues which they put before the voters and to ascertain whether the issues raised by a particular contestant fall in the line with issues raised by his political party. The idea behind interviewing the party functionaries was to see whether the party functionaries are in agreement with the party policies or they differ from it. Voters from different strata were questioned to assess the impact of party appeals on decision making process of the voters.

LIMITATIONS OF ELECTORAL DATA IN POLITICAL BEHAVIOUR RESEARCH

Use of electoral data as a tool of analysis to judge the political behaviour of the masses poses a number of problems. These problems do not arise from the data itself but flow from the low level of political consciousness of the masses. This phenomenon, in turn, results from the dominating role of social institutions in Indian elections. In such a situation voters do not understand the significance of the institution of election. For a majority of voters, elections remain a ritualistic act. Their decision to take part in election is governed by highly non-political issues raised by political forces operating at the local level. Even if this crucial limitation is ignored electoral data suffer from other limitations. Therefore, it would be pertinent here to analyse the applicability of electoral data as a tool of analysis to develop characterization about Indian political system.

The electoral process in India gets completed in three stages. In the first stage the lines for electoral contest are drawn. This phase of elections get completed before the polling dates. Obviously this would include notification, nomination, withdrawal, scrutiny and final selection of the candidates. The second stage is related to participation in the act of voting. A decision to vote or not to vote constitute an important aspect of the electoral process. The third stage is related to the voters decision to vote for a particular party/independent. It is this phase of election which determines the outcome of any electoral process.

Problems of using electoral data as a tool of analysis for political behaviour research arise at all the three stages and therefore, it would be significant to analyse them briefly.

The first problem relating to electoral data results from multiplicity of political parties in India. The dominating role of social attributes in political processes in India has resulted in the emergence of a large number of political parties. This happens because every social group feels insecure under the leadership of another dominating social group. This forces every group to express itself either in the form of a pressure group or a political party which is evident from the number of political parties which enter into the electoral fray. There are two disadvantages of this phenomenon. First, it introduces an element of fragmentation in the political system and secondly, it acts as a barrier in highlighting the national issues which should otherwise determine the outcome of elections. What really happens is that the issues of national importance are replaced by the parochial and sectarian issues raised by communal and obscurantist parties.

The second limitation arises from the low level of participation by the electorate. It is evident from Table 1.1 that the participation rate remained very low in different elections.

This is evident from Table 1.1 that electoral participation has remained at a low level. The highest rate of participation was achieved during 1977 elections which is attributed to a strong urge to participate in the elections, generated by the 21 months emergency rule which preceded elections. Inspite of the fact that a political wave was sweeping the country only 60.53 per cent of the electorate participated in the elections. This implied that a large number of electorate do not take part in the elections. In this situation in which a large chunk of population is not even represented in the elections, formulation of hypothesis regarding political system based on electoral data poses a serious problem.

TABLE 1.1: ELECTORAL PARTICIPATION

Election Year	Participation Rate
1952	45.7
1957	47.8
1962	55.4
1967	61.3
1971	55.3
1977	60.5
1980	60.4

Third difficulty with electoral data arises from the division of votes among different constestants. It is often seen that the votes among the candidates are so divided that the winning candidate gets only a fraction of valid votes polled.

It is evident from Table 1.2 that a large number of candidates are declared elected by minority votes. This is attributed to a large number of political parties which field their candidates into electoral fray making multiple contest in a large number of constituencies. The problem is further complicated by a large number of independent candidates who enter into the electoral battle for their partisan ends.

It is obvious from these limitations that electoral data is not adequate to make generalizations regarding Indian political system. However, keeping in view the constraints involved in generation of data on political processes, electoral data seems to be the only viable source of information to carry out any empirical analysis on political processes.

TABLE 1.2: SEATS WON BY MAJORITY AND MINORITY VOTES

Votes secured by winning candidates	Number of constituencies 1971	1977	1980
0-10 per cent	-	-	-
10-20 per cent	-	-	1
20-30 per cent	9	-	11
30-40 per cent	46	4	86
40-50 per cent	109	62	146
50-60 per cent	179	220	207
60-70 per cent	116	161	68
70-80 per cent	48	83	9
80-90 per cent	10	10	-
Unopposed	1	2	1
Total	518	542	529*

* Excludes 12 constituencies of Assam and 1 constituency in Meghalaya.

METHODOLOGY

The present study is based on the analysis of electoral data for the last three Parliamentary elections viz., 1971, 1977 and 1980. The analysis has been attempted at the parliamentary constituency level. There were 518 Parliamentary constituencies in 1971. But as a result of 1975 delimitation, their number rose to 542 in 1977 which remained same in 1980 (Fig.1). However, for 1980 this study is based on data of 529 constituencies only since elections to 12 constituencies in Assam and one constituency in Meghalaya were not held along with general elections.

I. The first variable which has been analysed is the seats won by different political parties. However, this did not require any statistical computation. The spatial patterns of seats won in 1971, 1977 and 1980 Parliamentary elections have been identified with the help of choropleth maps. Further, the patterns of majority and minority wins have been analysed to highlight the irrationality of Indian elections.

II. It is seen that a large number of candidates get elected by securing a strikingly low share of votes polled in a constituency. Therefore, a candidate may win a seat by polling 20 per cent of votes while another candidate may be defeated even after securing 49 per cent of votes. In such a situation winning of a seat by a party does not necessarily indicate its real strength. Therefore, in order to assess the real strength of a party it is necessary to determine its share in the total valid votes polled. For this purpose percentage of votes polled by each party in each of the constituency has been considered as an important variable. The votes secured by major parties viz., Communist Party of India, Communist Party of India (Marxist), Congress Party, Janata Party[51] and Janata(S) have been depicted on maps. The constituencies have been grouped into five categories i.e. above 70 per cent, 50-70 per cent, 30-50 per cent, 10-30 per cent and less than 10 per cent.

III. The mass following of political parties is not static and changes with the passage of time in view of the changed political climate on the eve of elections. However, impulses of the existing political situation vary over space. People do not perceive policies and programmes of political parties uniformly in different regions. In this perspective, political parties register swings of varying magnitudes in their votes. (The swing is a simple measure of determining the change in percentage of party votes.) However, if the elections are really on a national plane then one would expect the uniform swings across the country. But in case the swings are not uniform, it will reflect the fragmented political behaviour.

Swings in party votes have been calculated for all parties during 1971-77 and 1977-1980 by measuring the change in percentage of votes. The areas of negative and positive swings with varying magnitude have been identified. Constituencies have been grouped into 4 categories viz. above 30 per cent, 20-30 per cent, 10-20 per cent and below 10 per cent. Spatial patterns have been analysed with the help of choropleth maps.

IV. The changing pattern of voters' allegiance to political parties over time may be meaningfully analysed by attempting an analysis of party consistency. Generally, the pattern of consistency is analysed by considering the single variable either, seats won or percentage of votes polled. However, this researcher feels that a better picture of party consistency will emerge if the analysis of consistency is based on a composite score derived from a number of electoral variables of party strength. If a party continues to perform uniformly in different elections, it may be termed as consistent in that area. Therefore,

Fig. 1.1
India: Parliamentary constituencies

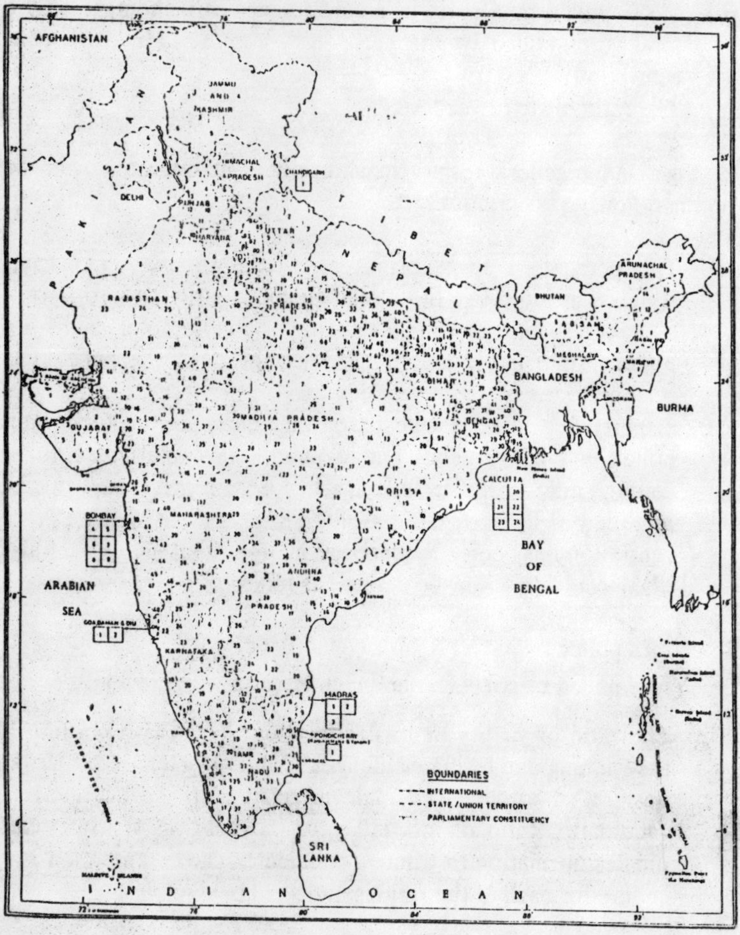

composite scores of different constituencies in each of the election have been compared for 26 political parties. The composite scores are derived from the following 3 variables:

(a) Votes polled by a party in a constituency as percentage to the total valid votes polled.
(b) Votes polled by a party in a constituency as percentage to the total votes polled by the party in the country (Index of concentration)
(c) The ratio of victory or loss.

Speaking in general terms, the choice of these indicators is based on the following assumptions:

(i) The percentage share of votes polled by a party in a constituency is indicative of its relative voting strength in that constituency. A high share of a certain party in the total valid votes polled would imply that the party holds a strong position in relation to the other contestants.
(ii) A party may have a high percentage share in the total votes polled in a constituency but its share in its total votes in the country may be quite low. Such a constituency may not be regarded as its stronghold at all. Therefore, the index of concentration has been considered as an important indicator. Index of concentration may be defined as follows:

$$\frac{\text{Votes polled by party (X) in a constituency}}{\text{Votes polled by party (X) in the country}} \times 100$$

(iii) The ratio of victory or loss reflects on the relative position of the winning and losing candidates. Ratio of victory indicates the position of winning candidate in relation to the nearest rival candidate. Ratio of loss indicates the position of losing candidates in relation to winning candidate. The computation procedure for each of the ratio is indicated below:

$$\text{Ratio of Victory} = \frac{\text{Votes polled by winning candidate}}{\text{Votes polled by nearest rival canidate.}}$$

$$\text{Ratio of Loss} = \frac{\text{Votes polled by a losing candidate}}{\text{Votes polled by a winning candidate}}$$

Thus if a party has won in a constituency its ratio will be greater than one and if it has lost, its ratio will be less than one.

These variables have been composited with the help of the modified principal components analysis. [52] However, in the present case the method has been further modified in order to make factor scores comparable over time. This is achieved through merger of each variable's 3 years vectors into a single vector as shown below:

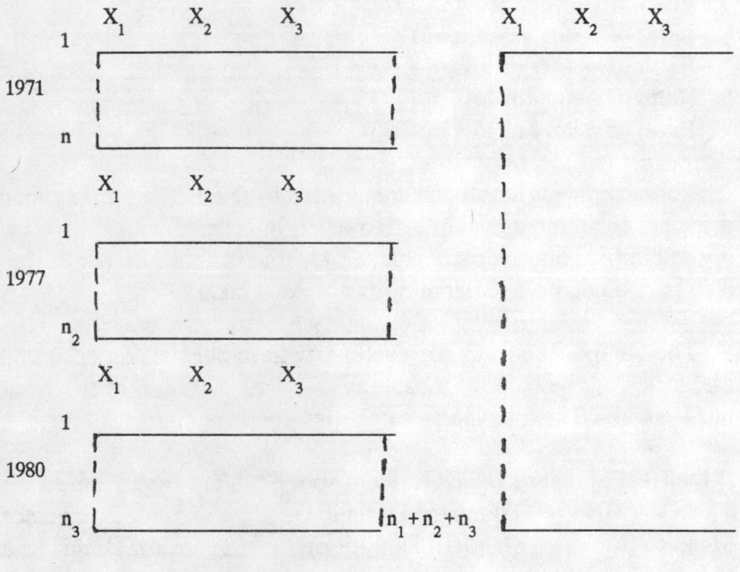

In the final analysis the composite scores for all the three years were separated and classified on the basis of mean and standard deviation of the composite scores. Four groups were obtained at the interval of 1 standard deviation. If a party retains its category in all the 3 elections in a constituency, it is regarded as consistent in that constituency. Similarly retaining of category in two elections has been viewed as partial consistency and the change of category in all the 3 elections has been regarded as the phenomenon of inconsistency. The pattern of consistency for 4 major parties have been analysed with the help of choropleth maps. The pattern of other parties has been analysed with the help of analytical tables.

V. Furthermore, the process of overall fragmentation has been analysed by identifying the pattern of party domains by considering the following 9 variables:

1. Percentage of votes polled by a party in a constituency in 1971.
2. Percentage of votes polled by a party in a constituency in 1977.
3. Percentage of votes polled by a party in a constituency in 1980.
4. Index of concentration in 1971.
5. Index of concentration in 1977.
6. Index of concentration in 1980.
7. Ratio of victory or loss in 1971.
8. Ratio of victory or loss in 1977
9. Ratio of victory or loss in 1980.

These variables have been composited by the method of modified principal components analysis. However, in order to make the composited indices of each party comparable, the variables were normalized by dividing each variable by its weighted mean.

The composite scores for each party have been classified into 4 categories on the basis of mean and standard deviation of the composite scores. The following 4 categories are recognized.

(Mean + 1 Standard Deviation) and above	Very High Dominance
Mean to (Mean + 1 Standard Deviation)	High Dominance
Mean to (Mean - 1 Standard Deviation)	Low Dominance
(Mean - 1 Standard Deviation) and below	Very Low Dominance

The categories for each party in a constituency have been compared. The party with highest category code has been recognized as a dominant party in that constituency.[54] Its category indicates its dominance level.

VI. The degree of political fragmentation highlighted by this study is a manifestation on the operation of centripetal and centrifugal forces in India. However, this argument has further been supported by developing an index of centrifugality using the electoral data of 1971, 1977 and 1980 Parliamentary elections.

The methodology adopted in this analysis is based on the assumption that the acceptability of party programmes and policies may be judged through people's support to political parties in the elections. It also presupposes that the parties may be arranged in a hierarchial order by assigning them the weightages based on their policies pertaining to the issues of (a) state autonomy and provision of President's Rule, (b) financial autonomy/centre state relations and (c) language issue. The stand taken by different political parties on these issues has been assessed through their election manifestos. However, besides the election manifestos, the information gathered through interviews have also been used to assign weightages. These interviews were conducted in November-December 1979 in Calcutta, Singhbhum, Bombay and Madras.

This analysis is based on electoral data of 41 political parties for three Parliamentary elections of 1971, 1977 and 1980. Percentage share of votes polled by a party in each of the election in a constituency has been multiplied by its weightage. These weighted indices for parties in a constituency have been added together and then divided by number of candidates. The resultant figures has been termed as centrifugality index. It may be expressed as follows:

$$C_i = \frac{\sum_{t=1}^{3} \sum_{j=1}^{41} W_j \quad X_{ijt}}{n}$$

where, C_i = centrifugality index for ith constituency;
W_j = weightage for jth party;
X_{ijt} = percentage votes polled by jth party in ith constituency in t election;
n = total number of party candidates in ith constituency.

The centrifugality indices have been classified into following 5 categories on the basis of their Mean and Standard Deviation by taking the interval of 0.5 Standard Deviation. The following categories have been recognized:

Above 41.35	Very High
29.80 - 41.35	High
18.24 - 29.79	Medium
6.68 - 18.23	Low
Below 6.68	Very Low

(Mean - 18.24; S.D.- 23.30)

List of political parties and their weightage are presented below:

Weightages	+3	+2	+1	0	-1	-2
Parties	APHLC,ADMK DMK, MRP NNO, PPC PPA, SAD TUJS, UDF, UFN, PHJ, JKD.	CPI, CPI(M) FBL, JKN KEC, KCP, MAG, PWP, RSP, VHP, JKP, SSN, SUCI, TPS.	JNP	CONG. CONG(O) CONG(U) PSP,SSP	JNP(S) Swa-tantra BKD, RPI,RPK	BJS HMS RRP

The weightages for political parties are determined on the basis of the proposed departure from the existing constitutional norms. A high weightage is given to those parties which favour drastic changes in the existing structure. If these proposed changes by a political party will result in weakening the power of the centre and strengthening the political authority of the states then a positive weightage is assigned to the party. However, if the proposed changes are such that they will further enhance the unitary tendencies then a negative weightage has been assigned. The policies of political parties are summarised in Chapter VIII, Table 8.4

NOTES AND REFERENCES

1. J.H. Hutton, *Caste in India* (Bombay: Oxford University Press, 1977), p. 1.
2. B. Subbarao, *Personality of India* (Baroda: M.S. University, 1958).
3. From Aristotle onwards it has been argued that in a society in which relatively few people live at the level of real poverty, the chances for the success of democracy are great.
4. Indeed the various aspects of socio-economic development such as industrialization, urbanization and education are closely related. This issue, in relation to democracy, has been discussed in, S.M. Lipset, *Political Man* (New Delhi: Arnold Heinemann India, 1973), pp. 55-57.
5. Lucian W. Pye and Sydney Verba (eds.), *Political Culture and Political Development* (Princeton: Princeton University Press, 1965), p. 525.
6. Gabriel A. Almond and G.B. Powell, Jr., *Comparative Politics - A Developmental Approach* (Boston, 1966), p. 313.
7. Gabriel A. Almond and Sydney Verba, *The Civic Culture* (Princeton: Princeton University Press, 1963), p.5.
8. Alexis de Tocqueville was the first major exponent of the idea that democracy involves a balance between the forces of conflict and consensus.
9. Although India has always been described as possessing "Unity in Diversity", it remains a notion only.
10. Surinder Suri, "Towards a Theory of Indian Politics: Some Implications of the Results of the General Elections," *Economic Weekly*, Vol. 14, December 1962, p. 1840.
11. E. Krehbiel, "Geographical Influences in British Elections," *The Geographical*

Review, Vol. 2, March 1961, pp. 419-432.

12. Richard Hartshorne, "The Functional Approach in Political Geography," *Annals, the Association of American Geographers,* Vol. 40, June 1950, p. 101.
13. *Ibid.,* p. 117.
14. The usage of voting behaviour to connote the political behaviour may be seen in an earlier study by Paul H. Appleby, *Policy and Administration* (Tusea loosa: Univeristy of Alabama Press, 1949).
15. The roots of the field may be traced in the work of A. Siegfried, *Tableau Politique de la France de l' ouest* (Paris: Armani Colin, 1913); E. Krehbiel, *op. cit.,* pp. 419-32; and C.O. Sauer, "Geography and the Gerrymander," *American Political Science Review,* Vol.12, 1918, pp. 403-26.
16. J.R.V. Prescottt, "The Functions and Methods of Electoral Geography", *Annals, Association of American Geographers,* Vol. 49, 1959, pp.296-304.
17. I.R. Mcphail, "Recent Trends in Electoral Geography," *Proceedings of the Sixth New Zealand Geography Conference,* Christ Church, 1917, Vol.I, pp.7-12.
18. See, R.L. Morril, *Spatial Organization of Society* (Belmont California: Woodsworth Publishing Company, 1970).
19. K.R. Cox, *Conflict, Power and Politics in the City: A Geographical View* (New York: McGraw Hill, 1973).
20. A. Siegfried *op.cit.*
21. E. Krehbiel, *op.cit.*
22. C.O. Paullin, *Atlas of the Historical Geography of the United States* (New York: American Geographical Society, 1932).
23. J.K. Wright, "Voting Habits in the United States: A Note on Two Maps", *Geographical Review,* Vol.22, 1932, pp. 666-672.
24. V.K. Dean, "Geographical Aspects of Newfoundland Referendum", *Annals, Association of American Geographers,* Vol. 39, 1949, pp. 70-77.
25. F.W.S. Crisler, "Voting Habits in the United States", *Geographical Review,* Vol. 42, 1952, pp. 300-301.
26. H.R. Smith and J.F. Hart, "The American Tariff Map". *Geographical Review,* Vol.45, 1955, pp. 327-346.
27. R.D. Dixit, "Retreat from Political Geography", *Area,* Vol.9, 1977, pp. 234-239.
28. M.A. Busteed, *Geography and Voting Behaviour* (London: Oxford University Press, 1975), p.54.
29. A.F. Burghardt, "The Bases of Support for Political Parties in Burgeland", *Annals, Association of American Geographers,,* Vol.54, 1964, pp. 372-390.
30. P.F. Lewis, "Impact of Negro Migration on the Electoral Geography of Flint, Michigan, 1932-62: A Cartographic Analysis", *Annals, Association of American Geographers,* Vol.55, 1965, pp. 1-25.
31. D.R. Reynolds and J.C Archer, "An Inquiry into the Spatial Basis of Electoral Geography," Department of Geography, University of Iowa, *Discussion Paper No.11.*
32. K.R. Cox, "The Voting Decision in a Spatial Context", in C. Board, R.J. Chorley and P. Hagget (eds.), *Progress in Geography,* Vol. I (London: Arnold, 1969), pp. 81-117.
33. I.R McPhail, "The Vote for Mayor in Los Angeles in 1969", *Annals, Association of American Geographers,* Vol.61, 1971, pp.744-758.
34. P.J. Taylor and R.J. Johnston, *Geography of Elections* (Penguin, 1979).
35. E.W. Soja, "A Paradigm for the Geographical Analysis of Political Systems," in K.R. Cox, D.R. Reynolds and S. Rokkan (eds.), *Locational Approaches to Power and Conflict* (New York: Halsted Press, 1974), pp.43-72.
36. K.R. Cox, "A Spatial Interactional Model for Political Geography", *East Lake Geographer,* Vol.4, 1948, pp.58-76.

37. K.Z. Amani, "Elections in Haryana, India: A Study in Electoral Geography," *The Geographer* Vol.4, 1970, pp.27-40.
38. K.Z. Amani, "Voting Patterns in Indian Elections: Uttar Pradesh, A Case-Study", *Geographical Review of India,* Vol.34, No.2, June 1972, pp.123-133.
39. K.Z. Amani,"Question Raised by a Map of the 1971 Indian Elections," *The Professional Geographer,* Vol.26, No.2, May 1974, pp.207-209.
40. Myron Weiner and John Osgood Field, *Electoral Politics in the Indian States,* Vol.I-IV (Delhi: Manohar Book Service, 1975).
41. Biplab Dasgupta and W.H. Morris-Jones, *Pattern and Trends in Indian Politics: An Ecological Analysis of Aggregate Data on Society and Elections* (New Delhi: Allied, 1975).
42. Rajni Kothari, "Congress System in India", *Asian Survey*, Vol.4, No.12, December 1964, pp. 1161-1173.
43. W.H. Morris-Jones, Parliament and Dominant Party: Indian Experiences," *Parliamentary Affairs,* Vol.17, No.3, Summer 1964, pp.296-307.
44. Gopal Krishna, "One Party Dominance - Development and Trends," *Perspectives,* Supplement to the Indian Journal of Public Administration, Vol.12, No.1, January-March 1966.
45. Rajni Kothari and Tarun Sheth, "Extent and Limits of Community Voting: The Case of Baroda East", *The Economic Weekly,* September 15, 1962, pp.1473-86.
46. Myron Weiner, "Village and Party Factionalism in Andhra: Ponnur Constituency," *The Economic Weekly,* September 22, 1962, pp.1509-1518.
47. Samuel Eldersveld, "The Developing Pattern of Party Preferences," *Monthly Public Opinion Surveys,* Vol.9, No.4, January 1964.
48. Harold A. Gould, "Traditionalism and Modernism in U.P.-Faizabad Constituency", *The Economic Weekly* August 18, 1962.
49. Henry Hart, "Urban Politics in Bombay: The Meaning of Community", *The Economic Weekly*, Special Number, June, 1960, p.985.
50. Paul R. Brass, "An Industrial Labour Constituency: Kanpur", *The Economic Weekly,* Special Number, July 1962, p. 1113, Rajni Kothari and Tarun Sheth, *op.cit.*, p. 1483.
51. The votes for the Janata Party in 1971 elections are derived by aggregating the votes polled by its constituents in 1971.
52. The modification has been introduced by Amitabh Kundu in "Methods of Regionalization and Their Application to the Study of Urban Processes in North-Western India - 1961-71" (Unpublished doctoral thesis of the Centre for the Study of Regional Development, JNU, 1977, p. 137). The modified principal components analysis differs from the principal components analysis in the sense that instead of using R matrix, it uses A Matrix which is defined as follows

$$A = \frac{\hat{X}'\hat{X}}{n}$$

Were $\hat{X}$ is the data matrix in Normalized form (division by mean).

53. In this case the normalization of the variable is not achieved by dividing them by their respective means. Instead, the normalization has been done by dividing each variable by their weighted mean. The weighted mean for a particular variable is obtained as follows:

$$M = \frac{M_1 n_1 + \ldots\ldots\ldots M_r n_r}{n_1 \;+\; n_r}$$

Where M = Weighted mean; M_1 = mean for party 1;
n_1 = number of observations for party 1.

This has been done in order to make the composite scores comparable for the different parties.

54. However, if two parties fell in the same category, the actual values of composite scores have been used for categorization.

TWO

FRAGMENTATION OF POLITICAL BEHAVIOUR IN INDIA A QUEST FOR THEORY

India today is in the process of nation building. However, her sheer size, the socio-cultural diversity and disparities in economic development, seem to have slowed down the process of nation building. The major task today is to bring about a harmonious integration of the disparate elements within the Indian polity.

The present situation suggests that there is a built-in tendency in the political system to treat national integration and the centralisation of political authority as synonymous. This poses a serious threat to the basic concept of unity in diversity. The tendency towards more and more concentration of power at the centre acts as a barrier in the process of nation building. A centralized or a unitary system is not suited to India. Such a system fails to promote the interests of the diverse elements at the regional levels. Moreover, it generates pulls and strains within the polity which inevitably give rise to disintegrative tendencies at the regional level.

The structure of the Indian polity may best be evaluated in the context of its evolution as 'India today is the outcome not only of the immediate past, but also of the thousands of years of the long story of country. Layer upon layer of thought, experience and action have conditioned us and made us what we are today.[1] Her history reveals a remarkable existence of regional particularism as streams of races, languages, cultures and religious groups have contributed to the evolution of her unified civilization. This had recognized India as a classic concept generally referred as 'Unity in Diversity'. In the words of Gandhi 'I believe that the civilization India has evolved is not to be beaten in the world'.[2]

The historically determined regional diversity finds an expression in the present-day Indian polity. The annals of various dynasties which rose to power evidently testify that it was their attempt to eliminate regional autonomy which contributed to disintegration of their respective empires and 'proved the conception of a United Hindustan to be a chimera'.[3] No factor other than the magnitude of her diversity could have contributed to such a phenomenon. Reacting on India's diversity Nehru commented:

> The diversity of India is tremendous; it is obvious; it lies on the surface and anybody can see it. It concerns itself with physical appearances as well as with certain mental habits and traits. There is little in common, to outward seeming, between the Pathan of the North-west and the Tamil in the South. Their racial stocks are not the same, though there may be common strands running through them; they differ in face and figure, food and clothing, and, of course, language ... The Pathan and the Tamil are two extreme examples, the others lie somewhere in between. All of them have their distinctive features, All of them have still more the distinguishing mark of India...[4]

The magnitude of diversity may be explained by the process of historical evolution which was influenced by physical parameters within the country. The wide alluvial plains, an older land mass of peninsular India with river basins separated by the Mountain ridges and forests have played a vital role in the evolution of historical regions. One may recognize three principal regions - Himalayas, the Indo-Gangetic Plain and the Peninsular Plateau. The Vindhyan complex in mid-India running from the west coast to the delta of Bengal acts as a transitional belt between the great plains of the north and the southern peninsula. The Peninsular India is drained by the great rivers, such as, Godavari, Krishna and Kaveri. These relief features have influenced the course of movement of streams of people who have penetrated the country at various points of time and have led to the emergence of perennial nuclear regions, the areas of isolation or *culs-de sac* and areas of relative isolation.[5]

The perennial nuclear regions were the principal river basins with their agricultural potential. These river basins were frequently penetrated and exploited by agricultural communities pushing the earlier settlers into the mountainous terrain and forested areas which were unfit for sedentary cultivation. These areas of isolation or *culs de sacs* served as refuge zones. In between these two lay the areas of relative isolation. The displacement, contraction and isolation theory of cultures suggests that the present day divergence in the country is attributable to differences in the cultural *mileau* of the first large scale agricultural communities in the different regions.

The existence of historico-cultural regions seems to have contributed to the existing diversity in India's personality.[6] The process of bringing a fundamental unity will have to be based upon this historically evolved framework. According to Nehru:

> We must look to the future and work for it purposively, and with faith and vigour, at the same time we must keep our van past inheritance and derive sustenance from it. Change is essential, but continuity is also necessary. The future has to be built on the foundations laid in the past and the present. To deny the past and break with it completely is to uproot ourselves and sapless dry up.[7]

The recognition of the importance of India's diversity in her regional structure does not imply that elements of diversity expressed through regional urges may be allowed to play unchecked. History has enough testimony to suggest that whenever the regional forces were allowed to operate uniterrupted, the country moved towards disintegration.

DIVERSITY IN REGION FORMATION

The basic foundation of the Indian polity lies in the coincidence of historically evolved regions with administrative political regions. This organic relationship had existed during a great span of time from the ancient to the medieval period. Evidence of this fact is contained in two important historical documents, the *Puranas*and the *Ain-i-Akbari*of Abul Fazl. Both these documents throw enough light on the territorial divisions of *Bharatwarsha*or Hindustan respectively.

The *Puranas*contain information regarding the *Janapadas of Bharatwarsha*.[8] The Janapadas were determined on the basis of a number of considerations such as ethnicity, dialect, social mores, geographical location and political status. The Vayu Purana contains information regarding 165 Janapadas which were grouped into seven regions.[9]

The *Ain-i-Akbari*of Abul Fazl describes the *Subahs*of Mughal Empire. It has been emphasised that the linguistic and cultural homogeneity received special concern in the delineation of the Subahs.[10] A comparison between the Janapadas of ancient India and the Mughal Subahs will reveal that there was a certain degree of coincidence which suggests that both the types of administrative organisation had a prime consideration for socio-cultural diversity within the sub-continent.

Distortions in the regional structure of India came to surface immediately after the decline of Mughal Empire when socio-cultural diversity of the sub-continent was ignored while delineating the administrative units. It was during the asendency of the British East India Company that the political map of India underwent drastic changes. The British India was organized into 9 Governor's Provinces, and 3 Chief Governors Provinces and covered only 56 per cent of the total territory; the remaining territory was divided into 562 princely states.[11]

The British Provinces were formed through the process of annexation and political and administrative strategies were given prime consideration. It may be state that the infrastructure of the polity that we inherited in 1947 was a confused mosaic created by a foreign imperial power unmindful of the valid basis for the territorial organization of the subcontinent.[12]

This brief description of the processes of formation of territorial administrative units in India suggest that the foundation of India's cultural unity lay more in its socio-cultural diversity throughout its history except during a spell of colonial rule. The regional structure of the Indian polity and various political processes associated with it may be examined in this historical context of region formation.

MANIFESTATION OF DIVERSITY

It is evident from the preceding paragraphs that the diversity of the subcontinent has played a significant role in region formation throughout history. Literary evidences suggest that India's history is one of expansion of powerful communities resulting in displacement of existing inhabitants. Various streams of immigrants which entered India at different periods, influenced, and were in turn influenced in their social and cultural traits as a result of their contact with new people. This resulted in the evolution of a complex cultural synthesis. It is the horizontal unity built by this cultural synthesis that has given rise to the fundamental unity of this sub-continent, based as it is on a common cultural heritage. Yet this very story of fundamental unity is neither complete nor valid, if we ignore the counteracting centrifugal forces-representing the "Provincial State within a National State or - to put it in another way - the forces of regionalism in contrast to a united state". [13] Therefore, inorder to get a true perspective of Indian hostory, it is necessary to examine briefly the operation of centripetal and centrifugal forces.

History reveals that whenever attempts were made to strengthen centripetal tendencies without recognizing centrifugal forces, the polity met with disintegration. This is particularly true from the period of the Mauryan Empire (C.320 B.C.). It has been observed that whenever the forces of cohesion operating from above became weak, the constituent units acquired separatist tendencies and became autonomous. The Ashoka Empire was, by and large, an achievement. His empire stretched from the Persian - Afghanistan plateau in the north-west to the Padma-Meghna in the east and from Sub-Himalayan region in the north to river Pennar in the South.[14] After the death of Ashoka the Mauryan Empire broke into two parts - the north with its capital at Pataliputra and the west with its capital at Ujjain. The disintegration of the Mauryan Empire was complete by the end of C.197 B.C. when Sindh, Gujarat, Rajasthan and Malva came under the control of the Kshatrapas. It was during the reign of Akbar that another phase of central authority began when a substantial part of India came under imperial control.[15] The Mughal Empire withered away after the death of Aurangzeb in 1707. It is significant to mention here that barring brief interlands many parts of the south remained outside the central authority.

It was during the British rule that an attempt was made to bring all parts of the country under a powerful central authority. The

British were able to consolidate politically the Indian sub-continent for more than a century preceding Independence in 1947. But unfortunately, administrative framework of the British warped the basic foundation of the Indian polity i.e., the coincidence of socio-cultural regions with administrative/political regions.

India under the British experienced a two-tier administrative set-up - the territory ruled directly by the British and that ruled by the Indian princely states. There were as many as 562 princely states with disparate constitutional, legal and fiscal practices and varieties of civil code. The political organisation in almost all these states continued to be feudal. At Independence it was found necessary to integrate these states into a single political system. However, despite the fact that these states were merged into unified larger states, the princely territories continued to suffer from a relatively slow pace of development. The development of political institutions lagged behind and the people in these states continued to be guided by pre-democratic political influences.

REGIONALISM AND REGIONALISATION IN CONTEMPORARY INDIA

India at independence had to face the problem of nation building, because her identity as a sovereign state depended upon this very process. This required a careful exercise as in India the Modern region forming process began with modernization and westernization, intensified in the 20th century by the rise of the nationalist movement.[16] The problem was further aggravated by the nature of Indian society. To quote Chakraborty:

> There is as much reality in subscribing to the view that the present Indian society is basically traditional as there is truth in reiterating the differing structural features, political styles, methods and identities as features of a modern society. Variance from region to region within India between what is traditional or modern is also no less real.[17]

In such a situation which was characterized by duality of social order, it was necessary to evolve such a system which can provide stability to the Indian polity. It was thought that a formula which considers regional sentiments inherent in her diversity will help in maintaining unity of the Indian people. Therefore, the national government tried to correct the distortions caused by the British imperial power in the regional structure of Indian polity. It was justified in view of the fact that the 'National Unity can genuinely flower out of a healthy reconciliation between regionalism and nationalism. However, it is evident that like national chauvinism, unhealthy regional or subregional patriotism is equally cancerous and disruptive both of creative regionalism as also of syncretic nationalism.'[18]

Regionalism was not a new phenomenon which emerged on the Indian scene all of a sudden. It is inherent in the diversity of the sub-continent. However, this did not surface as the conditions which promote regionalism were not mature. [19] The process of regionalism in India was further hastened by the fact that although Indian society was characterized by the co-existance of traditional and modern order 'the rules of contact between Europe and India had failed to evolve any pervasive praxis of modernity involving the broader Indian social order'.[20]

This coupled with the vast size of her polity and the nature of social heterogeneity imposed arduous constraints on the process of federal nation building.Rasheeduddin Khan assessed this problem in the following words:

> A viable and legitimate federal state authority in India would have to reconcile simultaneously the requirements of a modern state/structure (legitimised periodically by the consent of the governed) on the one hand, with the peculiar and specific problems of the federalising process endemic in a 'chronic' plural society on the other. An over sight or deliberate neglect of one or the other of the two factors would vitiate not only the democratic tenor of change but also might create more problems in its wake than it might solve. [21]

It was against this background and to meet the demands of regional sentiments that the national government considered reorganisation of the states. The State Reorganisation Commission was appointed in 1953 and most of its re-commendations were implemented through the State Reorganisation Act, 1956. Recommendations of the SRC were based on the following 4 criterion[22] (1) Preservation and strengthening of the unity and security of India; (2) linguistic and cultural homogeneity; (3) financial,economic and administrative viability and (4) the need to implement successfully planning under Five Year Plans. However, it argued that linguistic homogeneity is the only rational basis for demarcation of states. It was thought that if the states were reorganised on the basis of language, regional sentiments would be satisfied.

> It is obviously an advantage that constituent units of a federation should have a minimum measure of internal cohesion. Likewise, regional consciousness, not merely in the sense of a negative awareness of absence of repression or exploitation but also in the sense of scope for positive expression of the collective personality of a people inhabiting a state or a region(emphasis added) may be conducive to the contentment and well being of the community. Common language may not only promote the growth of such regional consciousness but also make for administrative convenience. Indeed, in a democracy the people can legitimately claim and the government have a duty to ensure that the administration is conducted in a language which the people can understand.[23]

However, it was ironical that the idea of sentimental unity based on linguistic homogeneity collapsed for the simple reason that if the language has a positive content of unity, it has a negative content too which may act against the fundamental principles of unity.[24] Despite the fact that language helps to create emotional unity, it may also become highly inflammable which was evident in Tamil Nadu riots. The linguistic issue in terms of regional language vs. Hindi vs. English led to such disturbing questions as 'can different states in India communicate with each other if English is withdrawn and Hindi does not emerge as a link language?'[25]

The reorganisation of states on the principle of linguistic homogeneity has created two problems. First, the relationship between majority and minority linguistic groups within a state; and secondly, the distribution of gains of economic development. Myron Weiner has analysed the problem of minority groups in the following words:

Whether the minority group is a tribe or a religious or linguistic group, it is often concerned with preserving its cultural identity and resisting assimilation into a larger regional culture. Regionalism, like its earlier counterpart, nationalism, has become a powerful loyalty within most of the states and has resulted in a degree of assimilation of related social group, but minorities are often even more protective of their status in the midst of growing regional sentiments. This protectiveness takes many forms: there is often a fight over representation in the governing Congress Party and in the state assembly, insistence upon a share of appointments in the state administration or a proportion of admissions and scholarships into colleges, technical schools and universities, and where the minority group has its own language, pressure for the use of the mother tongue as the medium of instruction of local schools and in the publication of state laws and administrative regulations.[26]

The economic aspect of the regionalism constitutes the crux of the problem. Experience has revealed that it is possible to contain regional pulls through better sharing of gains of economic development and well drawn political strategies. The Constitution of India incorporated the basic characteristic of federalism by dividing functions and powers between the States and the Union Government. All matters of legislation have been arranged under three separate lists in the Seventh Schedule of the Constitution - the Union List, the State List and the Concurrent List. However, the Constitution made some provisions which introduced a bias in favour of the Union Government and put the States in a disadvantageous position.

It is a well known fact that the Indian Polity is characterized by large inter-regional as well as intra-regional disparities. Despite planned economic development during last 35 years, many areas of the country suffer from chronic backwardness. Variations in the distribution of natural resource endowments coupled with the biases in the allocation of development resources have further accentuated this process. Therefore, demands for more economic benefits have, time and again, been voiced which have sometimes taken the form of mass movements. It may be mentioned here that the demand for new states was primarily a result of the unequal pace of development in multilingual states. [27] Areas having a sizeable proportion of

Scheduled Tribes offer another example of the same process. The charge of partisanship against the centre, scramble for heavy industries, the present-day conflict between migrants and sons of the soil, and the Shiv Sena's movement in Maharashtra emanate essentially from the persistent problems of unequal pace of economic development. One may not fully agree with Selig Harrison when he states :

> As population mounts, densely populated regions cry lebensraum at their neighbours. Bihari labourers flock to jobs in the mining and industrial towns bordering Bengal, and overcrowded Bengal protests in return that the towns should be the preserve of its own jobless. The tea plantations of Assam become a battle ground between rival groups of Assamese and Bengali unemployed. Tamilnad demands the border plantation land of Malayalam-speaking Travancore Cochin to protect Tamil collies from Malayalee competition. With each year and more and more people - made more and more group - conscious by scarcity compete ever more feverishly for limited economic spoils, the hope for ultimate escape from India's vicious circle grows more remote.[28]

Inter-regional pulls and pressures are inevitably caused by economic disparity. The demand for more and more autonomy to states and overriding problems in the north-east are manifestation of the uneven pace of economic development.

THE POLITICAL SYSTEM

The magnitude of the prevailing diversity in the country and the complexity of its social structure forced the leadership to evolve a political system aimed at fostering sense of unity among the Indian population living in diverse social environments. It was in due regard to this factor that the country opted in favour of a federal system of governance. It was thought that the federal system is the only way to keep India together as it maintains a balance between two opposite forces - forces of unification and forces of disintegration.

This leads one to recognise two fundamental aspects, First, India requires a consitution in which the central authority has enough power to hold together the subordinate units and to sustain a sense of national loyalty, and secondly, the constitution should be such as to guarantee enough autonomy to subordinate units so that there is a proper sharing of power. This may be achieved only through a federal system of governance. It is in this arrangement where the states become effective instruments of development within a national framework, that the economic imbalances and distortions which generate centrifugal tendencies may be checked and the foundations of national unity strengthened in the real sense.

As evident from the preceding paragraphs, the reorganisation of the states was done primarily to keep populations having a similar social ethos together. The system worked well under the dominating leadership. This is not to say that there was no divergence from the federal principle. But these diversions were subsumed under the dominating leadership of the Congress Party.

The Congress leadership under Nehru managed to create a semblance of stability by tackling the overriding centre-state problems within the framework of the party constitution and its tradition. The removal of Nehru from the scene exposed the real weakness of the system, when the political support which the party hitherto enjoyed was withdrawn to such an extent that the ruling party at the Centre became a pawn in the hands of the powerful state bosses who managed to overrule the Prime Minister in all important matters. The powers enjoyed by the 'Syndicate' within the Congress Party in the post 1967 period is a case in point.

However, the present day working of centre-state relations is somewhat different from what it used to be during its formative phase in the fifties and the early sixties. At that stage of development the ruling Congress was capable of maintaining a balance between national and regional goals and a unifying force. The leadership acted thus at two levels:

> In its effort of win, Congress adapts itself to the local power structure. It recruits from among those who have local power and influence... The result is a political system with considerable tension between a government concerned with modernizing the society and economy and a party seeking to adapt itself to the lo-

cal environment in order to win elections.[29]

The contemporary situation is altogether different. The Congress Party has lost its all-India character in the wake of the absence of a leadership which has a national image and can promote national integration. This has come in as a result of two processes operating simulatneously. Firstly, it was the result of increased will of participation by the rural elite in the game of power and secondly, the desire of ruling leadership to maintain its grip on Indian masses. This conflict forced the Congress Party to come to terms with sectional and parochial parties, and thereby legitimize the policies of destructive regionalism. The outcome was seen in a continous erosion in its mass base on one hand and the increasing influence of regional parties on the other. Imposition of internal emergency in June 1975 and the Janata's victory in March, 1977 Parliamentary Elections was the outcome of this on going process. Although, the Janata Party tried to foster the process of national integration and claimed itself as a party with a national perspective having an all India appeal, it failed miserably on this front due to its own inbuilt constraints. The Janata's capacity to emerge as an all India political phenomenon was restricted by a number of factors. The foremost among these factors was its fragmented mass base. In fact, the party did not have a mass base of its own - it operated through the network of its constitutent parties. This network in itself was highly fragmented and was confined to the north. Secondly, the components of the Janata Party had drawn their political strength from highly localized, parochial or sectional issues. They consisted of groups which were either the relics of the Congress _ Congress (U) and CFD - denuded of their political power and having no mass base at all or groups whose programme was specific to certain class or sectional interest. The Jan Sangh sustained itself on the support of the Hindu trading classes in urban areas of Hindi speaking north and the BLD represented and worked to preserve the interest of the middle ranking and land owning castes in the north. The socialists had enclaves of influences with a wider regional spread, but commanded little political hold on the masses. Thirdly, even after the emergence of Janata as a unified party, definitionally, the component groups failed to shed off their former identities and the group loyalties continued to be fragmented. This thwarted the very process of political assimilation of forces within the Janata Party and did not permit it to emerge as a cohesive all India force. Fourthly, lack of cohesion within the Janata Party, its major accent on north centric caste and kulak biased politics, and social approval of explicitly communal and obscurantist tendencies gave new lease of life to these forces and accelerated the process of social and political disintegration. Fifthly, the disappearance from the centre of a major cohesive political force which commanded wider control and carried with it the disparate social and ethnic elements within the Indian polity led to the rise of parochial forces which were particularly noted for their vigour on the periphery of the Indian Union. The resurgence of Akali Dal in Punjab and of the National Conference in J&K illustrates this point.

These forces facilitated the way for the collapse of the Janata Party. The process was completed in January, 1980 when the Janata Party was defeated at the hustlings of 1980 elections. The Congress (I) which emerged as majority party, since very beginning, started with tactics of concentration of power. Probably, the centralisation was considered as a precondition for national unity. It was not realized that concept of national unity is holistic as well as multi-dimensional. It is holistic because it involves polity, economy, society and administration. It is multi-dimensional because it involves integration of economy, polity, society and administration. In this perspective the tendency of centralisation of economic and political power acted as a constraint on the process of national unity. A centralised system is incapable of promoting country's personality and thus fails to check fissiparous tendencies. Since the government of the day ignored this aspect, it gave birth to chauvinistic and separatist tendencies. This process at work has undermined the basic foundation of Indian unity necessiating immediate remedial measures. It requires to be recognized that unity and diversity are not two ends of a continuum. They can not develop in isolation. History has enough testimony to show that attempts to bring unity by ignoring diversity have always met with frustration and therefore, the measures to forge unity on diversity sown by colonial rulers cannot succeed in contemporary India.

Indian electoral data provide enough evidence of this ongoing process. In a situation which is characterized by a low level of social integration and where primary associations based on caste and community have an edge over secondary associations, the political opinion continues to get polarized along social attributes. This coupled with the absence of a major cohesive force at the national level has contributed to a situation in which instead of mass following of the political parties there are framented sections of followers which reflect existing social fragmentation.

The phenomenon of fragmentation may be seen not only in the multiplicity of political parties, but also in the changing allegiance of the people to different political parties. This implies that no single political party commands a firm hold on public opinion in large areas of the country, and such parties do not retain political alliegence for a substantian period of time.

Electoral data reflect this continuing process of disunity. The democratic process instead of being an agent of cultural synthesis, has accentuated the inter-regional diversity in Indian polity. Whether elections have contributed to the unity in diversity or have promoted fragmentation of the Indian polity, therefore, constitute the crux of this analysis. It is in the light of this broad framework that the findings of this study should be viewed.

NOTES AND REFERENCES

1. Jawaharlal Nehru, 'Maulana Abul Kalam Azad Memorial Lecture, in 1959', cited in Indian Council for Cultural Relations, *Vision of India*, 1981, p.73.
2. Mahatma Gandhi, *Collected Works*, Vol. 10, p. 36.
3. K.N. Haksar and K.M. Panikkar, *Federal India* (London : Martin Hokkinson Ltd., 1930), p. 144.
4. Jawaharlal Nehru, *The Discovery of India* (New Delhi : Indian Council for Cultural Relations, 1981), p. 26.
5. B. Subbarao, *The Personality of India* (Baroda : M.S. University 1958), pp. 11-12.
6. The use of term 'personality' is based upon Subbarao's work. He used the term personality to connote diversity - both physical and social - of the subcontinent. *Ibid*., p. 1.
7. Jawaharlal Nehru, 'Abul Kalam Memorial Lecture'. *op.cit.*, p. 77.
8. Janapada was a territorial unit. A detailed account of Janapadas is contained in S.M. Ali, *Geography of Puranas* (New Delhi : People's Publishing House).
9. *Ibid*., p. 133.
10. This is not to suggest that linguistic and cultural homogenity was the only factor in the delineation of the Subahs. In fact the main architect of the Subahs, Raja Todar Mal, gave enough consideration to factor of revenue collection.
11. Carl. C. Taylor, et-al., *India's Roots of Democracy* (Orient Longmann, 1965), p. 5.

12. Rasheeduddin Khan, 'Regional Dimension', *Seminar*, 164, April, 1973, p. 38.
13. B. Subbarao, *op.cit.*, p. 20.
14. V.A. Janaki, *Some Aspects of the Political Geography of India* (Baroda : M.S. University, 1977), p. 54.
15. *Ibid.*, p.64.
16. Bernard S. Cohn, "Regions Subjective and Objective : Their Relation to the Study of Modern Indian History and Society" in Robert. I. Crane, *Regions and Regionalism in South Asian Studies : An Exploratory Study* (Duke University, 1973), p. 21.
17. Satyesh Chandra Chakraborty, 'Split-up modernization - its Relevance in the Study of Modern History and Society in *Essays in Honour of Prof. S.C. Sarkar* (New Delhi : People's Publishing House, 1976). p. 602.
18. Rasheeduddin Khan, *op.cit.*, p. 3.
19. Conditions which are prerequiste for the growth of regionalism are a symbol - pool, selection, standardization and transmission of symbols and establishments of Regional Elites. (Bernard S. Cohn, *op.cit*, pp. 22-30).
20. Satyesh Chandra Chakraborty, *op.cit*, p. 605.
21. Rasheeduddin Khan, 'Territorial Reorganisation', *Seminar*, 137, January, 1971, p. 28.
22. *Report of the State Reorganisation Commission* (New Delhi, Govt. of India, 1955).
23. *Ibid.*, p. 46.
24. The question of positive and negative aspects of language as cohesive/divisive force has been analysed by Rohit Dave (Rohit Dave, 'Regionalism in Maharashtra', *Janata* (13), March 23, 1958).
25. Selig S. Harrison, *India : The Most Dangerous Decade* (Madras : Oxford University Press, 1960), p. 9.
26. Myron Weiner, 'Political Development in the Indian States', in *State Politics in India* (Princeton : Princeton University Press, 1968), pp. 26-27.
27. Report of the State Reorganisation Commission *op.cit.*, p. 225.
28. Selig S. Harrison, *op.cit.*, p. 333.
29. Myron Weiner, *Party Building in a New Nation* (Chicago : University of Chicago Press, 1967), p. 15.

THREE

SEATS WON: SPATIAL PATTERNING OF PARTY POSITION

It is intended here to analyse a simple variable pertaining to the parliamentary elections in India viz.the seats won by a certain political parties. It is considered as a simple variable because any conclusion derived on its basis will be of a highly generalized nature. An attempt has been made to analyse the strength of political parties expressed in terms of seats won in three parliamentary elections of 1971,1977 and 1980. The chief value of this approach flows from the fact that it gives a clear insight into the spatial pattern of the party strongholds.[1] However, winning of a seat is not an indication of the real strength of political parties because quite often, as indicated earlier, a large number of the candidates get elected with a strikingly low share of valid votes polled in a constituency. In order to prove this point in depth, an analysis of majority and minority wins by politicals parties has also been attempted.

Winning of a seat by a party is not a reflection on the acceptability of its political programme. In a society, such as india's characterized by a low degree of awareness - social as well as political - masses do not understand the real value of their vote and their decision to vote for a particular party, generally, is shaped by highly superficial and narrow considerations. But generally, the chances of winning a seat depends upon a number of factors, such as the mass following of a certain political party, its image and mass base, its ability to reach the different strata of society through electoral campaign and the local relevance of issues raised by the party at the eve of a particular election. The relevance of the issue/issues raised by a political party and its capacity to capitalize on them often plays a crucial role in the final decision-making of the voters.[2] If the issues have wider appeal, and are not specifically local or parochial, the party may have a broad base cutting across caste, language and religious identities. In case the issues are local or regional and are relevant only to a section of the electorate, the party following is likely to be restricted.[3]

Most of the voting behaviour studies in India have highlighted the role of caste in the electoral politics of India. Its role may be judged both at the level of selection of candidates and in the process of polarization of political opinion during the electoral campaign. Most scholars argue that caste continues to play a critically important role in conditioning social and political values and behaviour in contemporary India.'[4] It is easily understandable that the villager, other things being equal, prefers to vote for his caste man.'[5] Though party spokesmen always denounce the role of caste in politics, and claim to be above caste politics, it has been commonly observed that political parties give serious consideration to the caste factor while assessing their electoral prospects. This applies even to the communist parties.[6] In the first place, caste and communal affinity is one of the criteria applied at the time of selection of candidates. In consituencies having numerical dominance of a certain caste group, political parties always pay attention to this fact at the time of nominating their candidates. In such a situation all parties tend to choose candidates from the same caste group. Existence of caste-based political parties, proves this argument further.

Indian society is largely organized along caste, community and linguistic basis which in turn have a regional dimension flowing from the processes of social evolution. This has contributed to the varied nature of mass following of political parties in the country. This provides the basic framework for the analysis attempted in the following paragraphs.

ALL-INDIA PATTERNS

The national pattern of the relative strength of the political parties can be understood with reference to the composition of Parliament and the constituencywise distribution of the elected members.

The 1971 mid-term poll was held in a changed political atmosphere altogether. The preceding period saw a high degree of political instability in the wake of the outcome of Fourth General Elections. In fact, the political scene in india started fast changing after the death of Nehru who had sucessfully acted as a reconcilier of internal conflicts within the Congress Party.[7] The factional fights within the Congress party led some leaders to quit the parent organization; this affected its prospects in 1967 elections, as become clear in the election results. A few but important regional parties gained significantly. For the first time in the electoral history of India a fragmented political party system emerged on the scene. The pattern of their mass following revealed that even the congress party ceased to be a national party in the true sense of the term.

The post 1967 events reveal that there was little effort on the part of political parties to win the confidence of different groups. Political parties continued to bank upon the support of specific groups and thus not only promoted social tension but also contributed further to political fragmentation. The process is continuing unchecked.

1971 Mid-Term Poll

Despite the great split in Congress in 1969, the Congress[8] contested the maximum number of seats and scored high success. The grand alliance, formed by the four parties, viz., Jana Sangh, Congress(O), Swatantra and SSP, could not generate much popular support as could be seen from their small gains. The Congress fielded 441 candidates and emerged victorious in as many as 352 constituencies (Fig. 3.1). Table 3.1 presents the position of different political parties at the all-India level.

It is evident that except the Congress other parties did not even contest a substantial number of seats. The failure to field a candidate is a clear reflection on the non-existence of its vaible base among the masses. Judged by this simple criterion, they cease to be the national parties despite the Election Commission's recognition to this effect. Their performance in the electoral context proves this point further.

The success of the Congress was not independent of the help from other parties and influential individuals. The party had to enter into electoral adjustments with parties like the Dravida Munnetra Kazhagam besides seeking support of ex-princely houses.

TABLE 3.1: SEATS CONTESTED AND WON, 1971

Party	Seats contested	Seats won
Bhartiya Jana Sangh	157	22
CPI	87	23
CPI(M)	85	25
Congress	441	352
Congress(O)	238	16
PSP	63	2
SSP	93	3
Swatantra	59	8
State Parties	224	40
Registered Parties	203	13
Independents	1,134	14
Total	2,784	518

Source: *Report on the Fifth General Elections to the House of the People in India, 1971* (New Delhi: Election Commission of India, 1974).

Table 3.1 shows that none of the political parties, except the Congress, fared well. The 'grand alliance' was routed. The CPI and the CPM(M) scored some success; but the success of the CPI was mainly in those constituencies where it was in alliance with the Congress and the CPI(M)'s success came mainly from West Bengal. Among other parties the DMK in Tamil Nadu and Telangana Praja Samiti in Telangana region of Andhra scored a significant success.

1977 Elections

If the period between 1967 and 1971 saw a high degree of political unstability, the subsequent period was characterized by the collapse of the democratic institutions. This provided the background for the polarisation of political forces in India. The process started with the formation of Bhartiya Lok Dal by a merger of seven political parties in August 1974.[9] The policy formulations of these parties suggest that they were mainly the parties of farmers. The need for united opposition was further felt in the wake of the internal emergency and as soon as the elections were announced, the four opposition parties viz., the Jana Sangh, the Congress(O), the socialists and the Bhartiya Lok Dal decided to contest from the same platform under the banner of the Janata party. The Congress for Democracy, a group of dissident Congressmen also joined hands with the Janata. In the changed political climate neither the Congress nor the Janata were sure of their victories and thus both the parties entered into electoral alliances with other parties. This ensured, by and large, a straight fight between the two main rivals. The Janata party won absolute majority in parliament. The Congress Party which contested the maximun of 492 seats had to satisfy itself just with 154 seats (Fig. 3.2). Table 3.2 shows the national picture in regard to all political parties.

Fig. 3.1
Seats Contested and Won: 1971 Parliamentary Elections

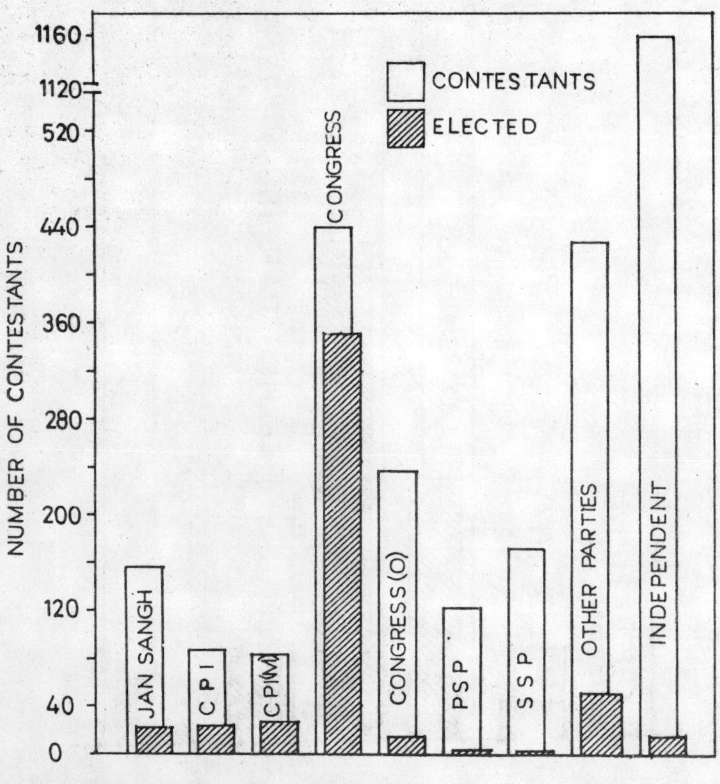

Fig. 3.2
Seats Contested and Won: 1977 Parliamentary Elections

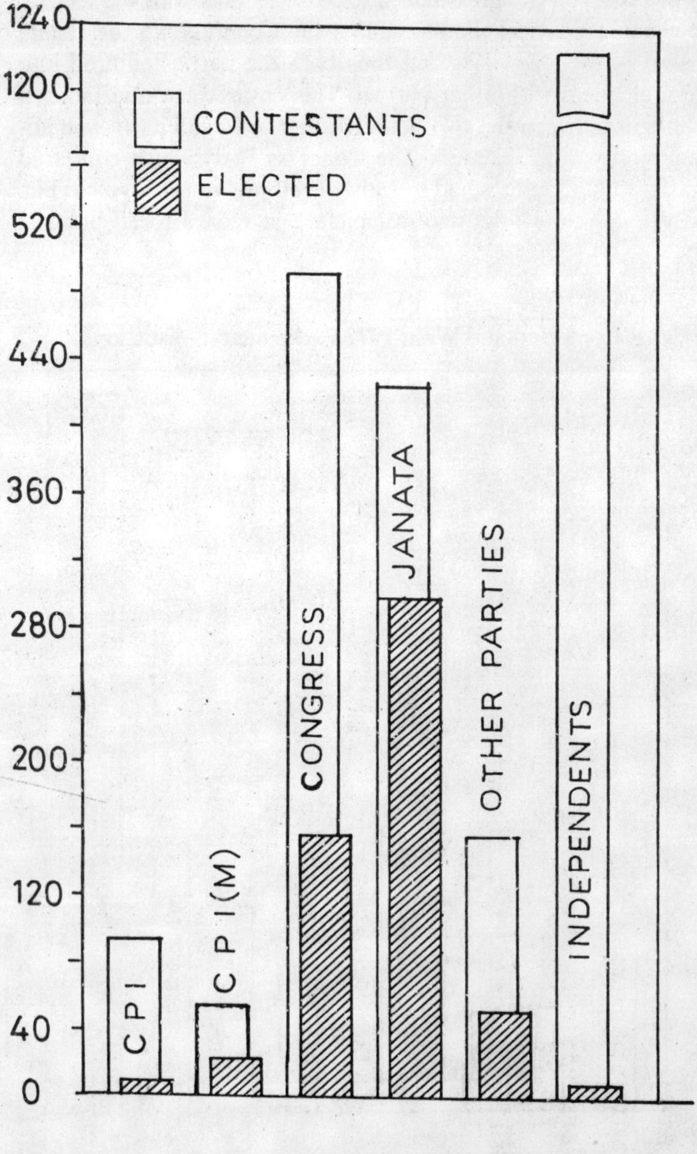

TABLE 3.2: SEATS CONTESTED AND WON, 1977

	Party	Seats contested	Seats won
1.	CPI	91	7
2.	CPI(M)	53	22
3.	Congress	492*	154*
4.	Janata	424	298
5.	State Parties	85	49
6.	Registered Parties	70	3
7.	Independents	1224	9
	Total	2439	542

* Includes seats contested and won under the Congress (0) symbol.

Source: *Report on the Sixth General Elections to the House of the People in India, 1977* (New Delhi: Election Commission of India).

Despite absolute majority gained by the Janata it could not make a significant dent in the Southern states which voted overwhelmingly in favour of the Congress. This created an unprecedented north-south divide. In the wake of this election, the regional parties got new lease of life. This suggests that the regional sentiments inherent in the ethno-lingual diversity of the country were quite strong. However, the emergency was the single contributory factor to this changing pattern of party politics. The CPI's reduced party strength, to a great extent, was due to its covert alliance with the Congress. The CPI(M)'s gain were mainly in West Bengal and Tripura. This brief analysis is a clear reflection of the political landscape of the country which suggests that all major parties emerged as regional parties having their following in specific areas of the country.

1980 Elections

The Janata rule was marked by inner party squabbles. Its constituent parties could not shed their individual identities and the Janata remained an conglomeration of political groups with basic ideological differences. The only unifying factor was lust for power. But even this could not keep them united and the result was the downfall of the Janata Government in the wake of the party split. The Bharatiya Lok Dal constituent along with some Socialists parted their way. Mr. Charan Singh leader of the Janata(s) Parliamentary Party, formed another government with the help of Congress (U).[10]

Unfortunately, this ministry could not prove its majority on the floor of the Parliament and therefore, the Parliament was dissolved entailing a mid-term poll.

The tenure of the Janata and the Janata(S) ministries was a complete failure on economic as well as social fronts. These parties could not satisfy the aspirations of different social groups which led to mounting social tension. Keeping in view the vast ethnolingual diversity of the country, a party must be capable enough to win the confidence of different social groups, and therefore, a socially flexible and non-conformist ideology is required. It was this character of the Congress Party[11] during the days of Nehru which gave it the status of an All India Party. What follows from this is that to be an All India Party, it cannot ignore the ethno-lingual diversity of the country.

The Janata and Janata(S) once again tried to capitalize the issue of emergency during the election campaign. The Congress reminded the people of their sufferings on the economic front and the mounting social tension in different parts of the country. The two Communist parties joined hands and focussed their campaign on the issue of safeguarding of democracy and threat of authoritarianism. The Congress(U) could not come out with any clear cut policy. The regional parties, as usual, raised the issues of local relevance.

The Congress secured a two-third majority. Both the Communist Parties achieved some success. The Janata was routed. The Janata(S) gained in the pockets dominated by middle class Jat peasantry. Regional parties with deep roots in their areas of operation scored gains. Table 3.3 presents the national scene.

TABLE 3.3: SEATS CONTESTED AND WON, 1980

Party	Seats contested	Seats won
CPI	48	11
CPI(M)	63	36
Congress	492	353
Congress(U)	212	13
Janata	432	31
Janata(S)	294	41
State Parties	106	34

Registered Parties	156	1
Independents	2826	9
Total	4629	529 *

* excludes 12 constituencies of Assam and 1 constituency of Meghalaya.

Source: *Seventh General Elections to the House of the People in India, 1980,* Abstract (Provisional) (New Delhi : Election Commission of India).

Fig. 3.3
Seats Contested and Won: 1980 Parliamentary Elections

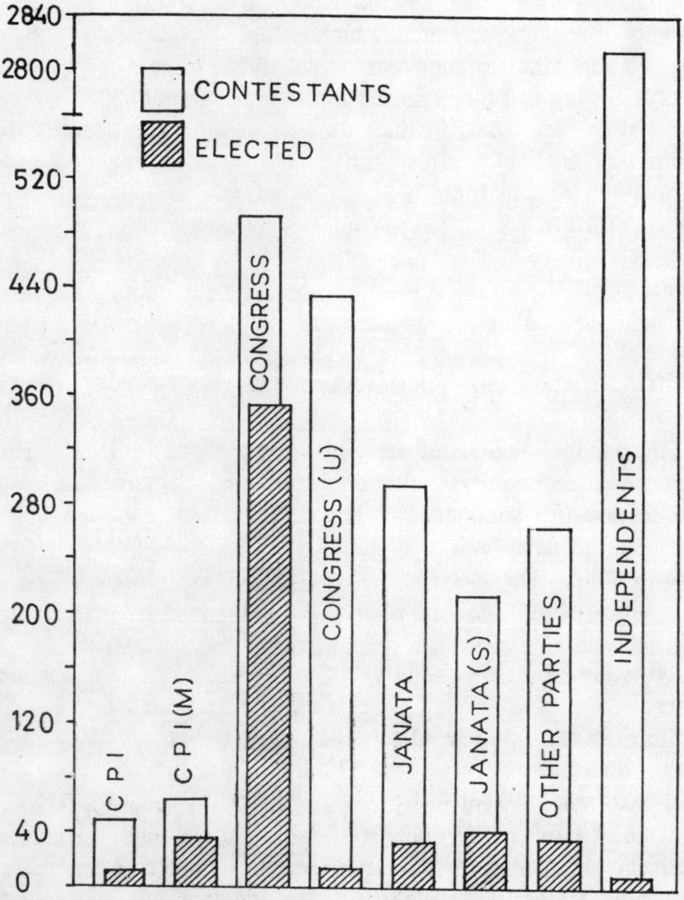

Judged by the criterion of party victories, it is evident that out of the 6 major parties only the Congress may be regarded as having an all India character (Fig. 3.3). But an insight into the pattern of its gains reveals that the party's following in the two populous states of Bihar and Uttar Pradesh was highly fluid. In West Bengal, Kerala and Tripura, it failed to make any significant dent. In Tamil Nadu, it had to seek the support of theDravida Munnetra Kazhagam. In this perspective even the Congress could not claim an all India character.

The preceding analysis of all India strength of political parties in the three elections clearly reveals that the party following expressed in terms of seats won, remains highly fluid. Despite calling themselves National Parties, they cease to satisfy the basic criterion of national following to be recognized as all India parties. The regional parties with their roots in their areas, continue to flourish. This preliminary analysis provides sufficient ground to assert that the political situation in India is highly fragmented. Firstly, because a number of major parties fail to contest a substantial number of seats which in the very first instance reflects on their restricted mass following. Secondly, even if a party secures majority of seats, its areas of strongholds remain restricted.

REGIONAL ANALYSIS OF PARTY GAINS

The regional analysis of party gains on the basis of their performance in different States and Union Territories of the Indian Union provides a better understanding about their areas of influence. It is seen that the performance of the parties varies significantly from State to State. The vast ethno-lingual differences among the states are manifested through the performance of the political parties.

Bhartiya Jana Sangh

Since its inception in October 1951, the Bhartiya Jana Sangh remained virtually a party of the 'Hindi Heartland'. Such a restricted mass base was inherent in its aim to establish a 'Dharma Rajya or the Rule of Law' and in doing so to 'abide by the highest traditions of Bhartiya Sanskriti, that bind all people together in ties of real amity and fraternity.'[12] With such an ideology the party could succeed mainly in Rajasthan, Uttar Pradesh, Madhya Pradesh, and

Bihar, where the society has deep orthodox moorings. Here the exploitation of the down-trodden is in the conformity with the caste-Hindu outlook and practices.The electoral data of 1971 elections clearly illustrate this point. The Party contested only 157 seats out of which 100 were in four states viz., Rajasthan, Uttar Pradesh Madhya Pradesh and Bihar. It could secure only 22 seats, half of them coming from Madhya Predesh, 4 each from Rajasthan and Uttar Pradesh, 2 from Bihar and 1 from Gujarat (Appendix IA).

CPI and CPI(M)

The Communists in India could succeed only in those areas where oppression, social or economic, has taken its worst form. With their greater accent on the question of 'socialism', the Communist Parties are deeply entrenched in these areas. The CPI and the CPI(M) are the two branches of the same parent organization which had split in 1964 on the question of extra-territorial loyalty.

The CPI finds its place mainly in areas where the exploitation of the landless has been very prevalent. It has strong roots in parts of Bihar, Kerala, Andhra Pradesh and Tamil Nadu. It contested 87 seats in 1971 and annexed in all 23 seats from Andhra Pradesh, Bihar, Kerala, Orissa, Punjab, Tamil Nadu, Uttar Pradesh and West Bengal. Its highest representation of 5 seats came from Bihar (Appendix IA). The CPI in this election was highly benefitted by its alliance with the Congress. In fact its main gains were in those areas only where it had an alliance with the Congress. If the CPI was benefitted from its cooperation with the Congress, in 1971, it had to pay a heavy cost for it in the 1977 elections. The party could win only 7 seats (4 in Kerala and 3 in Tamil Nadu) out of 91 contested. Drawing lessons from this election, the party reviewed its policy of cooperation with the Congress, changed its stand, and started to cooperate with other left parties. It joined hands with CPI(M) and other left parties in 1980 elections. It contested only 48 seats and secured 11 seats - 4 in Bihar, 3 in West Bengal 2 in Kerala and 1 each from Manipur and Uttar Pradesh. This shows that the party has its areas of stronghold basically in 3 states, i.e., Bihar, Kerala and West Bengal.

The areas of influence of the CPI(M) lay in Kerala, West Bengal and Tripura. But unlike the CPI, it is more prominent among industrial workers. In 1971 the party secured 25 seats out of 85 contested. Of these, 20 were in West Bengal, 2 each in Kerala and Tripura and 1 in Andhra Pradesh (Appendix IA). Its tally in 1977 elections came down to 22 but this was attributed to the fact that the party had alliance with the Janata and thus left a number of seats to it in the areas of its influence. It contested only 53 seats. In 1977, its highest share of 17 seats came from West Bengal. Besides it had representation in Maharashtra, Orissa and Punjab. Its performance was at its peak in 1980 elections when out of 63 seats contested, it secured 36 of which 28 were in West Bengal, 6 in Kerala and 2 in Tripura. It is evident the CPI(M) remains a party dominantly of West Bengal, Kerala, and Tripura.

Congress Party

The Congress of pre-1967 period and the Congress of post-1967 period were qualitatively different. Its dominating influence which was eroded in 1967 election could not be reestablished despite its big majorities in the elections of 1971 and 1980. Althouth it proved its strength in 1971 elections by winning 352 seats out of 441 contested, the party could not achieve success in many parts of the country. Its performance in Gujarat, Madhya Pradesh, Rajasthan, Tamil Nadu and West Bengal illustrates this point. The inclusion of Tamil Nadu in this category may look odd as it annexed all 9 seats contested but the fact remains that its success in 9 constituencies was possible only due to alliance with the Dravida Munnetra Kazhagam. In Telangana region of Andhra Pradesh too, the Congress failed to make significant dent. In this perspective even the Congress ceased to be a national party.

The failure of the Congress Party to control the national scene characterized by worsening economic conditions and rising social conflicts led to a catastrophic situation.The process culminated in the imposition of 'internal emergency' in June 1975. This contributed to the unification of four opposition parties in the name of the Janata in 1977 elections. The Congress contested 492 seats but could annex only 154, that too in southern states. In the north its rout was complete and thus the Congress emerged as a party only of South India.

Situation changed once again in 1980 elections.The non-performance of the Janata and the Janata(S)-Congress(U) coalition ministries was the main issue which the Congress put forward to the electorate. This weakness was well exploited by the congress party. It won 353 seats out of 492 contested. However, the success of the Congress came mainly from those areas where the people had no alternative but to vote for the Congress. Therefore, in the areas where the parties other than the Janata had strong following, the Congress was defeated. Its major victories came from Andhra Pradesh, Gujarat, Himachal Pradesh, Karnataka, Madhya Pradesh, Maharashtra, Orissa, Punjab and Delhi. Its following remained highly fluid in Bihar, Rajasthan and Uttar Pradesh. In Kerala and West Bengal its performance was altogether bad where it could secure 4 and 5 seats respectively (Appendix IA). This reveals that the Congress gains were confined to those areas where its hegemony had never been challenged by any political party during the electoral history of India.

3. Congress(O)

Ideologically the Congress(O) and the Congress were not different. Congress (O) was formed as a result of the 1969 split in the Congress in the wake of 'divergence of personalities and their struggle for power and supremacy.'[13] Basically the Congress(O) consisted of the old Congress stalwarts, who probably were against the style of Mrs Gandhi's working. But there is no doubt that the leaders of the Congress(O) failed to convince the masses that they belong to the real Congress. In fact they failed to generate any public opinion in their favour. The result was that their following remained centred around personalities - in Gujarat around Morarji Desai, in U.P. around Banarasi Das and in Tamil Nadu around Kamraj.Therefore, the party's success came mainly from those areas where these people commanded their influence. It contested 238 seats but could annex only 16 seats of which 11 were in Gujarat, 3 in Bihar and 1 each in Tamil Nadu and Uttar Pradesh (Appendix IA). This is sufficient to conclude that the party was denuded of its political base in the country.

Congress(U)

Similar to the Congress (O), the Congress (U) too was born out of another split in the Congress in January 1978. Once again personality conflict was the main issue occasioning the split. Its base, too, was centred around personalities of its leaders, and therefore had no mass base as such. The fact that it contested only 212 seats in 1980 elections reveals that the party did not project itself as a national alternative. It could secure only 13 seats of which 4 were in Bihar, 3 in Kerala and one each in Andhra Pradesh, Jammu and Kashmir, Maharashtra, Rajasthan, Goa, Daman and Diu and Lakshadweep.

Janata Party

The Janata party which came into being in January 1977 did not have a mass base of its own and had to operate through the mass base of its constituents. Thus the party's areas of influence coincided with the areas of influence of its constituents. Its constituents had a following only in the north with the exception of the Congress (O) which commanded its influence in Gujarat and Tamil Nadu. This is supported by the electoral data of 1977 Parliamentary elections which show that the party's success was confined mainly to the 'Hindi Heartland.' It contested 424 seats and won 298. In the four southern states of Andhra Pradesh, Karnataka, Tamil Nadu and Kerala it had a strength of only six. Its best performance was in Haryana, Himachal Pradesh, Uttar Pradesh, Chandigarh and Delhi where it won all the seats. In Bihar and West Bengal it secured all the seats it contested. It could not secure a single seat in Jammu and Kashmir, Kerala, Manipur, Dadra and Nagar Haveli, Goa, Daman and Diu and Pondicherry (Appendix IA).

The infighting among the Janata constituents, which was a major factor for its non-performance during the days of its power, was responsible for its complete rout in 1980 elections. Out of 432 seats contested it could secure only 31 from the states of Bihar, Gujarat, Haryana, Karnataka, Madhya Pradesh, Maharashtra, Rajasthan, Uttar Pradesh and Delhi. These victories were mainly due to the personal influence of the candidates which they commanded in their respective areas. Otherwise, probably it would have been completely wiped out from the electoral landscape of the country.This is a pointer towards the assertion that the party had no mass base of its own.

Janata (Secular)

The party with the aim of preserving the interest of middle class peasantry could find a place only in the Jat community of the the north. Outside their home region the party had no existence. This is seen from the 1980 election results: out of 294 seats contested its wins were only in 41 constituencies of which 29 were in Uttar Pradesh, 5 in Bihar, 4 in Haryana, 2 in Rajasthan and one in Orissa.

P.S.P. and S.S.P.

Although socialism as a political way of life has some emotional appeal in Indian society, the Socialists could not develop their mass base for the reason attributed to their leadership. The history of Indian Socialists is full of splits and mergers. The only difference between the PSP and SSP, which led to parting of ways after unification, was the issue of cooperation with other opposition parties. The major group of SSP led by Dr. Lohia favoured cooperation with all parties irrespective of their ideology; the other group which again formed PSP was against cooperation with Communists and communalists. Although the PSP had a wider mass base, it was not very effective. The PSP which contested 63 seats in 1971 could win only two (one each in Maharashtra and West Bengal).Similarly SSP could claim only 3 (two in Bihar and one in Madhya Pradesh) out of 93 seats contested. The SSP was merged in Bhartiya Lok Dal in 1974 and the PSP, renamed as Socialist Party, merged with Janata in 1977.

Swatantra Party

The Swatantra party largely stood for free private enterprise, for private ownership of land and other means of production with no interference from the state. The party accordingly got impressive support of big landlords and industrialists. In fact the brain behind formation of the Swatantra Party were three pressure groups, the Agricultural Fedration of India (an organization of rich landlords) the Forum of Free Enterprise, and the All India Manufacturers Association. The party attracted the ex-rulers who provided it a foothold in the areas of their influence. It fielded 59 candidates in 1971 elections and won in 8 constituencies (3 each in Rajasthan and Orissa and two in Gujarat).

Other Parties

The organization of the Indian society along caste, community and linguistic lines has given rise to formation of a number of political parties on these lines. This tendency is so deeply rooted that every group feels that its interest may be looked after only by the party belonging to their group. This feeling has developed mainly due to the failure of the major parties to contain the different social groups to their fold. The domination of socially stronger groups over the weaker sections has further accelerated this process. This attitude has become so intense that some political parties have questioned the very basis of Indian regional structure. It is noted that they thrive in peripheral states. It is also noticed that whenever political unstablity persists in the country, the regional parties get a new lease of life. Although there are a number of such parties, the important ones are National Conference in Jammu and Kashmir; Shiromani Akali Dal in Punjab; Jharkhand Party in Bihar; Dravida Munnetra Kazhagam and Anna Dravida Munnetra Kazgagan in Tamilnadu; Maharashtrawadi Gomantak party in Goa, Daman and Diu and a number of tribal parties in the the north-east. Performance of these parties in all the 3 elections is presented in Appendices IB, IC and ID.

In the 1971 elections, there were 427 candidates belonging to these other the parties of which 53 were successful. In view of the need to avoid multiple contest their number came down to 155 in 1977. Of this 52 were successful. The number of candidates belonging to these parties swelled to 261 in 1980. But only 35 were successful. The distribution of these seats in all the 3 elections reveals that the regional parties have been most strong in Jammu and Kashmir, Tamil Nadu, Goa and the north-east. The Akali Dal found strong expression in Punjab in 1977.

GEOGRAPHIC PATTERNING OF PARTY GAINS

The geography of party strongholds, gives a new dimension to studies in voting behaviour. Unlike studies in political science and sociology, geographical studies emphasise the spatial aspects. Here, thus, the study is oriented towards regional variations in the framework of India.

The electoral statistics provide data pertaining to electorates, voters, valid votes, rejected votes, votes polled by candidates and obviously winning candidates in each constituency. A simple statistical approch is the analysis of the spatial pattern of seats won by various parties with the aid of choropleth maps.[14] Its limitation lies in the fact that quite often candidates get elected by minority votes and in which case discussion on the basis of gains alone fails to reveal the political leanings within a constituency.[15] However, the significance of this lies in the fact that it gives a comparative picture of major party strongholds. Keeping in view this aspect, the following paragraphs attempt to present a geography of seats won in three elections of 1971, 1977 and 1980 (Figs. 3.4., 3.5 and 3.6).

1971 Elections

A perusal at Fig. 3.4 reveals the fragmented nature of the mass following of political parties. It belies the hegemonic or dominating influence of the Congress Party. It is seen that Udaipur-Gwalior region, lower Ganga plain,Telangana and the deep south encompassing Tamil Nadu and Kerala remained out-side the pale of the Congress influence. Further the rise of a number of intervening pockets of the other parties especially at the periphery of the Indian Union further questions the dominant nature of the Congress Party. This was possible because a party representing their interest existed in these areas.

The Jana Sangh emerged in Udaipur-Gwalior region cutting across the boundary of Madhya Pradesh and Rajasthan. This region with deep roots of Hinduism and feudal in character continues to be under the domain of ex-princely houses. This favoured rise and success of the Jana Sangh. The Baghelkhand region too became the Jana Sangh stronghold. The basic cause for this lay in influence of the prince of Rewa:Martand Verma. Five other pocket of Jana Sangh consisting of one constituency each arose in the Gangetic Plain.

The CPI strongholds were not extensive and were in the form of enclves in different parts of the country. These enclaves lay in southern Punjab, eastern Uttar Prdesh, Bihar, Tamil Nadu and Kerala. It is observed that these enclaves correspond with the areas of agrarian crisis expressed in terms of landlessness and exploitation of agricultural labours in its worst form.

Fig. 3.4
India: 1971 Parliamentray elections: Seats Won by Political Parties

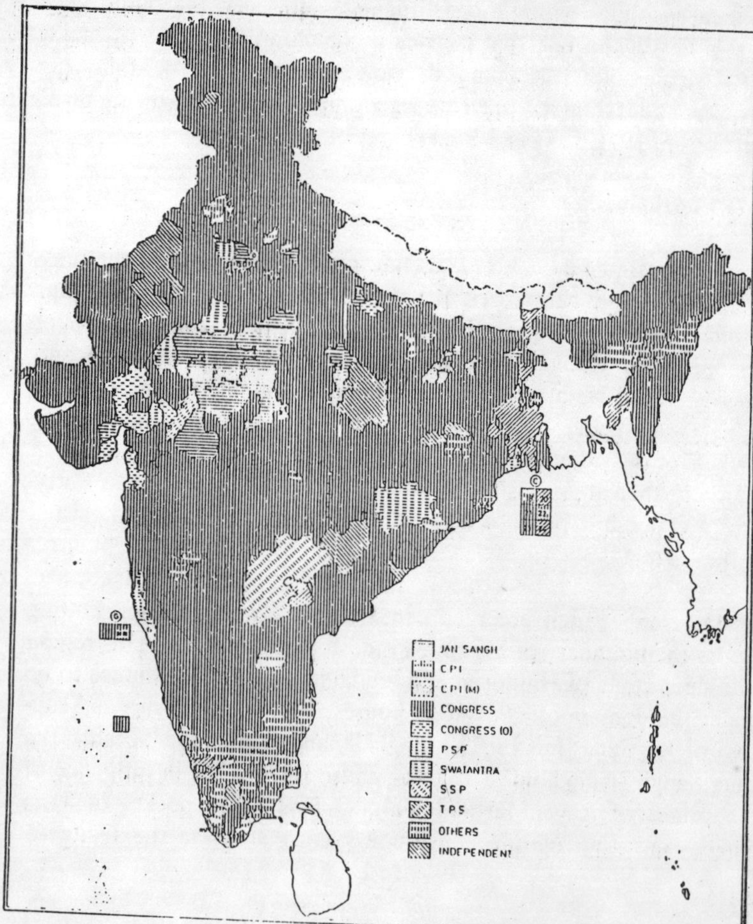

The lower Ganga Plain and Tripura fall under the dominant influence of the CPI(M). Unlike CPI, the party has a strong appeal among the industrial workers and thus its area of influence corresponds mainly with the industrial nodes where there is a strong party organisation. The CPI(M) also has a strong base in Kerala. The 1964 CPI split considerably reduced the prospects of both the Communist Parties. Its lone pocket outside West Bengal, Tripura and Kerala, lay in Andhra Pradesh.

The spatial pattern of the Congress (0) seats was evident enough to support the view that the party was a Gujarat based party. Its failure to project itself as a mass based party led to make it a small party with activities centred around a few personalities; its focus was in Gujarat. Its alone pocket in the deep south in the homeland of Kamraj again illustrates that it was a personality based party. The success of the Swatantra, PSP and SSP, was highly fragmented and was in the form of a few enclaves.

Among the regional parties the Shiromani Akali Dal, Vishal Haryana Party and Bhartiya Kranti Dal had their enclaves of one constituency each in Punjab, Haryana and Uttar Pradesh respectively. The Jharkhand Party had its stronghold in Singbhum, and the Utkal Congress in Kendrapara constituency of Orissa. The Telangana Praja Samiti, which advocated for separate statehood for Telangana region found a strong expression in Telangana sweeping most of the seats in this region. And so was the Dravida Munnetra Kazharam in Tamil Nadu.

1977 Elections

The political landscape in the wake of 1977 elections changed drastically. It seemed that the Indian polity was compartmentalized between the north the south with the Vindhyas largely acting as the dividing line (Fig. 3.5). The emergency was the major or even the sole factor which led to merging of four political parties to form the Janata. The Janata belt extended all over the Hindi heartland, also over parts of Gujarat and Maharashtra in the West and South West, and Orissa in the south-east. In West Bengal, Assam and the south the Janata had pockets of stronghold. The Congress following was mainly in Karnataka, Andhra Pradesh and Assam. Its enclaves were also present in Jammu and Kashmir, Sikkim, Arunachal Pradesh, Manipur, Tripura, Meghalaya, eastern Gujarat, Vidarbha, western Maharashtra, Tamil Nadu and Kerala. In the Hindi belt the party was represented only in two pockets of one constituency each in the states of Madhya Pradesh and Rajasthan. The both Indian islands groups voted the Congress. The CPI(M) influence was confined mainly to southern West Bengal. Besides, the party had 5 other pockets of one constituency each (3 in Maharashtra and one each in Punjab and Orissa). The CPI was represented in 7 constituencies (4 in Kerala and 3 in Tamil Nadu) as pockets in different areas.

The emergent pattern came in response to the history of existence of political parties. The constituents of the Janata Party had their roots only in Hindi speaking areas of the north. Their eagerness to see Hindi as the national language largely acted as a barrier in their expansion to the south. The socialists had their enclaves in Konkan region which returned the Janata. The only constituent which commanded some following in the southern region was the Congress(O) which had a strong base in Tamil Nadu. The Utkal Congress and the Swatantra had a good base in Orissa. The re-emergence of the Congress in Karnataka, Andhra and Assam was due to lack of any organized party in this area. The Congress was benefited in Telangana by the merger of Telangana Praja Samiti.

The emergence of regional parties in many parts of the country indicates the rise of regional forces. The National Conference emerged in the Kashmir valley. The party finds a strong place among the Muslim population which is in overwhelming majority in the valley proper. The Shiromani Akali Dal emerged as the winning party in Punjab. This party which finds a strong place in the Jat-Sikh peasantry, largely because of its emotional demand for a separate state for Sikhs re-emerged after its debacle in 1971. The Jharkhand party (All India) continued to enjoy its stronghold in Singhbhum. The Jharkhand Party with its demand for a separate state for the tribals has been successful in rallying the support of the masses in this area. But more so, its influence was due to its leader Bagun Sumbrui, considered as Messiah of the tribals. Peasants and workers Party (PWP), a peasants organization was represented in 5 constituencies of Maharashtra. Of these 3 were in Marathwada and one in Kolaba. The scene in Tamil Nadu was dominated by Anna

Dravida Munnetra Kazhagam, a splinter group of the DMK having the same ideology but a less rigid attitude towards the question of autonomy. The party was benefited by the serious charges of corruption against the DMK leaders. Besides, a number of other parties were also represented in a few constituencies in different parts of the country (Appendix IC. Fig. 3.5).

Fig. 3.5
India: 1977 Parliamentary Elections: Seats Won by Political Parties

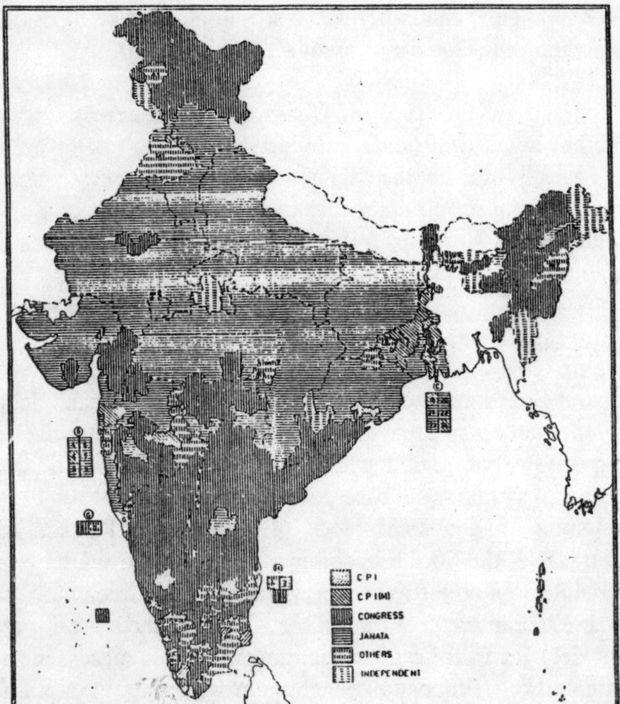

Fig. 3.5

1980 Elections

Power patterns changed once again in 1980 elections. The Congress reemerged as a majority party by gaining what it lost in 1977. But despite its unprecedented victory the party failed to achieve much success in several parts of the country as could be seen from Fig. 3.6. It is evident that Jammu and Kashmir, West Bengal, the north-east, and Kerala remained outside its influence. The situation in Uttar Pradesh and Bihar remained highly fluid. The case of Tamil Nadu is an exception where the party could achieve success with the help of the DMK. This pattern of Congress seats illustrates the nature of the Congress-base in India. If one analyses the event further it becomes clear that wherever a strong alternative to the Congress was present, the Congress candidate was defeated.

The splinter group of the Congress, the Congress(U), could not make any significant dent. The party's gains do not reveal any pattern basically due to the fact that whatever success it achieved, it came in response to personality factor. The success of Karan Singh in Jammu and Kashmir and Y.B. Chavan in Maharashtra illustrate this point.

The Janata was the worst sufferer in this election. The party was more or less, wiped out from the Indian political scene. However, wherever the Janata's constituents had a very strong and deep rooted base, the party was capable of achieving some amount of success. In Udaipur-Gwalior region where the Jana Sangh constituent of the party had a strong mass base due to the influence of princely houses, the Janata, had a solid block of 5 seats. In Konkan region of Maharashtra, the Socialists commanded a very strong base, and thus the Janata was able to win in this region. In Bombay too, the party was able to capture 5 of the six seats. Similar factors were attributed to its victories in Bihar. But the reason for this success in the tribal dominated constituency of Singhbhum was purely the political lead of personality. Bagun Sumbri, the tribal leader of this region, defected to Janata leaving his parent organization- the Jharkhand Party. This helped the Janata. Its lone victory in the south came from the Bangalore constituency in Karnataka.

The spatial pattern of the Janata(S) seats is an expression of a factor which contributed to its gains in certain areas of the north Indian plain. The party has a contiguous pocket in the Western Uttar Pradesh in the area where the Jat peasantry are a significant force. Its another pocket in the eastern Uttar Pradesh further illustrates its mass base. In Bihar the party was represented in 5 constituencies. Rajasthan too returned two of its candidates. The party's only victory outside this region was in Orissa. But this was a personal victory for Biju Patnaik.

The CPI was able to capture much of its lost following in this election. Its major victories were in Bihar. It is significant to note that all these seats were in north Bihar and around the region in which the Janata and Janata(S) find representation. Its pocket in Uttar Pradesh lay in eastern Uttar Pradesh. The party was represented in 3 constituencies of West Bengal, 2 in Kerala and 1 in Manipur. The CPI(M) continued to enjoy its supremacy in West Bengal and Tripura. However, the party was able to expand its influence in Kerala.

Among the regional parties, only those with strong ethno-lingual base were successful. National Conference in Kashmir valley, Jharkhand party in Khunti constituency of Bihar, Sikkim Janata Parishad in Sikkim and Maharashtrawadi Gomantak Party in Panaji (Goa, Daman and Diu) emerged victorious.

Besides these parties, a few other parties had a strong following in some parts of the country. They include Forward Block, Revolutionary Socialist Party, Muslim League and Kerala Congress. The former two find an expression in West Bengal and Kerala while the latter two are represented in Kerala only. However it is important to note that the Muslim League of Kerala is qualitatively different from that of the north India.

The analysis of party victories in all the three elections brings out the fragmented character of Indian polity. It is seen that the major party patterns do not change much over time. The political parties with strong social base continue to enjoy their supremacy. It also reveals that the party following expressed in terms of seats won continues to be fragmented and therefore all parties cease to be the National Parties.

Fig. 3.6
India: 1980 Parliamentary Elections: Seats Won by Political Parties

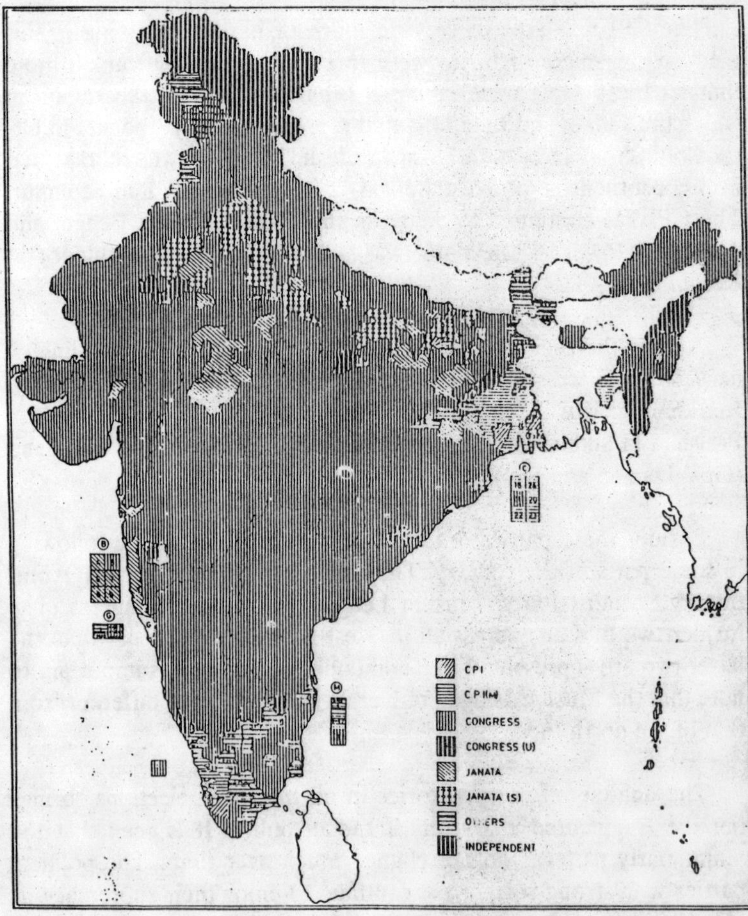

MAJORITY AND MINORITY WINS

Any assessment of party following based on seats won will lead to a possible faulty conclusion because of the peculiar character of Indian elections where a large number of candidates are declared elected with a strikingly low share of valid votes polled in a constituency. In other words, they get elected on the basis of votes which form a minority of the total. The phenomenon is attributable to the multiplicity of electoral contest where a large number of candidates are in the electoral fray and the total votes get shared by them. The winning candidate as such gets only a minor share in the total votes polled. Table 3.4 shows the all India position in this regard in all 3 elections.

TABLE 3.4: SEATS WON BY MAJORITY AND MINORITY VOTES

% of Votes secured by winning candidates to the total votes polled	Number of constituencies		
	1971	1977	1980
0-10 per cent	-	-	-
10-20 per cent	-	-	1
20-30 per cent	9	-	11
30-40 per cent	46	4	86
40-50 per cent	109	62	146
50-60 per cent	179	220	207
60-70 per cent	116	161	68
70-80 per cent	48	83	9
80-90 per cent	10	10	-
Unopposed	1	2	1
Total	518	542	529*

* Excluding 12 constituencies of Assam and 1 constituency of Meghalaya.

It is seen from Table 3.4 that the number of candidates declared elected by minority votes was least in 1977. This was attributed to a sharp decrease in number of contestents. The 1977 elections were distinct for electoral alliances which resulted in direct contest between two main rivals. In 1971, 164 candidates were elected by minority votes. This number swelled to 244 in 1980. This shows the increasing irrationality of Indian elections.

Fig. 3.7
Majority and Minority Wins: 1971, 1977 and 1980

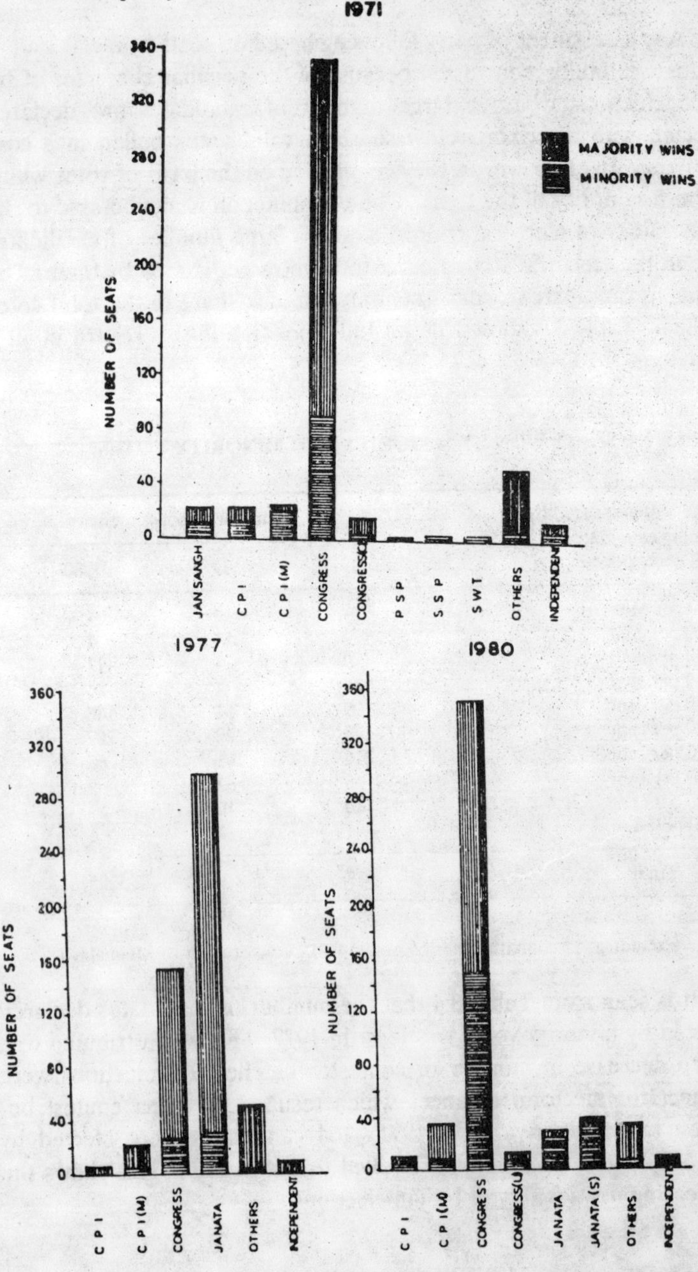

At the state level the distribution of these seats reveals that the highest number of seats (in relation to total seats in state) with minority votes were in West Bengal in 1971 and 1977. But in 1980, Bihar had the distinction of falling in this category. This phenomenon in Bengal is attributed to the keen contest between the two main rivals but in Bihar a large number of aspirants in each constituency contribute to this phenomenon. In 1980, the Bihar state returned 46 out of 54 candidates with minority votes.

Appendices IIA to IIG show the division of seats won by majority and minority votes among the different political parties.

AN OVERVIEW

The spatial analysis of party positions reveals the fragmented character of the Indian polity. It is observed that despite the big majorities commanded by the ruling parties in the three Parliamentary elections of 1971, 1977 and 1980, their areas of influence remained restricted. In this perspective, all these major parties cease to be termed as National parties irrespective of the Election Commission's recognition in this direction.[16] The analysis indicates that the peripheral areas of the Indian Union continue to be dominated by political forces other than those ruling at the centre.

The analysis exposes the irrational character of the Indian elections. It is noted that a large number of candidates get elected by strikingly low share of votes. This phenomenon is attributable to the multiplicity of electoral contest where a large number of candidates are in the electoral fray and the total votes are shared by them. The winning candidate as such gets only a minority share in the total votes polled.

NOTES AND REFERENCES

1. M.A. Busteed, *Geography and Voting Behaviour* (London : Oxford, 1975), p. 25.
2. Electoral campaign during the last General Elections has proved this point beyond any doubt.During the 1977 elections, the Janata's capacity to capitalize the issues of emergency led to its victory. While in 1980 elections, the Congress(I)'s capacity to harp upon the issue of "non-performance of the Janata Government" yielded good results.
3. This point is well illustrated by the mass following of the National Conference.

The party has an overwhelming following in the Kashmir valley which is a Muslim majority area. But in Jammu region the party's base is comparatively weak.

4. Norman D. Palmer, *Elections and Political Development* - The South Asian Experience (New Delhi : Vikas, 1976), p. 281.
5. M.N. Srinivas, *Report of the Seminar on Casteism and Removal of Untouchability* (1965), p. 137.
6. Salig S. Harrison, "Caste and the Andhra Communists", *The American Political Science Review*, Vol. 50, June 1956, pp. 378-404.
7. Myron Weiner, *Party Building in a New Nation - The Indian National Congress* (Chicago : University of Chicago Press, 1967), pp. 11-13.
8. Hereafter the Congress refers to the Congress(R) in 1971; the Congress in 1977 and the Congress(I) in 1980.
9. The constituent parties of the Bhartiya Lok Dal were the Bhartiya Kranti Dal, Swatantra Party, Utkal Congress, Samyukta Socialist Party, Rashtriya Lok Tantrik Dal, Kisan Mazdoor Party and Punjab Khetihari Majdoor Union.
10. The Congress(U) was formed by another split in the Congress Party in January 1978 on the question of leadership. A faction of the Congress Party which was opposed to the then leadership of the Congress Party and was critical of the emergency policies and programmes left the party and formed Congress(S). Later it was renamed as Congress(U) when Mr. Dev Raj Urs became its president.
11. S.N. Sadasivan, *Party and Democracy in India* (New Delhi : Tata McGraw-Hill Publishing Company Ltd., 1977).
12. Shyama Prasad Mookerjee, "Why Bharti‸a Jana Sangh," *Presidential Address to the Opening Convention of Akhil Bhar‸ya Jan Sangh* (Delhi : Delhi Bharat Mudranalaya, 1951), p. 4.
13 S.N. Sadasivan, *op.cit.*, p. 172.
14. M. Kinnear, *The British Voter : An Atlas and Survey Since 1885* (London : Batsford, 1968).
15 M.A. Busteed, *op.cit*, p. 27.
16. The Election Commission emphasised the need urged to change the norms for the recognition of the National parties. It has proposed that to be called a National Party, a party should have representation in half of the states and should secure more than 10 per cent of valid votes. At present if a party secures at least four per cent votes in not less than four states it is entitled to be recognized as a National party. "Parties' Recognition Norms May Change," *The Hindustan Times*, July 25, 1981.

FOUR

VOTES SECURED : SPATIAL PATTERNING OF PARTY FOLLOWING

The winning of seats by a particular party does not indicate its real strength. This is established in the preceding chapter which revealed that a large number of candidates get elected by securing a small fraction of the valid votes polled. A more rational way of analysing the party strength is, therefore, to analyse the percentage share of votes polled by a political party. The percentage share of votes polled by a party is indicative of its voting strength in relation to the other contestants in the field. A high share of votes would imply that the party holds a strong position in relation to other contestants. In this chapter an attempt has been made to analyse this aspect.

The analysis of party following is a significant aspect of electoral studies because it is through political parties that the masses not only come closer to the political system but also the political parties come to terms with the political realities at the grass root level. The election thus 'initiate a process of creative interaction between the political parties and the people.'[1] This process of interaction, which is shaped by the ideological framework of the political parties, is the very basis of the existence of political parties in modern democracies. In the Indian context where the polity is characterized by a 'low level of social integration' the political parties act as 'mediating agencies between the largely traditional and politically diffused electorate and the modern state system.'[2]

Elections afford an opporunity to the political parties to assess the real strength of their mass base and thus check the acceptability of their programmes by the electorate. But in a society, such as India's where the level of political consciousness is, by and large, of a low order, the programmes of political parties carry little meaning for the electorate and thus remain mostly ritualistic. They are meant for consumption among the educated sections of the electorate and the intelligentia. In fact, the programmes are very often meant as propaganda, with little or no intention towards implementation. The illiterate electorate soon gets disillusioned by such election manifestos. In the absence of a well-spelt out programme it is the impact of the more articulate pressure-groups which matters in the process of decision making. The multiplicity of political parties and a large number of the so-called 'independent' candidates in the electoral fray in India is an illustration of this phemomenon. Evidently, it discourages the process of polarization of political forces.

The territorial extent of the mass base of a political party is an inherent phenomenon in all democracies. This is a function of its capacity to wield influence on the people and widen its social base for which it has to influence, shape or accept the social preferences and social claims.[3] The capacity to have a strong base depends upon the way the agents of a viable party interact with the masses over a considerable period of time. It is on the basis of this interaction that the parties build their image. In India, this process of interaction is more or less conscpicuous by its absence and, therefore, there are very few parties which have succeeded in building their mass base with stability.

PARTY STRENGTH IN STATES

It is interesting to note the overall position of the various political parties in terms of their share in valid votes polled. It reveals a big discrepancy between the percentage share of votes polled and seats won (Fig. 4.1, Table 4.1).

It is evident from Table 4.1 that the party with majority of the seats in the Parliament was elected with minority of votes. At no time did the ruling party secure majority of votes. On the other hand, the other parties polled more votes than seats won. E.P.W. da

Costa conceptualized this relation of seats won to votes polled as a 'multiplier'[4] which has always worked in favour of the majority party. It is also evident from Table 4.1 that the strength of the majority party fluctuated around plus or minus 43 per cent of valid votes. However, there are marked variations from state to state (Appendix IIIA).

TABLE 4.1 PERCENTAGE OF VALID VOTES POLLED AND SEATS WON BY POLITICAL PARTIES : ALL INDIA PATTERN

	1971		1977		1980	
	% votes polled	% seats won	% votes polled	% seats won	% votes polled	% seats won
Bhartiya Jana Sangh	7.36	4.25	-	-	-	-
CPI	4.73	4.44	2.82	1.29	2.59	2.07
CPI (M)	5.12	4.83	4.30	4.06	6.14	6.80
Congress	43.68	67.95	34.52	28.41	42.69	66.72
Congress (O)	10.42	3.09	-	-	-	-
Congress (U)	-	-	-	-	5.28	2.45
Janata	27.23*	-	43.04	54.98	18.95	5.86
Janata (S)	-	-	-	-	9.41	7.75
PSP	1.04	0.39	-	-	-	-
SSP	2.42	0.58	-	-	-	-
Swatantra	3.07	1.54	-	-	-	-
State and Registered Parties	13.48	10.23	9.83	9.59	7.62	6.61
Independents	8.37	2.70	5.50	1.66	7.35	1.70

* derived from votes polled by the Janata's constituents.

The difference between percentage of seats won and percentage of votes polled by political parties are more pronounced at the state level (Table 4.2). It is evident from Table 4.2 that the Janata Party secured 100 per cent seats in Uttar Pradesh in 1977 by polling 68.08 per cent votes. Similary the Congress' share of votes in Andhra Pradesh during 1980 elections was just 56.24 per cent despite 97.61 per cent seats at its command. The Congress Party in Uttar Pradesh could not win a single seat in 1977 even after securing 24.99 per cent votes. It reveals that a party which secures majority of seats in a state always polls less per cent of votes.

Fig. 4.1
Seats-Votes Variations: 1971, 1977 and 1980

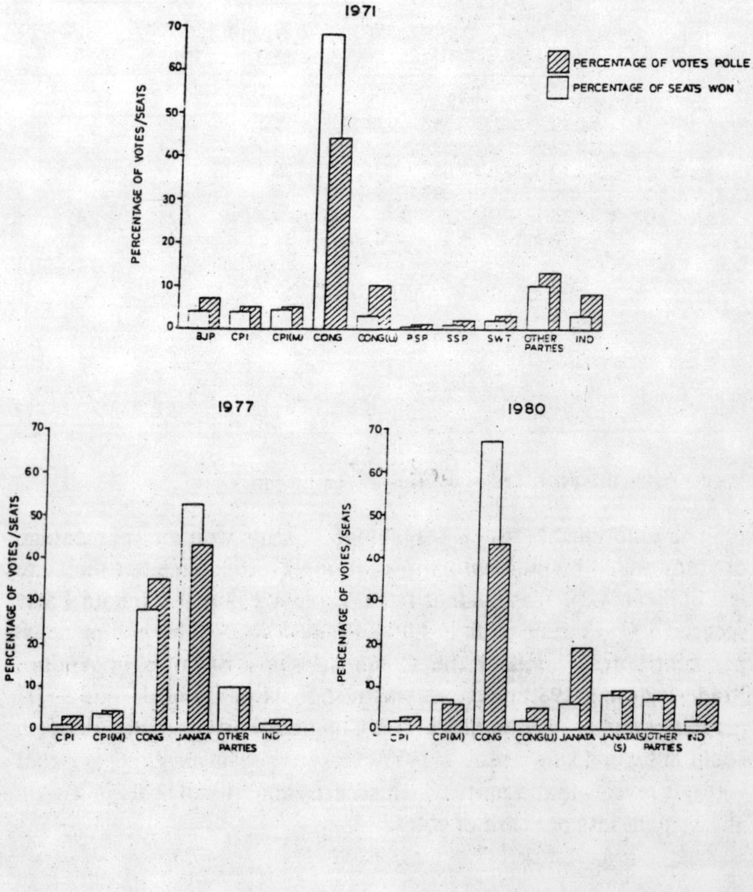

TABLE 4.2 : VOTES-SEATS VARIATIONS, SELECTED STATES

Party	1971		1977		1980	
	%votes polled	%seats won	%votes polled	%seats won	%votes polled	%seats won
			ANDHRA PRADESH			
CPI	5.94	2.93	2.67	-	3.68	-
CPI (M)	2.82	2.43	4.72	-	3.56	-
CONG	53.73	68.29	57.36	97.61	56.24	97.61
JNP	12.00	NA	32.33	2.38	15.23	-
			BIHAR			
CPI	9.85	9.43	5.63	-	7.29	7.40
CPI (M)	0.76	-	0.20	-	0.94	-
CONG	40.06	73.58	22.90	-	36.44	55.55
JPN	35.39	NA	64.98	96.29	23.55	14.81
JPN (S)	-	-	-	-	16.59	9.25
			MADHYA PRADESH			
BJS	33.56	30.55		-	-	
CONG	45.60	58.33	32.47	2.50	47.20	87.50
JNP	38.18	-	57.90	92.50	31.30	10.00
			MAHARASHTRA			
CPI	1.91	-	0.67	-	0.50	-
CPI (M)	0.48	-	3.56	-	1.36	6.25
CONG	63.18	93.33	47.02	41.66	53.30	81.25
JNP	12.74	-	31.39	39.58	20.42	16.66
			TAMIL NADU			
CPI	5.43	10.25	4.60	7.69	3.59	-
CPI(M)	1.64	-	1.56	-	3.21	-
CONG	12.51	23.07	22.27	35.89	31.62	51.28
JNP	40.62	-	17.78	7.69	7.96	-
DMK	35.25	58.97	18.06	2.56	23.01	41.02
ADK	-	-	30.59	46.13	25.38	5.12
			UTTAR PRADESH			
CPI	3.70	4.70	1.10	-	1.63	1.17
CPI (M)	0.19	-	0.10	-	0.10	-
CONG	48.56	85.88	24.99	-	35.90	60.00
JNP	38.09	-	68.08	100.00	22.57	3.52
JNP (S)	-	-	-	-	29.02	34.11
			WEST BENGAL			
CPI	10.56	0.75	6.49	-	4.28	7.14
CPI (M)	34.30	50.00	26.15	40.47	39.91	66.66
CONG	28.23	32.50	29.37	7.14	36.51	9.52
JNP	10.00	-	21.46	35.71	4.53	-

Jana Sangh

The Jana Sangh secured 7.36 per cent votes at all India level in 1971. However, its share was as high as 33.56 per cent in Madhya Pradesh and as low as 0.73 per cent in the Union Territory of Goa, Daman and Diu (Appendix IIIA). Its performance was above the national average in the states of Bihar, Haryana, Himachal Pradesh, Jammu and Kashmir, Rajasthan, Uttar Pradesh and Union Territories of Chandigarh and Delhi.

Communist Parties

The CPI's best performance was in Manipur in all the three elections. Kerala followed the pattern in 1971 and 1977, but in 1980, Bihar showed the second best performance in regard to the CPI. The CPI(M) scored its high success in Tripura followed by West Bengal and Kerala in all the three elections (Appendix III-A). In other states the party commanded very little influence.

Congress Party

The Congress party does not reveal consistent pattern in its following. In 1971 it secured 43.42 per cent of votes at all India level but its best success was in Karnataka where it annexed 70.87 per cent of valid votes. On the other hand it could poll just 12.51 per cent of votes in Tamil Nadu. The Congress suffered a set back in 1977 elections and its share in total votes declined to 34.52 per cent. It achieved highest amount of success in Union Territory of Lakshad weep followed by Andaman and Nicobar Islands, Andhra Pradesh and Karnataka. Its worst performance was in Jammu and Kashmir. The Congress' share in valid votes rose to 42.69 per cent in 1980 elections. However their exists a high degree of variation among the states. It achieved the highest amount of sucess in the state of Meghalaya followed by Pondicherry. Its worst performance was in Goa,Daman and Diu. The states in which its performance was above the all India average include Andhra Pradesh, Assam, Gujarat, Himachal Pradesh, Karnataka, Maharashtra, Manipur, Orissa, Punjab and Union Terriotories of Andaman and Nicobar Islands, Arunachal Pradesh, Chandigarh, Dadra and Nagar Haveli and Delhi. This reveals that in Hindi speaking states its performance in terms of valid votes polled was below the national average.

Congress(O) and Congress(U)

The Congress(O) secured 10.42 per cent of votes in the 1971 elections at all India level. It achieved the highest success in Gujarat, securing 39.70 per cent of votes. The Congress(U) could poll just 5.28 per cent of votes in 1980. However, it secured as much as 56.37 per cent votes in the union territory of Lakshadweep. This is an enough proof to suggest that both the splinter groups of the Congress party which came into existence in 1969 and 1978 were denuded of their political strength.

Janata Party

The Janata Party which came into existence at the eve of the 1977 elections polled 43.04 per cent votes at all India level. If one adds the votes polled by the Janata's constituents in 1971 elections, it becomes evident that the party registered an increase of 15.81 per cent over its 1971 performance. This reveals that despite its overwhelming victory, the party could not widen its mass following. The point which emerges is that unity among political parties in elections is capable enough to change the political equations. This polarisation also reduces the chances to win with a minority votes. The analysis of majority and minority wins illustrated this point.

The share of Janata in total valid votes varied significantly from state to state (Appendix IIIA). In 1977 its highest success came from Haryana with 70.35 per cent votes to its credit. In the other 3 Hindi speaking states of Bihar, Rajasthan and Uttar Pradesh it secured more than 60 per cent of votes. The Union Territories of Chandigarh and Delhi too fall in this category. In Madhya Pradesh its share was 57.90 per cent. The worst performance of the Janata was in Kerala where the party's share was just 7.20 per cent. This small share of votes was attributed mainly to the fact than it contested only 3 seats out of 20, leaving others to its allies. This probably indicates that the Janata was a party of northern-Hindi-speaking states.

The Janata party suffered a setback in 1980 elections. Its votes declined to 18.95 per cent. The highest share of 39.78 per cent was in Lakshadweep followed by Delhi, Gujarat and Himachal Pradesh. It could secure just 0.97 per cent of votes in Tripura. The states in which its performance was above the national average were Bihar, Haryana, Himachal Pradesh, Gujarat, Karnataka, Madhya Pradesh, Maharashtra, Rajasthan, Uttar Pradesh, Delhi, Lakshadweep and Pondicherry.

The analysis of the Janata votes reveals its variegated mass base. At no point of time has the party commanded a uniform following. Its area of influence broadly correspond with north-centric ideology of the Janata's constitutent groups, particularly the Jana Sangh, which had an appeal in this region. This appeal has no place in the south and the Indian periphery.

The Janata(S) which came into existence in the wake of Janata's split in July 1979 polled 9.41 per cent of total votes. However, it achieved a significant success in Haryana and Uttar pradesh by securing 33.52 and 29.02 per cent votes respectively. In Orissa and Bihar its tally was 19.60 and 16.59 per cent. Its worst performance was in Tamil Nadu, Andaman and Nicobar Islands and Chandigarh where its share was less than 1 per cent. This indicates that the party's main following lay in Uttar Pradesh and Haryana. Probably, this was due to a comparatively high proportion of Jat population in these two states.[5]

Socialists and Swatantra party

The socialists commanded a very little influence which is evident from the fact that the PSP and SSP secured 1.04 and 2.42 per cent votes respectively in 1971. However, the SSP commanded a sizeable following in Bihar (9.47 per cent votes in 1971). The Swatantra Party faired comparatively bettter (3.07 per cent votes). Its following was mainly in Orissa and Rajasthan where it polled 15.91 and 14.65 per cent votes respectively in 1971.

Regional Parties

Besides, a number of regional parties have flourished in India in the regions where the ethnic, cultural or religious forces find a strong place. Generally speaking the areas where regional parties are the strongest are along the Indian periphery. The states where they are strong include Jammu and Kashmir (National Conference), Punjab (Shiromani Akali Dal), Tamil Nadu (DMK and ADMK) and Goa, Daman and Diu (Maharashtrawadi Gomantak Party). A number of tribal parties flourish in the northeast.

Despite the fact that these parties have a definite social base their strength in terms of votes polled by them has varied over time depending on the national political situation. It is observed that whenever the forces of national integration become weak, the regional parties get a new lease of life. However, some of these parties have emerged as strong forces even when the nationalist forces were strong. The state of Tamil Nadu falls in this category. There were certain political parties which emerged at a particular time and suddenly disappeared from the political scene either by self disintegration or by merger with other parties. The Bhartiya Kranti Dal, Telangana Praja Samiti, Telangana Congress, Utkal Congress etc. fall in this category. Basically there are four regional parties which command a sizeable following. They are National Conference, Akali Dal, Dravida Munnetra Kazhagam and Anna Dravida Munnetra Kazhagam.

The National Conference reemerged on Indian political scene in 1977 Lok Sabha elections. Despite its alliance with Congress, it polled 33.92 and 36.88 per cent votes in 1977 and 1980 respectively. The Akali Dal has seen ups and downs in its following. Its tally of 30.85 per cent in 1971 rose to 42.30 per cent in 1977. But again it came down to 23.37 per cent in 1980. The DMK commanded a share of 35.25 per cent in Tamil Nadu in 1971. But in the wake of the party split in the subsequent period its votes declined to merely 18.06 per cent in 1977. But once again it improved its position in 1980 by securing 23.01 per cent of votes. The ADMK emerged as the significant political forces in Tamil Nadu in 1977 by securing 30.59 per cent of votes. However, the party failed to maintain its projected image in national politics and therefore suffered a set back in 1980 elections. This is seen from its share in votes which declined to 25.30 per cent.

The success of these parties in their respective states is due firstly, to their well defined social base and secondly, to their capacity to project themselves as the champion of the cause of their regional community. Therefore, while the Akali Dal enjoys the support of Jat Sikh peasantry in Punjab, National Conference to a great extent banks upon the muslim votes in the Kashmir valley and the DMK and ADMK find a place in upper non-Brahmin castes of Tamil Nadu. The performance of other parties is presented in Appendices IIIB, IIIc and IIID.

Summing Up

The analysis of party strength in states reflects the nature of mass base of Indian political parties. It is evident that even the majority party in parliament did not have the support of the majority of the people. Although, this phenomenon is attributed to multiplicity of contest, the unidentified social base of most of the parties further adds to this situation. The only exception to this phenomenon are the communist parties to some extent. The analysis further supports the view that no political party is capable of being giving the status of 'National Party' in true sense of the term. The broad regional patterning of the party votes indicates that the parties' main strength lay in specific areas of the country. The distinct feature of political behaviour of the north, the south and the periphery is brought out by this analysis.

THE GEOGRAPHIC PATTERNING OF PARTY FOLLOWING

The state level patterns of the party following do not really throw much light on the territorial strength of political parties. All the areas within a state do not respond uniformly to a political party and thus have variegated pattern in regard to party support. Generally speaking the organization of social forces in an area plays a significant role in determining the support of a political party but the factors like the perception of the local people about the party performance also play an important role. Considering the fact that the social composition of the India's population differs significantly from area to area and the image of a party also varies in accordance with the local environment, the party following continues to be highly fragmented. There is not even a single party which commanded a uniform support in any state over a period of time. However, the regional parties have less fragmented mass following because their social base has a limited geographical contiguity. It is in regard to these factors that an attempt has been made to identify the territorial hold of political parties in terms of percentage valid votes polled by them.

Bhartiya Jana Sangh

The Bhartiya Jana Sangh - a strongly religion oriented organization - remained a party of the north only and had no roots in the south.[6] However, its mass base was highly variegated in the constituencies of India. Table 4.3 shows its strength in different constituencies in 1971 elections.

TABLE 4.3 : NUMBER OF CONSTITUENCIES CLASSIFIED BY VOTING STRENGTH, BHARTIYA JANA SANGH

Percentage of votes polled	Number of constitutencies
Above 70 per cent	-
50 to 70 per cent	11
30 to 50 per cent	47
10 to 30 per cent	77
Below 10 per cent	22
Total	157

It is evident that the party had a majority following only in 11 constituencies out of which 8 were in Madhya Pradesh and 3 in Rajasthan. The distribution of these constituencies reveals that they form a strong pocket in the Udaipur-Gwalior region cutting across the boundary of Madhya Pradesh and Rajasthan. The party secured 30 to 50 per cent of votes in 47 constituencies out of which 29 were in Madhya Pradesh and Uttar Pradesh. The remaining 18 constituencies were in Bihar (8), Haryana(2), Maharashtra (2), Rajasthan (2) and Delhi (4). This is a reflection of the party's mass following. The distribution of other constituencies in order of voting strength is presented in Appendix IVA.

Communist Parties

Traditionally the Communist Parties have commanded a strong following in West Bengal,[7] Tamil Nadu, Kerala,[8] and Andhra Pradesh.[9] However, the contemporary evidence in the form of election statistics reveals that the Communist Parties have expanded their following outside the traditional strongholds. It is seen that the parties command a sizeable base in industrial townships and the areas of peasants' unrest.

While in industrial townships they have widened their following through the network of trade union, in the regions of peasant unrest they have penetrated by taking the cause of the agricultural labourers. It is through the latter that they have also a sizeable following in parts of Bihar, Punjab, Uttar Pradesh and Tamil Nadu. However, the 1964 split in the Communist Party has considerably affected the Communist following. In the following paragraphs an attempt has been made to assess their mass following in the three elections of 1971, 1977 and 1980.

(a) Communist Party of India (CPI)

The CPI could not emerge as a significant political force in any part of the country despite its cooperation with the ruling Congress for quite some time.This fact is brought out by Table 4.4 which shows its strength in different constituencies during the three elections.

TABLE 4.4 : NUMBER OF CONSTITUENCIES CLASSIFIED BY VOTING STRENGTH, COMMUNIST PARTY OF INDIA

Percentage of votes polled	Number of constituencies		
	1971	1977	1980
Above 70 per cent	-	-	-
50 to 70 per cent	11	7	5
30 to 50 per cent	21	6	13
10 to 30 per cent	37	33	10
Below to per cent	18	45	10

It is evident from Table 4.4 that the party secured less than 30 per cent votes in more than half of the constituencies in all the three elections. It could secure above 50 per cent votes only in eleven constituencies in 1971, out of which 3 were inTamil Nadu, two each in Bihar, Kerala, and Uttar Pradesh and one each in Andhra Pradesh and Punjab. The spatial pattern of these constituencies (Fig. 4.2, Appendix IVB) reveals that they form separate pockets. Out of 21 constituencies in which the party secured 30 to 50 per cent of votes, 12 were in West Bengal and Bihar. These constituencies in West Bengal were located in southern part around the Calcutta metropolis. There are two other contiguous pockets of constituencies in which the party's strength was between 10 and 30 per cent. One of these pockets lay in the Assam valley and the other in

Fig. 4.2
India: 1971 Parliamentary Elections: Spatial Pattern of Party Votes - Communist Party of India

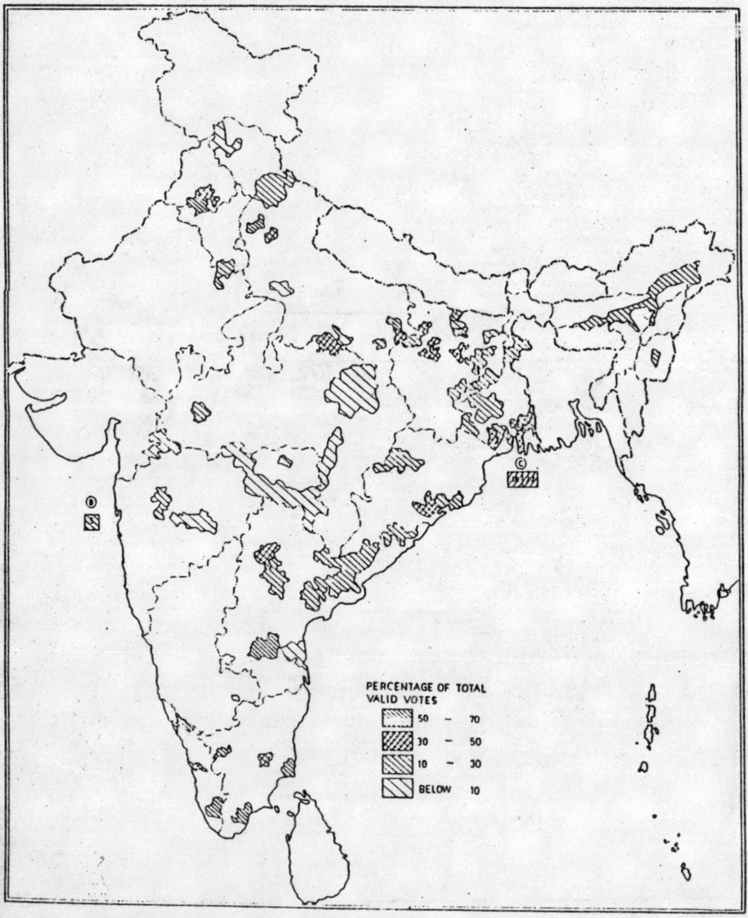

Fig. 4.3
India: 1977 Parliamentary Elections: Spatial Pattern of Party Votes - Communist Party of India

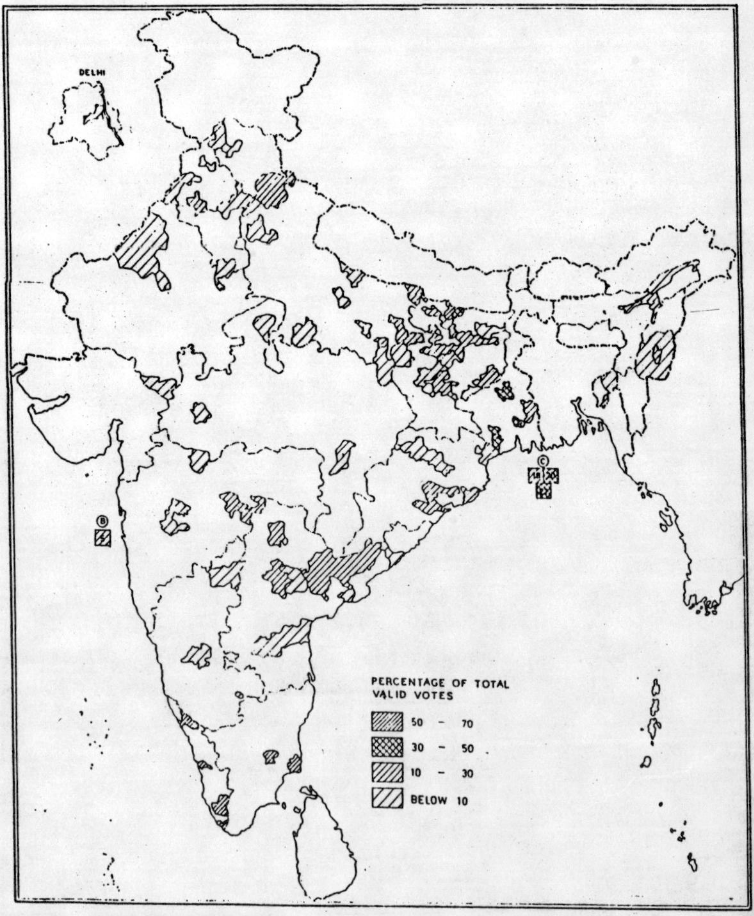

Andhra Pradesh. The distribution of these constituencies in Bihar and Bengal reveals that they are mainly in the areas of coal mines. The constituencies in which the party's voting strength was negligible lay in Andhra Pradesh (1), Bihar (2), Himachal Pradesh (1), Karnataka (1), Madhya Pradesh (3), Maharashtra (6), Tripura (2) and Uttar Pradesh (2). Barring Andhra Pradesh and Bihar all these states never gave a sizeable support to the Communist parties. The failure of the Communist Parties to create a conducive atmosphere for their expansion in these states lay in the organization of the social forces which are opposed to Marxist ideology.

The mass base of the CPI was eroded considerably in the 1977 elections which is evident from the fact that the party could secure more than 50 per cent votes in only 7 constituencies (4 in Kerala and 3 in Tamil Nadu) and its share remained less than 10 per cent in as many as 45 constituencies. Only 6 constituencies were in the category of 30 to 50 per cent. The spatial pattern of its following (Fig. 4.3, Appendix IVB) reveals that the party had a highly fragmented mass base. There were only two contiguous pockets in which it secured 10 to 30 per cent of votes. The first one lay in north Bihar and the second in Telangana.

The CPI was able to rebuild its following in the 1980 elections. It was able to secure 50 to 70 per cent votes in 5 constituencies out of 48 contested. Two of these were in Kerala and 3 in West Bengal. In another 13 constituencies the party's share was between 30 and 50 per cent. Of these 6 were in north Bihar, two in eastern Uttar Pradesh, one each in Andhra Pradesh and Kerala and three in Tamil Nadu (Appendix IVB). There are two contiguous pockets of the constituencies in which the party's strength was between 10 and 30 per cent (Fig. 4.4). The one pocket lay in the coal belt of Bihar and the second in the Telengana region. Constituencies of negligible following (even less than 10 per cent of votes) were in Himachal Pradesh (I), Madhya Pradesh (3) Bihar (1), Meghlaya (1), Gujarat (1), Maharashtra (1), Karnataka (1) and Delhi (1).

The spatial analysis of the party's following reveals that its main base lay in Bengal, Bihar and Kerala. However, its following remained highly fragmented as the areas of party following formed separate enclaves.

Fig. 4.4
India: 1980 Parliamentary Elections: Spatial Pattern of Party Votes - Communist Party of India

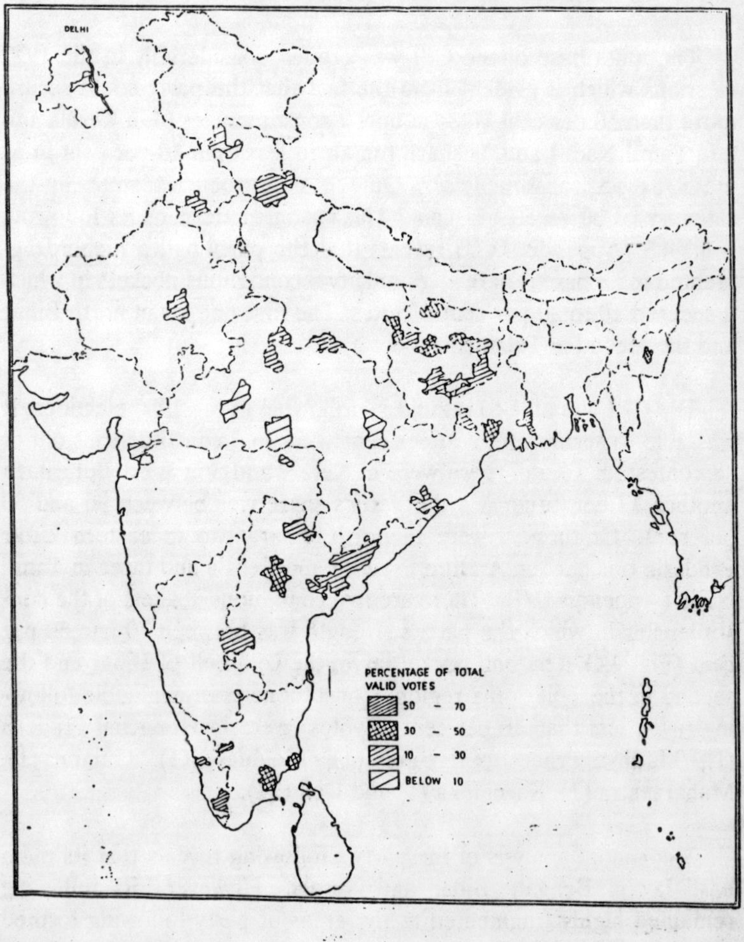

(b) Communist Party of India (Marxist)

Although the CPI(M) commanded a comparatively stronger following, its mass base was narrower than the CPI. This was basically because the party operates mainly through the network of trade unions and has very little impact in the agrarian regions of the north. Table 4.5 shows its voting strength in different constituencies during the elections of 1971, 1977 and 1980.

TABLE 4.5 : CONSTITUENCIES CLASSIFIED BY VOTING STRENGTH, COMMUNIST PARTY OF INDIA (MARXIST)

Percentage of votes polled	Number of constituencies		
	1971	1977	1980
Above 70 per cent	-	1	-
50 to 70 per cent	5	16	28
30 to 50 per cent	32	25	18
10 to 30 per cent	30	2	10
Less than 10 per cent	18	9	6
Total Contested	85	53	62*

*Excluding two constituencies in Assam.

The CPI(M) has improved its position over time. This is brought out by Table 4.5 which shows that the number of constituencies with high voting strength has gone up. The spatial pattern of the party votes in 1971 (Fig. 4.5) reveals that out of 5 constituencies of high voting strength 4 were in West Bengal and one in Kerala. All the constituencies in West Bengal were in the zone of industrial concentration. The constituencies with a voting strength between 30 and 50 per cent form a contiguous belt in West Bengal as well as in Kerala. In West Bengal they incorporate the whole of the central part while in Kerala they formed a long belt. Both the constituencies of Tripura fell in this category (Appendix IVC). There was only one more constituency in this category which lay in Telangana. In West Bengal constituencies with voting strengths between 10 and 30 per cent encircle the zone of high voting strength. The region corresponds with areas where agriculture is the main economic activity. Except one constituency each in Bihar and Punjab,the party polled less than 10 per cent votes in all the constituencies in the north.

Fig. 4.5
India: 1971 Parliamentary Elections: Spatial Pattern of Party Votes - Communist Party of India (Marxist)

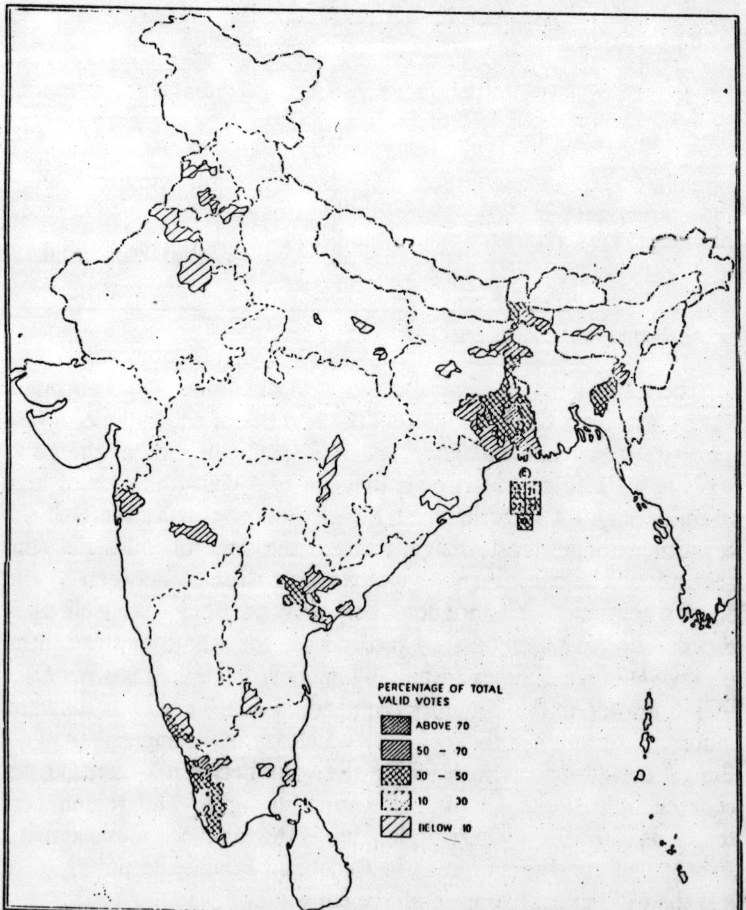

Fig. 4.6
India: 1977 Parliamentary Elections: Spatial Pattern of Party Votes - Communist Party of India (Marxist)

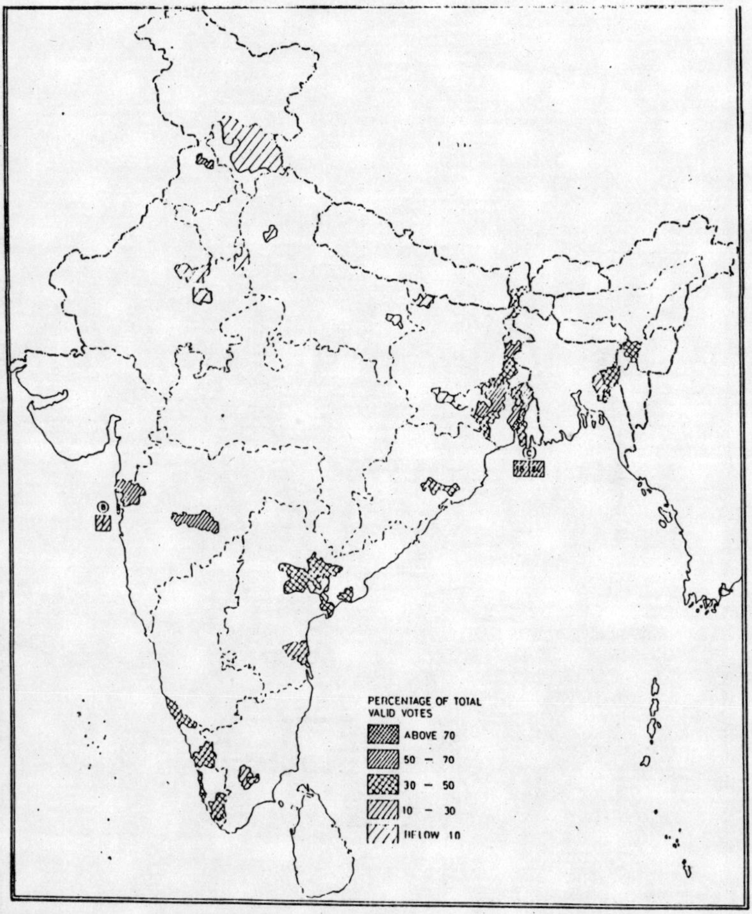

Fig. 4.7
India: 1980 Parliamentary Elections: Spatial Pattern of Party Votes - Communist Party of India (Marxist)

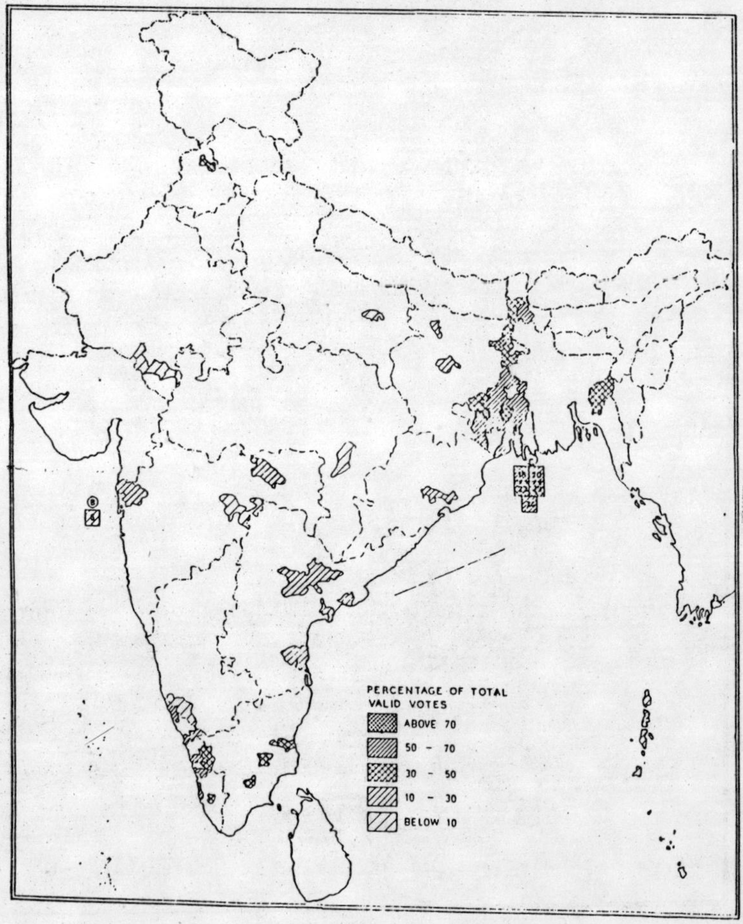

In 1977 elections the party was able to secure above 70 per cent votes in one constituency of West Bengal. It's share was between 50 and 70 per cent in as many as 16 constituencies. Of these, 12 were in West Bengal,3 in Maharashtra and one in Punjab (Appendix IVC). Its better performance in Maharashtra and Punjab was mainly due to the support it received from the parties like Janata in the wake of electoral adjustments. The spatial pattern of these constituencies (Fig. 4.6) reveals that in West Bengal they form two clusters. The party emerged as a significant force in Telangana by securing 30 to 50 per cent votes in 4 constituencies. In Kerala, the constituencies of this category lay divided in 4 pockets. Only in two constituencies its strength varied between 10 and 30 per cent (one each in Tripura and Tamil Nadu). In all the constituencies of Himachal Pradesh, Rajasthan, Uttar Pradesh and Bihar its share was less than 10 per cent.

The CPI(M) further improved its position in the 1980 elections by securing 50 to 70 per cent votes in as many as 28 constitutencies of which 23 were in West Bengal and 5 in Kerala (Appendix IVC). The spatial pattern of these constituencies (Fig. 4.7) reveals that in West Bengal, except for one constituency in the north, all form a single block encompassing most part of southern Bengal. This indicates that with the passage of time the party has been able to infiltrate into the rural areas of the state. However, in Kerala they are represented in 5 isolated pockets. Except one constituency of Punjab where its share was between 30 and 50 per cent, all constituencies in this category were in Kerala and West Bengal. In the remaining constituencies of all the states, it secured below 30 per cent votes.

This analysis indicates that the CPI(M) commands a sizeable following only in West Bengal, Tripura and Kerala. However, in terms of territorial expansion, its hold is extensive only in West Bengal. But with its increasing hold in West Bengal, its base has further narrowed down in other states except Tripura and Kerala.

Congress Party

The success of the Congress Party lay in the role it played in the country's freedom struggle. It is for this role that the party was not considered, initially, as a political organization but as a National Movement. The credit for the formation of the Congress goes to Allen Octavian Hume, who, highly perturbed by the miserable conditions of the people due to colonial oppression, conceived necessity of a National Union. But viewing the nature of the Sanskrit knowing Hindu Orthodox who believed in self isolation and the English oriented masses, too eager to seek employment in subordinate services, Hume thought that "if only fifty men, good and true can be found to join as founders, the thing can be established and the further development will be comparatively easy."[10] His wishes were fulfilled when at 12 noon on December 28, 1885, the First National Congress met at Gokul Das Tejpal Sanskrit College, Bombay. The first voices heard were those of A.O. Hume, S. Subrahmania Aiyer and K.T. Telang who proposed, seconded and supported the election of the first president-W.C. Banerjee.

However, the Congress remained as a party of bourgeoisie interest when it was used by middle class educated persons to solve their grievances. It was only after 1899 that it started working as a political organization with the objective of attaining Independence. It emerged as an all-embracing mass organization accommodating all sections of society from capitalists to communists, feudalists to socialists, reactionaries to revolutionaries and from conservative to radical. In view of its umbrella character it was considered as having no parallels in the world and representing every conceivable interest and type of personality.[11]

This character of the organization which continued even after Independence, forced the party to develop an ideology which was federal, flexible and non-conformist. [12] It is in response to this factor that the party emerged as an all-embracing political entity. As long as there was no shift from this basic character, the party performed well. But when the leadership of the party failed to accommodate the varying interests in the party it was challenged by emergent political forces. The electoral data of the last 3 elections provide enough testimony. Table 4.6 shows its performance in different constituencies of India.

1971 Elections : It is evident from Table 4.6 that the Congress Party had a highly variegated mass base in the country. The party secured majority votes in 261 constituencies in 1971. In 54 constituencies its share was more than 70 per cent. Of these 41 were in 3 states of

TABLE 4.6 : CONSTITUENCIES CLASSIFIED BY VOTING STRENGTH, CONGRESS PARY

Percentage of votes polled	Number of constituencies		
	1971	1977	1980
Unopposed	1	2	-
Above 70 per cent	54	7	7
50 to 70 per cent	207	120	197
30 to 50 per cent	154	197	239
10 to 30 per cent	25	162	45
Below 10 per cent	-	4	1
Total	441	492	489*

* Excluding 2 constituencies of Assam and 1 constituency of Meghalaya.

Andhra Pradesh, Karnataka and Maharashtra (Appendix IVD). The spatial pattern of party votes (Fig. 4.8) reveals that the constituencies with above 70 per cent of votes in Andhra Pradesh were mainly in coastal areas. This area, where the Kammas are a significant force, was a strong Communist hold. But with the split in the Communist Party and with increasing representation of Kammas in the Congress, the area has become a strong Congress hold. In Karnataka, the constituencies of this category form a contiguous pocket in the southern part which corresponds mainly with the old Mysore state. In Maharashtra the constituencies of this category form two pockets lying in Western Maharashtra and the Vidarbha.

The Congress emerged as a majority party securing 50 to 70 per cent of votes in 207 constituencies. The areas where these constituencies form clusters include Jammu and Kashmir except Srinagar constituency, Punjab except Faridkot and Patiala, U.P Himalayas, eastern Uttar Pradesh, western Bihar, Brahmputra valley, the Aravallis of Rajasthan, south-west Gujarat, central Madhya Pradesh, Mirjapur plateau, Chattisgarh, part of Maharashtra, part of Rayalseema and part of coastal Karnataka. This pattern indicates that in all these areas the Congress has enjoyed its hegemony because the forces opposed to the Congress were inactive in all these areas.

Fig. 4.8
India: 1971 Parliamentary Elections:
Spatial Pattern of Party Votes - Congress Party

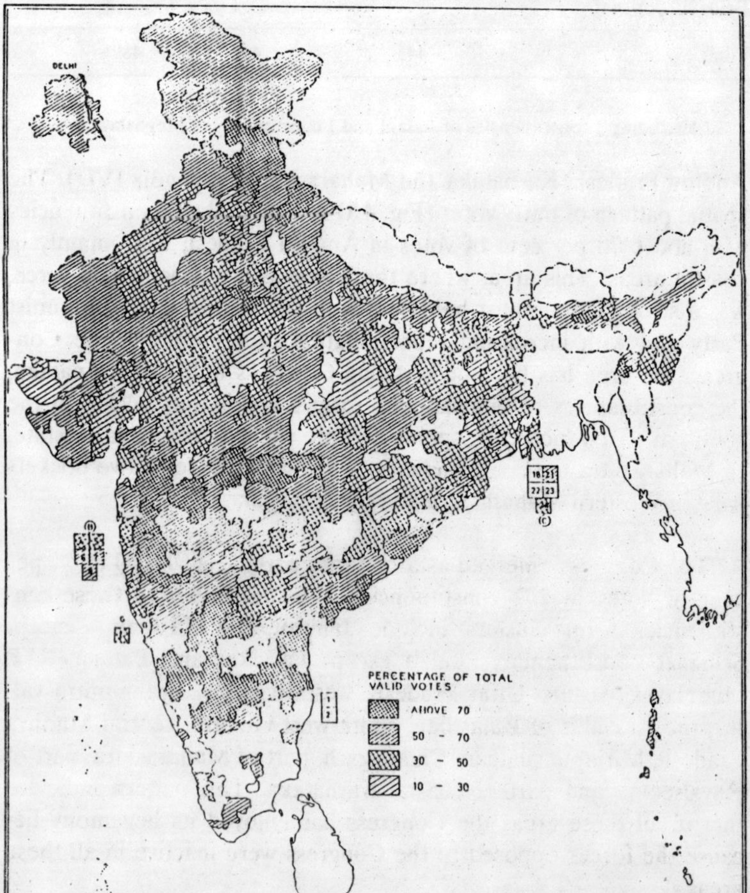

In 154 constituencies the party's strength varied between 30 and 50 per cent. The major concentration of these constituencies was in adjoining parts of Madhya Pradesh, Rajasthan and Gujarat, Chotanagpur plateau, West Bengal and most of Orissa. Viewing these regions in terms of political culture one observes that in Madhya Pradesh the Jana Sangh was a significant political force. In Gujarat, the Congress(O) commanded a wider following, becoming a political obstacle to the then Congress(R). The Bhartiya Kranti Dal was a significant political entity in Western Uttar Pradesh because the region is characterized by the dominance of the Jat peasantry. The Jharkhand Party in tribal belt of Bihar and the Socialists in the plains of Bihar were capable enough to reduce the Congress influence. The CPI(M) in West Bengal and Utkal Congress in Orissa succeeded in reducing the Congress strength.

There were only 25 constituencies in which the party secured 10 to 30 per cent votes. The distribution of these constituencies was : Andhra Pradesh 3, Bihar 7, Madhya Pradesh 4, Orissa 3, West Bengal 4 and Gujarat, Manipur, Tripura and Uttar Pradesh one each.

1977 Elections : The Congress Party suffered a great setback in the elections of 1977. The bad performance of the Congress in this election may be visualised from the fact that in as many as 363 constituencies it polled less than 30 per cent votes. Only in 7 constituencies its share was above 70 per cent and in 120 between 50 and 70 per cent.

The spatial pattern of the Congress votes in 1977 (Fig. 4.9) reveals that the constituencies of very high strength were only in 4 states *viz.* Maharashtra (3), Andhra Pradesh (2), Karnataka and Tamil Nadu (1 each). Constituencies in which its strength was between 50 and 70 per cent incorporated most of Andhra Pradesh and Karnataka with a few exceptions. These two states together with Kerala (8) and Tamil Nadu (13) accounted for as many as 78 constituencies (Appendix IVD). Maharashtra has a share of 15 of the constituencies in this category. Their distribution reveals that they form two big clusters in Vidarbha and Marathwada. In Gujarat too, the Congress had 9 constituencies in this category of which 7 form a cluster in the areas adjoining Madhya Pradesh and Maharashtra. In the north-east there were 9 constituencies in this category (Assam 8,

Fig. 4.9
India: 1977 Parliamentary Elections: Spatial Pattern of Party Votes - Congress Party

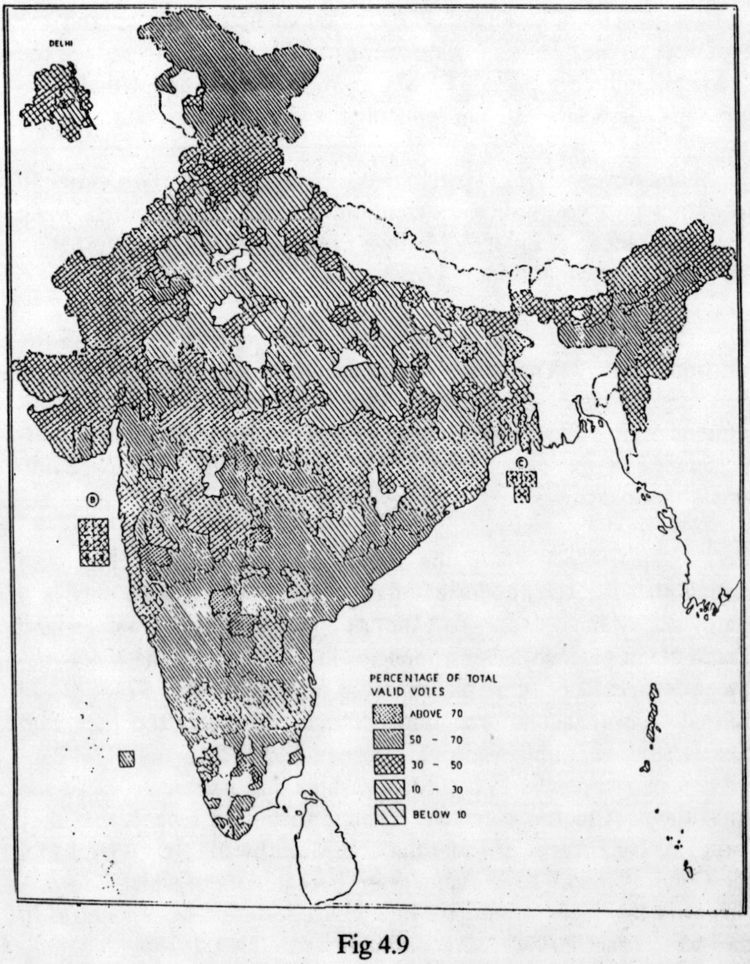

Fig 4.9

Megalaya 1). Out of the remaining 5, two were in Jammu and Kashmir and one in Rajasthan (Nagaur). Nagaur was the only constituency in the whole of the Hindi speaking belt where the Congress share in valid votes exceeded 50 per cent. In Lakshadweep and Andaman and Nicobar Islands too, its share was between 50 and 70 per cent.

Constituencies in which the party's share was between 30 and 50 per cent have a very distinct pattern. They were mainly in the mid-Indian tribal belt. The Konkan and eastern Marathwada, the lower Ganges plain, Himachal Pradesh and most of the Punjab plain also fall in this category. In the north-east, Arunachal Pradesh, Manipur, Nagaland, Mizoram and Tripura were also in this category.

The areas of its insignificant following (10 to 30 per cent votes) covered most of the north Indian plain leaving Punjab plain and lower Ganges plain. There were 162 constituencies in this category. The party had a negligible following in only 4 constituencies. They were Ferozepur in Punjab, and Samastipur, Maharajganj and Aurangabad in Bihar.

The geographic patterning of the Congress votes is in close corroboration with the geography of India. One can easily visualize tne three broad regions consisting of northern plain, the central India and the southern plateau. The pattern is also in close conformity with the ethno-lingual diversity of the country.The pattern thus evolved is not different qualitatively from the general political environment of the country. Once again the Congress emerged as an all embracing political force in those areas which have been Congress monolith and have not seen the rise of any other significant political force. However, what emerges from this analysis is that the party following of the Congress was fragmented in its nature. The anlysis also reveals that the Congress was reduced to a mere regional party with its strong following in Andhra Pradesh and Karnataka in the context of territorial extent.

1980 Elections : Although the Congress re-emerged as a most important political force on the Indian political scene in the 1980 elections, its performance was not to the level of 1971. This is evident from Table 4.5 which shows that its share was above 70 per cen only

Fig. 4.10
India: 1980 Parliamentary Elections: Spatial Pattern of Party Votes - Congress Party

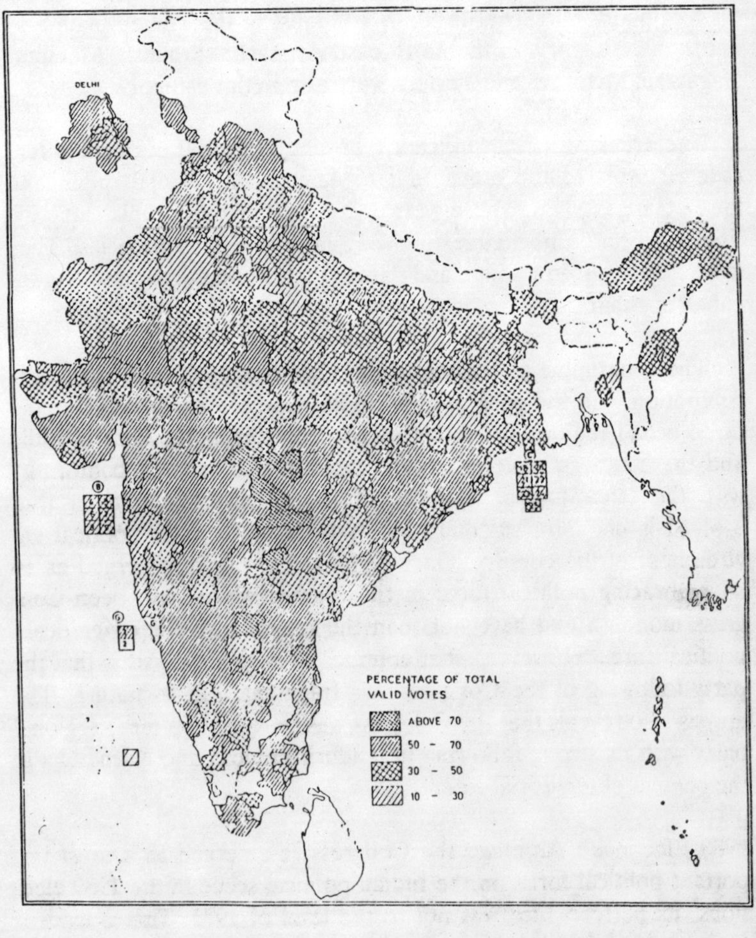

in 7 constituencies as against 54 in 1971. Similarly in 197 constituencies its votes varied between 50 and 70 per cent as against 207 in 1971. The spatial pattern of Congress' votes in 1980 (Fig. 4.10) reveals that the party's mass following was highly fragmented. There were 4 constituencies in Andhra Pradesh and 3 in Maharashtra in which its share was above 70 per cent. Out of 197 constituencies in which its votes were between 50 and 70 per cent, 141 were in the six states of Andhra Pradesh, Gujarat, Karnataka, Maharashtra, Orissa and Tamil Nadu. Three constituencies of Himachal Pradesh and 8 of Punjab were also in this category (Appendix IVD).

A majority of 239 constituencies in which its votes were between 30 and 50 per cent were in Rajasthan, Madhya Pradesh, Uttar Pradesh, Bihar and West Bengal. These 5 states together accounted for 173 constituencies. Maharashtra, too had a share of 13 constituencies (including 6 of Bombay).

There were only 45 constituencies in which its votes were between 10 and 30 per cent. Of these, 32 were in Uttar Pradesh and Bihar (19 and 13 respectively). Out of remaining 13, 4 each were in Haryana and Rajasthan and one each in Maharashtra, Manipur, Tripura, West Bengal and Goa, Daman and Diu. It secured less than 10 per cent votes only in Lakshadweep Islands.

Summing up

The spatial pattern of the Congress' following in three Parliamentary Elections of 1971, 1977 and 1980, contradicts the political formulation of the political scientists who have described the Indian system as that of one party dominance.[13] It is difficult to agree with the view that the Congress was a 'party of consensus'[14] because this consensus was forced by Nehru taking the advantage of his personality.[15] The fact that the process of transforming the Congress from a movement to the status of a ruling political party began by eliminating the organized groups within the Congress which were not amenable to control by the leadership[16] is a reflection on forceful consensus. Two major events in the Congress, the 1969 and 1978 splits further illustrate the point that the Congress can not be considered a party of consensus.

The analysis also reveals that despite its big majority in Parliament in the 1971 and 1980 elections, the party's mass following was highly fragmented. Its extensive following was confined mainly to two states of Karnataka and Andhra Pradesh. This is attributed to the polarisation of dominant social forces in both the states in favour of the Congress. This very process, restricted the other parties from making any significant dent in these states.

Congress(O) and Congress(U)

The Congress(O) came into existence in the wake of the 1969 split in the Congress and the Congress(U) was the result of the same process in 1978. On an average the Congress (O) in 1971 secured 10.42 per cent votes at all-India level. However, there existed large variations in different constituencies. The performance of the Congress(U) in 1980 was very poor by any criterion. Table 4.7 shows the distribution of constituencies by different categories of voting strength.

TABLE 4.7 : CONSTITUENCIES CLASSIFIED BY VOTING STRENGTH, CONGRESS (O) AND CONGRESS (U)

Percentage votes polled	Number of Constituencies	
	Congress (O) 1971	Congress (U) 1980
Above 70 per cent	-	-
50 to 70 per cent	11	7
30 to 50 per cent	66	19
10 to 30 per cent	71	63
Below 10 per cent	90	121
Total	238	210*

* Excluding two constituencies of Assam.

Table 4.7 reflects the nature of mass following of both the parties. The Congress(O) secured 50 to 70 per cent votes only in 11 constituencies of which 9 were in Gujarat and 1 each in Bihar and Tamil Nadu (Appendix IVA). It emerged as a significant political force by securing 30 to 50 per cent votes in 66 constituencies of which 28 were in Tamil Nadu, 9 in Gujarat and 8 in Bihar. In the remaining 161 constituencies its votes were less than 30 per cent. This reveals that the party's main following was in Gujarat followed by Tamil Nadu and Bihar. A look into the composition of the party leadership will reveal that its stalwarts were mainly from two states of Gujarat and Tamil Nadu who were capable enough to mould the public opinion in the favour of the party.

The Congress(U) failed to gain significant mass support which is evident from the fact that in only 7 constituencies its share in votes exceeded 50 per cent. Out of 7 constituencies, 3 were in Kerala, where the party was a partner in left front and 1 each in Jammu and Kashmir, Maharashtra, Goa, Daman and Diu,and Lakshadweep. The high share of votes in these constitutencies was mainly due to the personality of the candidates - Karan Singh in Udhampur (Jammu and Kashmir), Y.B. Chavan in Satara (Maharashtra), Edurado Martinho Faleiro in Mormugao (Goa, Daman and Diu) and Muhammad Sayeed Padannatha in Lakshadweep. The distribution of 19 constituencies with a voting strength between 30 and 50 per cent was : Andhra Pradesh 5, Bihar 4, Karnataka 1, Kerala 3, Maharashtra 4, and Rajasthan 2 (Appendix IVF). Its share of less than 30 per cent in 184 constituencies out of 195 contested shows that the party was denuded of its political strength.

Janata Party

The Janata Party was a gift of the internal emergency imposed on June 25, 1975. This provided an opportunity to the leaders of the opposition parties to keep aside their significant ideological differences and to fight the ills of the emergency unitedly. In the wake of this, as soon as the elections were announced on January 18, 1977, the four opposition parties - Jana Sangh, Bhartiya Lok Dal, Congress(O) and Socialist Party decided to contest the election from a common platform and on January 23, 1977 the Janata Party was formally launched. Its election manifesto promised to provide "both bread and liberty"[17] without a solid economic policy.[18] Despite this the party's main emphasis during election campaign was on the emotional issues such as "emergency excesses." The Janata Party emerged as the largest party with a clear majority in Parliament but its popular support was limited to just 43.04 per cent votes. This indicated an increase of 15.81 per cent on the combined votes of its constituents in 1971. The party failed on major economic fronts during its rule and was completely routed by the masses in the 1980 elections in the wake of the downfall of Charan Singh Government. In 1980, its votes declined to nearly 18.95 per cent. However, there existed large variations in the constituencies of India in regard to its share in valid votes. Table 4.8 shows number of constituencies in different categories of voting strength in 1971,[19] 1977 and 1980.

TABLE 4.8 : CONSTITUENCIES CLASSIFIED BY VOTING STRENGTH, JANATA PARTY

Percentage of votes polled	Number of constituencies		
	1971	1977	1980
Above 70 per cent	3	82	1
50 to 70 per cent	55	186	5
30 to 50 per cent	192	134	131
10 to 30 per cent	133	21	233
Below 10 per cent	78	1	60
Total Contested	460	424	430*

* Excluding two constituencies in Assam.

Note: Votes polled by the Janata Party in 1971 have been derived from its constituents

An analysis of the spatial pattern of the Janata votes in 1971, derived from its constituents, is necessary to understand the pattern of its strength in 1977 and 1980 elections. The spatial pattern of the Janata votes in 1971 reveals that the party's strong following was in the adjoining areas of Madhya Pradesh, Rajasthan and Gujarat (Fig. 4.11, Appendix IVE). In western Uttar Pradesh too, the party had a strong base. The areas of moderate following (30 to 50 per cent votes) include Tamil Nadu, Uttar Pradesh and parts of Rajasthan, Madhya Pradesh and Bihar. The party had little following in Andhra Pradesh, Karnataka, Kerala, Maharashtra, Punjab, Himachal Pradesh, Jammu and Kashmir, West Bengal and the north-east. This reveals that the party's main following was confined to Hindi speaking north and Orissa. South of Vindhyas, the party commanded very little influence except in Tamil Nadu where the party had moderate following.

The spatial pattern of the Janata following in the 1977 elections reveals that the Janata emerged as a strong political force only in the Hindi speaking states of the north (Fig. 4.12). The fact that out of 82

Fig. 4.11
India: 1971 Parliamentary Elections: Spatial Pattern of Party Votes - Janata Party

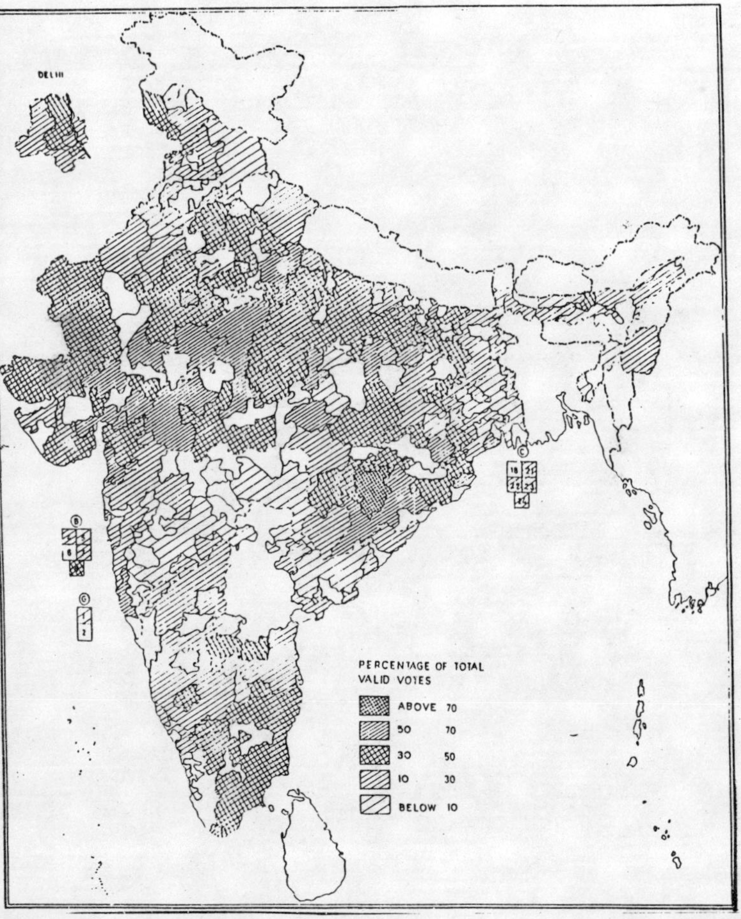

Fig. 4.12
India: 1977 Parliamentary Elections: Spatial Pattern of Party Votes - Janata Party

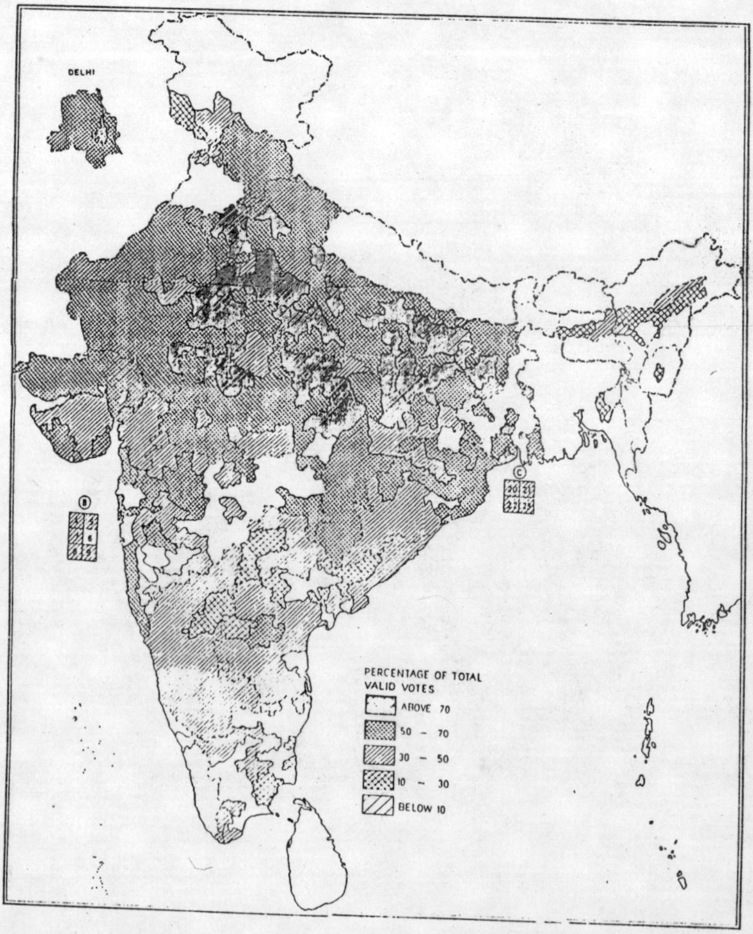

constituencies in which the Janata's share exceeded 70 per cent, 50 were in these states (Bihar 21, Haryana 5, Madhya Pradesh 8, Rajasthan 8, Uttar Pradesh 36, and Delhi 2) illustrates this point. The remaining two constituencies were in West Bengal. Although the party did not have a strong base in West Bengal, its success in some of the constituencies was due to its alliance with the left parties in this state. Further, out of 186 constituencies in which the Janata secured 50 to 70 per cent votes, 125 were in the states of Bihar (24), Himachal Pradesh (4), Haryana (4), Madhya Pradesh (24), Rajasthan (16), Uttar Pradesh (48), Chandigarh (1) and Delhi (5). In the south, the party could achieve this extent of success only in 4 constituencies - two in Tamil Nadu and one each in Andhra Pradesh and Karnataka. The remaining 57 constituencies were in Maharashtra, Gujarat, Punjab, Orissa, West Bengal and Assam. The majority of the constituencies in which the party's share was between 30 and 50 per cent were in non-Hindi speaking states. However, all the constituencies in which the Janata had insignificant following (between 10 and 30 per cent votes) were in Jammu and Kashmir, Maharashtra, Assam, Manipur, Karnataka, Andhra Pradesh and Tamil Nadu. There was only 1 constituency (Manipur outer) in which the party's share was less than 10 per cent.

This analysis helps to identify the following regions: (a) The Hindi heartland characterized by strong party following; (b) The south where the Janata emerged as a significant force. This is comprised of Andhra Pradesh and Karnataka; (c) The periphery which includes Jammu and Kashmir, Punjab, Tamil Nadu, Kerala, West Bengal and the north-east except Assam. In this region the Janata had very little following.The polities of these areas are characterized by strong regional forces. In most of these areas the Janata contested a very few seats. (d) The transitional areas consisting of Maharashtra, Gujarat, Orissa and Assam characterized by enclaves of high following along with the enclaves of low following.

The performance of the Janata Party in the 1980 elections was worse than the combined performance of its constituents in 1971 (Appendix IVE). Its share was above 70 per cent in only one constituency - Rajapur (Maharashtra) and between 50 and 70 per cent in 5 constituencies which included 4 constituencies of Bombay metropolis and Aurangabad (Bihar). The Janata Party emerged as a

Fig. 4.13
India: 1980 Parliamentary Elections: Spatial Pattern of Party Votes - Janata Party

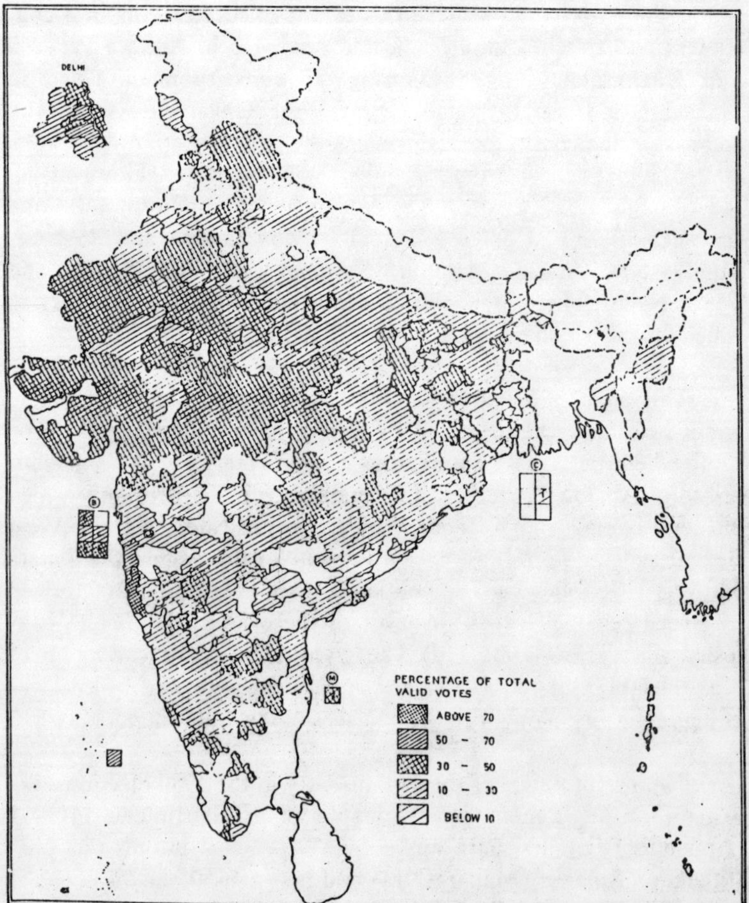

significant force securing 30 to 50 per cent votes in 131 constituencies majority of which lay in Himachal Pradesh, Rajasthan, Madhya Pradesh and Gujarat (Fig. 4.13). In most of the constituencies of West Bengal (32 constituencies out of 35 contested) and in Tripura, the party secured less than 10 per cent of votes. The pattern thus reveals that the Janata's following remained confined, by and large, to those areas only where either the Jana Sangh or the Congress(O) were significant political entities before their merger into the Janata Party.

Janata (Secular)

The Janata(S) as indicated earlier, was born as a result of the split in the Janata Party in August 1979. The party was constituted mainly by the erstwhile BLD group but some socialists also joined the party. The main mass following of the party centred around Charan Singh. Electoral data reveals that the Janata(S) emerged as a party of those areas where the Jat peasants are a numerically significant force. Table 4.9 gives the number of constituencies classified by voting strength.

TABLE 4.9 : CONSTITUENCIES CLASSIFIED BY VOTING STRENGTH, JANATA(S): 1980

Percentage votes polled	Number of constituencies
Above 70 per cent	-
50 to 70 per cent	5
30 to 50 per cent	57
10 to 30 per cent	107
Below 10 per cent	125
Total	294

Table 4.9 shows that the party emerged as a strong political force securing 50 to 70 per cent votes in only 5 constituencies (two each in Bihar and Haryana and one in Uttar Pradesh). The Party commanded significant following in 57 constituencies of which 28 constituencies form a continguous belt (Fig. 4.14) spreading over Haryana, Rajasthan and Uttar Pradesh. Out of remaining 29 constituencies, 15 were in Uttar Pradesh, 10 in Bihar, 3 in Orissa and 1

Fig. 4.14
India: 1980 Parliamentary Elections: Spatial Pattern of Party Votes - Janata (S)

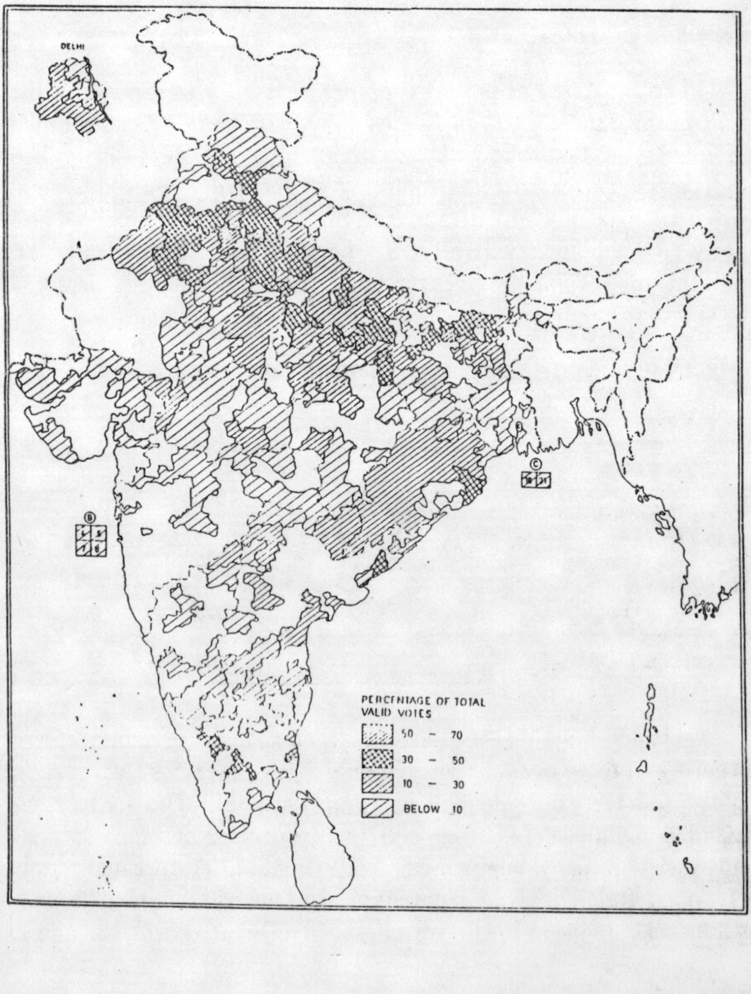

in Andhra Pradesh. The party's share in valid votes was between 10 and 30 per cent in 108 constituencies, majority of which were in Haryana, Rajasthan, Uttar Pradesh, Bihar and Orissa. In another 125 constituencies the party's share was less than 10 per cent. The majority of the constituencies in this category were in Gujarat, Madhya Pradesh, West Bengal, Maharashtra, Karnataka, Andhra Pradesh and Tamil Nadu. The reasons for the success of the Janata(S) in certain parts of the country flow from the character of the party emanating from the ideology of the erstwhile Bhartiya Kranti Dal which believed in right of private property as a must for the furtherance of the democracy.[20]

PSP, SSP and Swatantra Party

The socialists (both the PSP and the SSP) were the strong propagators of decentralization of power and a socialist economy which only can evolve a social order free from all kinds of exploitation.[21] Although there was general harmony in the policies of the PSP, and SSP, the SSP had a more radical programme of action.[22] The Swatantras on the other hand believed that "the progress, welfare and happiness of the people depend upon individual initiative, enterprise and energy and maximum freedom for the individual and minimum interference by the state."[23]

TABLE 4.10 : CONSTITUENCIES CLASSIFIED BY VOTING STRENGTH, PSP, SSP AND SWATANTRA PARTY, 1971

Percentage votes polled	Number of constitutencies		
	PSP	SSP	Swatantra
Above 70 per cent	-	-	-
50 to 70 per cent	-	1	5
30 to 50 per cent	6	9	19
10 to 30 per cent	11	35	22
Below 10 per cent	45	48	13
Total Contested	62	93	59

It is obvious that the socialists had a very attractive programme but the splits and merger of parties did not allow them to emerge as a significant political entity. The Swatantra Party emerged as an important political force where they got the support of big industrialists and agriculturalists who were in strong favour of private enterprise. Table 4.10 shows the performance of these three parties in 1971 elections.

It is evident from Table 4.10 that among all these three parties, the Swatantra has comparatively strong following which was confined to the states of Gujarat, Orissa and Rajasthan. Appendix IVA reveals that all the 5 constituencies in which its votes were between 50 and 70 per cent were in these states. Similarly 10 out of 19 constituencies in which its share was 30 to 50 per cent were also in these states.The PSP and SSP, although commanded a wider base but this was too small to have much significance.

Other Parties

Other parties in the course of this discussion include both the state as well as Registered Parties.[24] These parties have their origin in the existing social plurality. They represent the interest of certain social groups and therefore are based on caste, religious and linguistic identity. It is generally observed that these parties have flourished mainly on the Indian periphery in the wake of the ruling party's failure to contain the divergent social interests. Although there are a number of parties in this category, the important among them are Jammu and Kashmir National Conference,Shiromani Akali Dal , Dravida Munnetra Kazhagam, Anna Dravida Munnetra Kazhagam Forward Bloc, Peasant and Workers' Party, and Revolutionary Socialist Party. Appendix IVG shows their performance in constituencies of India.

It may be seen from Appendix IVG that these parties have fared well in all the 3 elections. This is attributed to their well defined social base which has a geographical expression and thus define the party geography. The National Conference is confined to the State of Jammu and Kashmir but finds a strong expression in the Muslim electorate of the valley; the Akali Dal has strong following among the Jat Sikh peasantry of Punjab and the Dravida Munnetra Kazhagam and Anna Dravida Munnetra Kazhgam have a strong following in the non-Brahmins of Tamil Nadu. The Peasants and Workers Party represents the interest of small farmers in Maharashtra and the Forward Bloc and Revolutionary Socialist

Party have their areas of influence mainly in Kerala and West Bengal.

AN OVERVIEW

The preceding analysis of the voting strength of the political parties reveals the fragmented character of Indian polity. None of the major parties have an extensive mass base of a decisive nature. The areas of strong following are in the form of enclaves. The analysis reveals that even the majority party in Parliament does not have strong following in extensive areas. It is evident that their areas of influence lay divided in specific parts of the country. In the wake of their fragmented mass following these parties can hardly be described as 'national'.

It is noted that although the voting strength of major political parties registered ups and downs during these three elections the emergent patterns are in close confirmity with the historical process which have shaped the Indian polity.

The analysis exposes the incoherent logic of the concept of 'one party dominance' put forward by a number of political scientists. [25] The concept of dominance based on numerical strength in Parliament seems to be a disputable concept because winning of a seat cannot be an indicator of dominance. However, in the contemporary situation where the party with majority of seats rules the country, the concept has its own validity. It is noted that the majority party in Parliament does not emerge as a political force having following in all parts of the country. Their following is region specific.

NOTES AND REFERENCES

1. Surinder Suri, *op.cit.*, p.1849
2. Gopal Krishana, "One Party Dominance - Development and Trends," *Perspective*, Supplement to the Indian Journal of Public Administration, Vol. XII, January-March 1966, pp. 9-11
3. S.N. Sadasivan, *op.cit.*, p.190.
4. E.P.W. da Costa, "The Congress Multiplier in 1971," *Monthly Public Opinion Surveys* of the Indian Institute of Public Opinion, Vol. XVI, January-February 1971, p.9.
5. The association of the Jats with Janata(s) was for two reasons : firstly, its leader was Mr. Charan Singh who finds a strong place in the Jat peasantry of

these states and secondly, the party projected itself as a champion of peasants.

6. The history and experience of these two regions of the country vary significantly. The Hindus in the north have taken various organized measures to resist the Islamic impact ever since the days of the predatory expeditions of Mohammad of Gazani. The south was comparatively free from this impact. In the subsequent period which saw a long period of Muslim rule, the society took a different shape. The Hindus took advantage of British Rule in outstripping the Muslims. This conflict between politically organized Hindu population and politically organised Muslim population have helped the organisations of Hindus in the north. (S.N. Sadasivan, *op.cit.*, p.6). North saw a large influx of refugees in the wake of the partition. These refugees who really experienced the outcome of the partition became a strong propagator of Hindu nationalism. It is important to note that while Hindu communalism was regarded as nationalism, Muslim communalism was treated as separatism.
7. One of the explanations for the strong base of Communist Parties in West Bengal is as follows; The Bengalis were not very happy from the outcome of the Independence. In fact they had to satisfy themselves with the bifurcation of the Bengal. Their suffering further increased when their leaders did not get the share they deserved in the power structure. This forced them to organize themselves in order to oppose the Congress which they did by joining Marxist organisations. The long history of economic exploitation by the British on the one hand and other trading classes on the other further helped the Marxist organisations to establish their roots. A sizeable strength of workers from outside Bengal created conducive conditions for the leading communities, the Brahmins, the Vaidyas and the Kayasthas to gain their lost predominance by providing new leadership through active unionization of the labour. The Marxian philosophy of class-struggle helped them to get consolidated under the banner of Marxist organization. The reluctance of the middle class workers to accept menial jobs drive them into the clutches of the Marwari Banias of the urban areas who are active in money lending. The way they exploit these middle class families bring them to pauperism. This has significantly boosted the expansion of the Marxian parties. Even by nature, the Marxists are opposed to Gandhism which they consider as an act of convenience. Marxism provides them a great stimuli for an action as they are highly emotional people with an strong intellectual urge (S.N. Sadasivan, *op.cit*
8. The most important factor which led to strong Communist following in Kerala is the pattern of social conflict. The pattern of social conflict in Kerala is governed by the basic objective of social equality. The lower castes like Ezhavas and the untouchables have constantly fought the Nairs and the Christians. Since the Ezhavas are socially more advanced than the untouchables they were the source of inspiration to the leaders of the oppressed classes. See, E.M.S. Namboodiripad, *The National Question in Kerala* (Bombay : Peoples Publishing House, 1952), p. 101. D.R. Mankekar noted that "Taking full advantage of an adult franchise democracy, they are smashing down the caste barriers. They have precipitated a veriatble social revolution." *The Red Riddle of Kerala* (Bombay : Manaktalas and Sons, 1965), pp. 16-62.

   The Ezhavas were forced to adopt Marxism in order to counterbalance the two other strong communities of the Nairs and the Christians who were rallying behind the Congress. It is this communal triangle of the Ezhavas, the Nairs and the Christians which is a motivating force of the Kerala politics. This has resulted in making the political parties in Kerala as projection of these communal groups. Communal consciousness takes the place of political life in Kerala. See, Jitendra Singh, *Communist Rule in Kerala* (New Delhi : Divan

Chand Information Centre, 1959), p.11.

9. In Andhra Pradesh too, the Communists have benefitted by the social conflict among the two rival social groups. The Kammas in Andhra have used the weapon of Marxism to neutralise the political supremacy of the Reddys. The Kammas community look into history which reminds them of the way their Kakatiya dynasty was overthrown by the Mohammedan invaders in 1327 A.D. with the support of the Reddys.
10. B. Pattabhi Sitaramayya, *The History of the Indian National Congress* (1885-1935), Vol. 1 (New Delhi: The Working Committee of the Congress, 1935), pp.11-12.
11. *Ibid.*, Annie Besant quoted, p. 27.
12. Schuster and Wint wrote that, "Like Hinduism itself, it finds room for every opinion, every class and every eccentricity." George Schuster and Guy Wint, *India and Democracy* (London, MacMillan & Co., 1941), pp. 165-66.
13. Rajni Kothari, "The Congress System in India," *Asian Survey*, Vol.IV, No. 12, pp. 1161-73; W.H. Morris-Jones, "Parliament and Dominant Party : Indian Experience," *Parliamentary Affairs*, Vol. XVII, No. 3, Summer 1964, pp. 296-307.
14. Rajni Kothari, *op.cit.*, pp. 1161-73.
15. Sisir Gupta, "The Political Outlook," *Souvenir : 66th Session of the Indian National Congress* (Bhavnagar : 1961), part 1, p.55).
16. This led to the resignation of Acharya Kriplani from the Presidentship of the Congress. See Nehru's note to some members of the Congress Working Committee on the question of relationship between the Government and the Congress Party, dated July 15, 1947, cited in G.S. Austin, *The Indian Constitution* (Oxford : 1966), pp. 16-17. Also see, Acharya Kriplani's statement on this subject in *The Indian Express*, August 3, 1965.
17. Janata Party, *Election Manifesto*, 1977, p.1.
18. The statement on economic policy was adopted only during November 11-14, 1977. See, Janata Party, *Statement on Economic Policy* (New Delhi: 1977), p.1.
19. The votes for Janata in each constituency for 1971 are derived by adding the votes of its constituent groups. The votes for Bhartiya Lok Dal which was formed in 1974 are derived from its 7 constituents namely, Bhartiya Kranti Dal, Samyukta Socialist Party, Swatantra Party, Utkal Congress, and Kisan Mazdor Party. Other two constituents *viz.*, Rashtriya Lok Tantrik Dal and Punjab Khetikari Mazdoor Union did not contest in any of the constituency.
20. *Aims and Principles, Bhartiya Kranti Dal* (Lucknow: the BKD, 1971), pp. 22-23.
21. *Policy Statement* (adopted by the Second National Conference of the PSP held at Gaya, 26-29 December, 1955) (New Delhi: The PSP, reprint, 1956), p.8.; See also, *Economic Situation in 1957* (report adopted by the General Council of the PSP at Delhi, November 2-3, 1957) (New Delhi : the PSP), p.8.
22. *Samyukta Socialist Party: Statement of Principles, Programmes and Political Line* (adopted at the Second National Conference at Kota on April 3-6, 1966), pp. 16-33.
23. *Swatantra Party: Statement of Principles* (Bombay : The Swatantra Party, 1959), p.1.
24. The State and Registered parties are the term used by the Election Commission of India to classify the political parties under different heads on the basis of their performance in the last election.
25. Gopal Krishna, *op.cit.*, pp. 9-11; Rajni Kothari, *op.cit.*, pp. 1161-73; W.H. Morris-Jones, *op.cit.*, pp. 296-307.

FIVE

SWINGS IN PARTY FOLLOWING

Popular support to political parties is not static and changes from election to election depending upon the political situation prevailing on the eve of elections. In accordance with the existing climate a party may register either an increase or a decrease in its popular support depending upon its capacity to put forward its appeals and programme before the electorate. This change on a long scale in voter allegiance to political parties between two consecutive elections is termed as '*swing*'. Thus, it is a measure of the extent of change in a party's mass following from one election to the next. In the present chapter an attempt has been made to study the spatial variations in the swings in party following during 1971-1977 and 1977-1980 elections.

The basic significance of the analysis of swings lies in the fact that it is a direct reflection of a party's capacity to influence the voters through its electoral campaign. Therefore, if a party registers a heavy swing in its favour then it will imply that it has succeeded in turning a vast majority of the voters in its favour. On the other hand, negative swing will show an erosion in the party's mass base. However, in societies, such as India's where not only is the majority of the electorate illiterate, but also has a low level of political consciousness,a positive swing is no indicator of an increasing acceptance of its programmes. Similarly, a negative swing may not be termed as rejection of its programmes, although it suggests erosion of its influence.

Despite its obvious significance in the study of political systems, this aspect of voting has remained, by and large, untouched by the scholars working in the field of Indian voting behaviour. The only study on India which touched upon this aspect of research is that of Biplab Dasgupta who used party swings as indicator to determine party consistency.[1]

Scholars have used various statistical techniques to study the swings. Stokes used analysis of variance to determine the nature of swings.[2] He applied this technique on 5 Congressional elections in the USA between 1952 and 1960.[3] Green has used the Factor Analysis Model to study party swings in two British cities, Leeds and Sheffield, for the council elections between 1951 and 1966.[66]

It is significant to note that all the methods to study party swings refer to the electoral data of Britain and USA. In these countries the voters, who are highly conscious about the happenings in the country, are directly influenced by the programmes and policies of political parties and thus swings are of uniform nature. This requires sophisticated tools to analyse the nature of swings. On the other hand in the Indian situation the swings are of such a nature that they speak for themselves and therefore do not require any advanced statistical techniques. In this analysis the nature of swings in different constituencies has been studied simply with the help of choropleth maps. However, the coefficients of variations have been computed for selected parties to develop a comparative framework for the analysis of variations in party swings.

THE CONCEPTUAL FRAMEWORK

Elections are a national event in all democratic systems where broad-based parties compete to capture national power. In such a situation the issues related to the national problems will have a prime importance and a uniform swing across the country will show that the elections are really a national event. But in case, forces having a local relevance only, are at work, the swings will fluctuate considerably over space implying that the national forces are of secondary importance and the elections cease to be a national event. This will indicate the existance of a fragmented political system.

The Indian scene as indicated earlier, is characterized by vast ethnolingual diversity with a high degree of segregation of social groups. This has resulted in a highly fragmented society in which social forces get polarized along caste, community, linguistic and religious lines. This process is especially intense in those areas where the exploitation of the weaker social groups has been a common phenomenon. This has forced them to adopt a new political strategy for protection through an organization, which is a political party, having a sectarian or regional appeal. In all such areas the local issues have an edge over national issues.

Swings in party following usually occur in the wake of a changed political environment to which different groups do not react uniformly. It depends upon the way the electorate perceive this climate in different social environments. The political climate on the eve of the 1977 elections was characterized by a high degree of terror in the wake of various measures taken during the Emergency. This was felt more vigourously in the Hindi speaking states of the north particularly as a reaction to the implementation of family planning programme. The atmosphere of coercion was less evident in the south, therefore, the electoral campaign in 1977 was centred around the gains and losses of emergency. However, the peripheral states saw a different atmosphere characterized by the predominance of local issues varying from state autonomy to opposition to Hindi as a national language. If the people's reaction to these issues were homognous, then a uniform swing would be expected throughout the country. However, in case people's reaction to these issues is not similar, swings will be far away from the national average. The former situation is an indication of the forces of nationalism and the latter is an indication of the process of regionalism.

PARTY SWINGS IN STATES

The swings in party following bring out a significant aspect of Indian elections. It is noted that despite the sharp increase and decrease in seats won by the political parties, the swings in their following have been relatively of a low order. This may seem to be an indication of the irrationality of the Indian elections. The phenomenon is attributed to a number of factors. firstly, the multiplicity of contest makes it possible to annex seats by securing a strikingly low share of votes and secondly, the wide differences in party support in different parts of the country create a situation in which swings cannot be of high magnitude at a broad level. Finally, the polarization of social forces takes place in such a way that if a party loses support of one group, it gains by registering the support of the other thus creating a situation in which the party votes do not bring about substantial swings between two elections.

It is significant to note that the Congress Party which contested maximum seats in all the three elections registered a swing of minus 9.16 per cent between 1971 and 1977 and of 8.11 per cent between 1977 and 1980. Table 5.1 shows the swings registered by different political parties at national level.

TABLE 5.1 : PARTY SWINGS IN INDIA

Year	CPI	CIP(M)	Cong ress	Janata	Other parties	Indepen dents
1971-1977	-1.91	-0.82	-9.16	+15.81	-3.65	-2.87
1977-1980	-0.23	+1.84	+8.17	-24.09	-2.21	+1.85

It is significant to note that the Janata Party has registered two extremes. It registered the highest increase (15.81 per cent) in 1977 and the highest decrease (24.09 per cent) in 1980. The single factor which contributed to this phenomenon was that the party has no mass base of its own. It operated through the network of the constituent groups. Whatever increase it registered in its percentage votes in 1977 came in the wake of opposition to the authoritarian forces represented by the Congress during the emergency period[5] The Janata Party could not build its mass base mainly because the party could not develop an effective leadership[6]and truly merge the identities of the constituent parties. As a result,its constituent groups remained busy in pursuing the line of infighting and thus failed to make the Janata a political party with a common interest and goal.[7] All this culminated in the failure of the Janata Party in tackling the problems confronting the nation, and in making the masses aware of its non-performance. It was in response to these factors that the party registered a high negative swing in 1980.

Communist Party of India

The CPI registered negative swings between 1971 and 1977 and during 1977-1980. The factors responsible for both these swings were entirely different. The negative swing of 1.91 per cent in 1977 came, largely, in the wake of its cooperation with the Congress in the pre-1977 period. But a further decrease of 0.23 per cent in 1980 was the result of the reduced number of seats contested because of its alliance with other left parties in the country. However, the patterns of swings at the state level reveal that in 1977 the party registered an increase of o.32 and 1.29 per cent in Karnataka and Kerala respectively. In the remaining states it registered negative swings. The highest decrease in the votes was in West Bengal (4.87 per cent).followed by Punjab (4.57 per cent). It is evident from Appendix VA that the party did not register uniform swings. Although, the CPI registered a negative swing between 1977 and 1980 at the national level, it was able to record an increase in percentage votes in the states of Andhra Pradesh, Bihar, Himachal Pradesh, Madhya Pradesh, Manipur, Rajasthan and West Bengal. The highest positive swing of 1.66 per cent was in the case of Bihar. On the other hand, the highest negative swing was in the case of Kerala (-3.86 per cent). This trend of party swings in Kerala is quite significant but easily understandable in terms of political happenings in the state. The CPI was highly benefitted in 1977 by is alliance with the Congress.[7] But the setback came in the wake of polarisation of political forces. The highest gain of the CPI in 1980 was in Bihar (1.66 per cent). It is evident from Appendix VA that the CPI could not regain its mass following.

Communist Party of India (Marxist)

The CPI (M) registered a negative swing of 0.82 per cent between 1971 and 1977 and a positive swing of 1.84 per cent during 1977-1980. But the negative swing was not a result of loss in of credibility but occurred in the broad framework of national interest which forced the political parties to forge alliances in order to avoid division of votes. Therefore, the party contested only 53 seats in 1977 against 85 in 1971. The positive swing in 1980 came in the wake of larger political trends which were in favour of left democratic forces, particularly in those areas where the left parties have a strong organizational network. The state level pattern of the swings reveals that the party registered positive swings in the states of Andhra Pradesh, Bihar, Maharashtra, Orissa and Punjab. The party's share in valid votes decreased in the remaining states. This reveals that wherever the party had a strong base, it registered a negative swing and in the areas characterized by a weak base, it registered a positive swing. This phenomenon is attributed to electoral adjustments with other parties which left few seats for the party in areas of low following at the cost of seats in areas of high following. The 1980 elections were unique for a broad understanding among the left democratic forces. It was for the first time that the left parties united together to fight the rightist forces which were creating social and regional tensions in different parts of the country. Obviously, the CPI (M) was the dominant party in this alliance and, in fact, was the architect of this united front. In view of this, major gains went to CPI (M) reflected in its swings during 1977-80. It is evident from Appendix VA that the party registered a positive swing in all the states where it had a strong organizational network. This includes Assam, Bihar, West Bengal and Tripura. It is significant to note that the party registered a negative swing in Kerala. Probably it was due to loss of Muslim support in the wake of forced resignation of the Koya Ministry.[10] The CPI(M) registered a negative swing in other states indicating erosion in its mass base which was highly superficial and came to its fold in the wake of its alliance with the like minded parties in 1977.

Congress Party

The Congress Party which registered a negative swing in 1977 and a positive swing in 1980 had a highly variegated patern of swing in different states. Despite a negative swing of 9.16 per cent, at the aggregative level, the party registered a positive swing in Andhra Pradesh, Gujarat, Kerala, Manipur, Tamil Nadu, West Bengal, Dadra and Nagar Haveli and Goa, Daman and Diu. The highest positive swing (15.55 per cent) was in Goa, Daman and Diu followed by Manipur (15.29 per cent). On the other hand, the lowest magnitude of swing was in Chandigarh followed by Jammu and Kashmir (AppendixVA).

Similarly, despite a gain of 8.17 per cent at all India level in 1980 elections, the party registered a negative swing in Andhra Pradesh, Karnataka, Kerala, Manipur, Tripura, Andaman and Nicobar Islands, Arunachal Pradesh, Goa, Daman and Diu and Lakshadweep. Among these, the Union Territory of Lakshadweep had the dubious distinction of registering the highest loss of 54.74 per cent. The most significant thing to note is that the states like Andhra Pradesh and Karnataka which are considered as the monolith of the Congress, registered a negative swing. However, one may understand the loss to the party in view of the 1978 Congress spilt. The positive swing was of highest order in Meghalaya[11] followed by Chandigarh and Delhi.

Janata Party

The magnitude of swings registered by the Janata Party in 1977 and 1980 elections indicates that the party had an ephemeral mass following. It registered a positive swing of 15.81 per cent during 1971-77 and a negative swing of 24.09 per cent between 1977 and 1980. These massive shifts were in conformity with the general political climate prevailing in the country. There is no doubt that the Janata was benefited by the issue of emergency in 1977, but to make emergency again an issue in 1980 election caused heavy loss to the party.[12] The electorate who were suffering on economic fronts were not interested in the old issues and moreover were highly disgusted with the Janata's non-performance. Although, the party tried to satisfy the voters by showing its achievements but this too was done with an emphasis on ridiculing the Congress (I) for telling lies.[13]

The state level pattern reveals that the swings were of different magnitude. Despite a heavy positive swing at national level in 1977, it recorded a negative swing in Jammu and Kashmir, Manipur, Tamil Nadu and Dadra and Nagar Haveli. The highest negative swing was in the case of Tamil Nadu. Although, Tamil Nadu had strong following of one of the Janata's constituent-the Congress (O)-but it was wiped out after the death of Kamraj leaving the party with a negligible following in the state.[14] Its other constituents, more or less, had no following in this state. The same is true for other areas with a negative swing. the pattern of positive swings reveals that the highest gain was in the state of Haryana (44.37 per cent) and the lowest in Gujarat (0.48 per cent). This shows the range of variation in the pattern of swings registered by the party.

The Janata Party registered negative swings in all the states and Union Territories except Manipur during 1977-1980. However, there were large variations in state to state which varied from 0.40 per cent in Jammu and Kashmir to 56.83 per cent in Chandigarh. But the heaviest loss in the context of size of electorate,in its mass following was in Uttar Pradesh and Bihar where the party registered negative swings of 42.21 per cent and 41.43 per cent respectively.

Other Parties

The pattern of party swings in regard to other parties is also not uniform. Appendix VB shows the swings in party following in regard to some of the important (state and registered) parties. It is seen that only Forward Bloc and Revolutionary Socialist Party have registered a positive swing during 1971-1977 and 1977-1980 in West Bengal. No other party had this distinction in any of the states. However, both these parties registered negative swings in both the elections in Kerala.

The Akali Dal increased its strength of votes by 11.45 per cent during 1971-1977. However, the party suffered a setback in 1980 when its share in votes declined by 18.93 per cent. The decrease of 18.93 per cent in 1980 is an indication of the hollowness of it mass base. The most important factor which contributed to this was the faction fighting within the Akali Dal.[15]

The DMK registered a decline in 17.19 per cent votes in 1977 but gained by 4.95 per cent in 1980. While the former was attributed to loss of its credibility in the wake of the findings of the Sarkaria Commission, the latter was due to its fine organizational network, down to the village level.[16]

The negative swing in the case of Anna Dravida Munnetra Kazhagam in 1980 was due to its performance during its tenure of government after 1977. The government did not have anything to show on the positive side except some social welfare measures. Another factor which contributed to this phenomenon was sustained agitation by Tamil Nadu Agriculturists Association which has great influence in districts like North-Arcot, Coimbatore, Salem, Ramanathapuram, Dharmapuri and Tirunelveli.[17] The similar reasons were responsible for the negative swing in Maharashtrawadi Gomantak Party's votes in Goa, Daman and Diu.[18]

SPATIAL PATTERNS OF PARTY SWINGS

A more rational pattern of the party swings emerges at the Parliamentary constituency level. It is seen that constituencies have a highly variegated pattern of party swings. The swings in party following in constituencies differ from the national average which shows that the different constituencies are not influenced uniformly by the various factors operating on the eve of elections. This phenomenon probably indicates that even the Parliamentary elections cease to be national. This may be attributed to the fact that the regional issues have an edge over the national issues involved in the elections. The following analysis attempts to analyse the spatial variations in the swings in party following of selected political parties during 1971-1977 and 1977-1980 at the Parliamentary constituency level.[19]

The Communist Party of India

The spatial pattern of swings in the CPI'S following during 1971-1977 (Fig. 5.1) reveals that despite a negative swing of 1.91 per cent at the national level, the party registered a positive swing in 3 constituencies. Table 5.2 shows the magnitude of swings in different constituencies of India during 1971-1977 and 1977-1980.

TABLE 5.2: SWINGS IN PERCENTAGE VOTES, COMMUNIST PARTY OF INDIA

Percentage change	No. of constituencies with negative swings		No. of constituencies with positive swings	
	1971-77	1977-80	1971-77	1977-80
Above 30 per cent	7	-	-	-
20 to 30 per cent	4	-	-	3
10 to 20 per cent	8	-	1	10
Below 10 per cent	17	7	2	7
Total	36	7	3	20

Fig. 5.1
India: Swings in Party Votes: 1971-1977-Communist Party of India

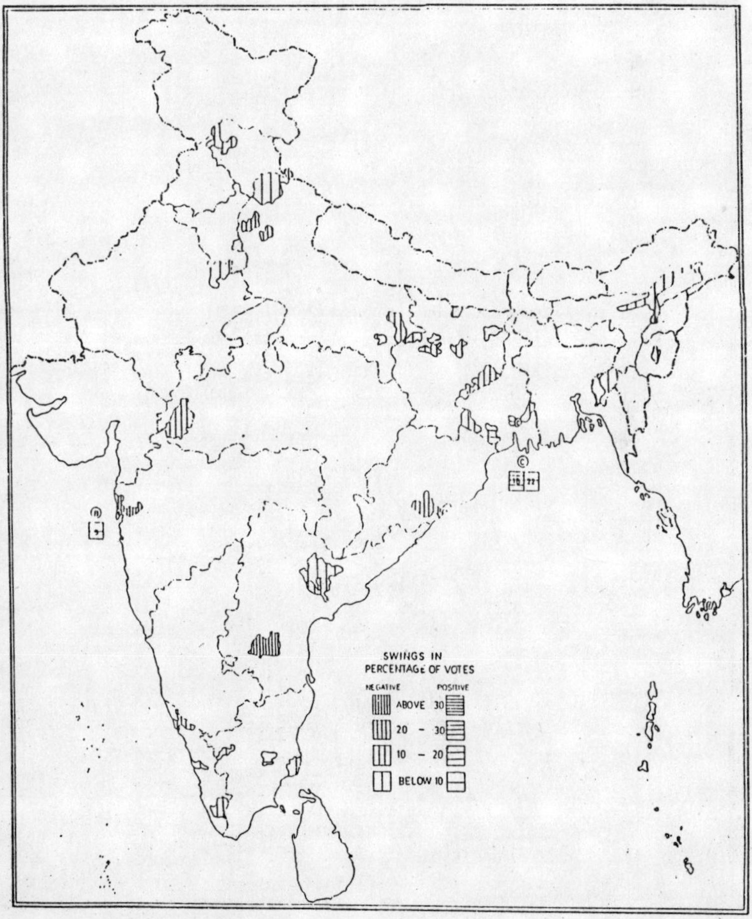

Fig. 5.2
India: Swings in Party Votes: 1977-1980-Communist Party of India

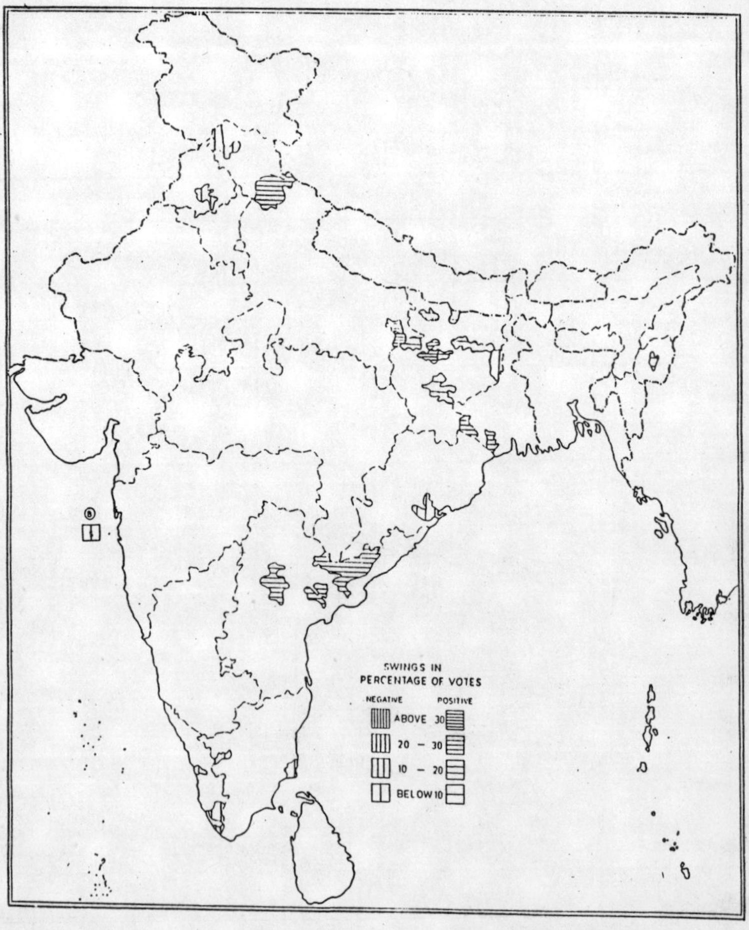

It is evident from Table 5.2 that the swings fluctuated considerably from the national average during 1971-1977. In Midnapore constituency of West Bengal, the party's share increased by more than 10 per cent. Two other constituencies, one each in West Bengal and Tamil Nadu registered a positive swing of less than 10 per cent. Altogether 36 constituencies registered negative swing out of which in 7 constituencies the loss was more than 30 per cent. Of these, 3 were in Uttar Pradesh, 2 in Bihar and one each in Andhra Pradesh and Maharashtra. However, the distribution of constituencies in different classes of party swings do not reveal any pattern.

During 1977-1980 the party registered an increase in its votes in as many as 20 constituencies. However, no constituency registered a swing of more than 30 per cent either on the negative side or on the positive side. In 3 constituencies the swings varied between 20 and 30 per cent. The distribution of constituencies reveals a significant pattern (Fig. 5.2). The majority of the constituencies with positve swings were in the middle Gangetic plain. The party's share declined in 8 constituencies of which only one constituency (Giridih - Bihar) was in the northern plain. It is significant to note that remaing 7 constituencies with negative swing were in Kerala (4), Tamil Nadu, Maharashtra and Orissa. This reveals that the party has been able to strengthen its mass base in the agricultural regions. The positive swings of 20 to 30 per cent in 3 constituencies of Telangana illustrate this point further. The negative swings in the constituencies of Kerala deserve attention. There are two probable explanations for this phenomenon. The first explanation could be that the CPI (M) did not work for the candidates of the CPI.[20] The second explanation could be that the Nair and Ezhava communities together voted for the United Democratic Front candidates.[21] But it seems that the second explanation is more rational because the parties of Nair, and Ezhava communities (NDP and SRP) were partners in the United Demoratic Front led by the congress (I).

Communist Party of India (Marxist)

Although the CPI(M) too registered a negative swing at all-India level during 1971-1977, the party managed to increase its share in valid votes in 33 constituencies. Its votes declined only in 6 constituencies. Table 5.3 gives the distribution of these constituencies in different categories of percentage change.

TABLE 5.3 : SWINGS IN PERCENTAGE VOTES, COMMUNIST PARTY OF INDIA (MARXIST)

Percentage change	No. of constituencies with negative swings		No. of constituencies with positive swings	
	1971-77	1977-80	1971-77	1977-80
Above 30 per cent	-	2	6	-
20 to 30 per cent	1	2	6	2
10 to 20 per cent	2	3	9	4
0 to 10 per cent	3	12	12	12
Total	6	19	33	18

The distribution of these constituencies reveals that out of 6 constituencies with a negative swing during 1971-1977, 2 each were in West Bengal and Kerala and one each in Tripura and Rajasthan. The majority of the constituencies with positive swings were in West Bengal (Fig. 5.3). However, only 2 out of 6 constituencies with a positive swings of more than 30 per cent were in West Bengal. The other 4 constituencies were in Maharashtra (2), Orissa (1) and Andhra Pradesh (1)

The pattern of swings during 1977-1980 reveals that there were 19 constituencies with negative swings and 18 constituencies with positive swings. The party did not register swings of more than 30 per cent in any constituency. Only in two constituencies (Tripura West and Barrackpore) the increase in votes was between 20 and 30 per cent.

The distribution of the constituencies (Fig. 5.4) reveals that in West Bengal the party registered negative swings in as many as 10 constituencies. However, in Kerala its votes did not decline in any constituency. All constituencies of Andhra Pradesh, Orissa, Maharashtra and Punjab registered negative swings. It is significant to note that despite a negative swing at the state level in Kerala, its votes did not decline in any constitutency. This was contributed by the shifts in seats contested. The analysis suggests that on the one hand the party continued to strengthen its mass base in Kerala, West Bengal and Tripura, on the other hand it suffered a setback in other parts of the country. It is also evident that the change in per cent votes highly fluctuates from one constituency to another.

Fig. 5.3
India: Swings in Party Votes: 1971-1977-Communist Party of India (Marxist)

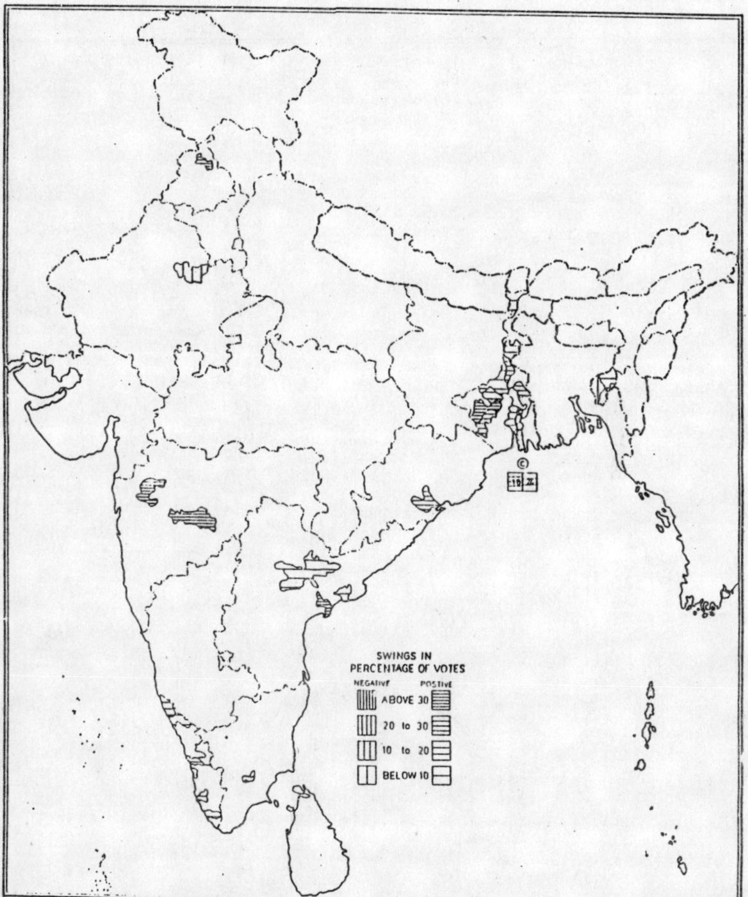

Fig. 5.4
India: Swings in Party Votes: 1977-1980-Communist Party of India (Marxist)

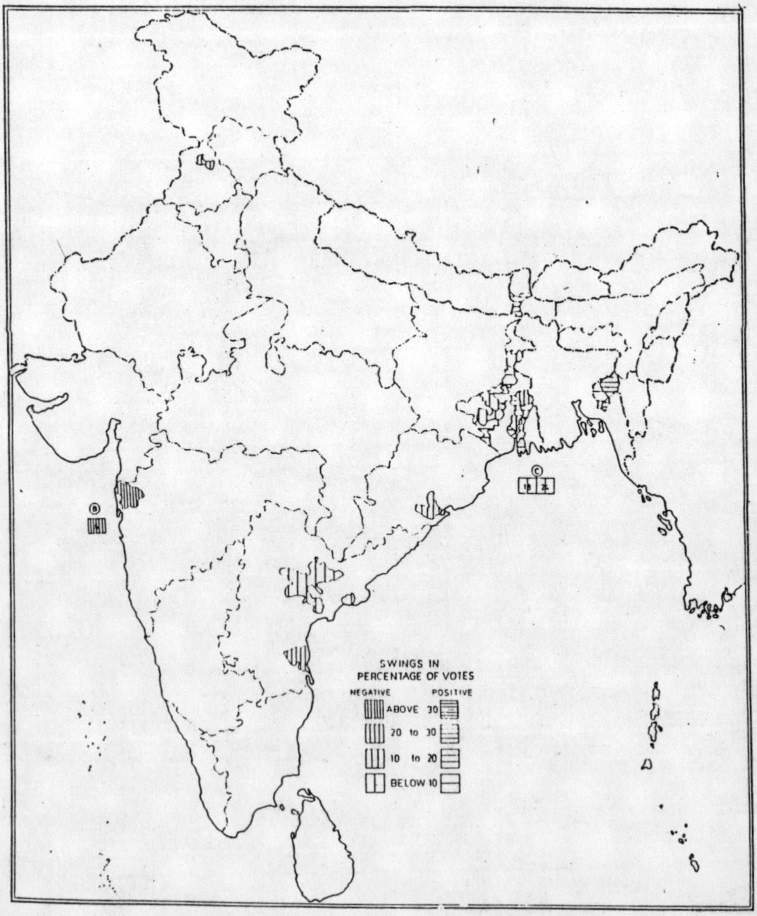

Congress Party

The Congress Party which had the honour of governing the country for nearly 30 years received a serious blow in the elections of March 1977. The party registered an all time negative swing of 9.16 per cent at all-India level. However, this was certainly not a big loss in the existing political climate which was characterized by strong anti-Congress feelings due to the internal emergency. But the constituencies of India tell a different story. It is seen that in many parts of the country the loss was of varying order. The party lost more than 30 per cent votes in as many as 80 constituencies. Table 5.4 shows the pattern of swings in the Congress following.

It is significant to note that despite the anti-Congress wave in 1977 the party managed to increase its strength in 68 constituencies out of which in 3 constituencies its share increased by more than 30 per cent. These constituencies were Shillong (Meghalaya), Peddapalli and Warangal in Andhra Pradesh (Fig. 5.5). There were 6 constituencies in which the party registered a positive swing of 20 to 30 per cent of which 4 were in Andhra Pradesh. Other two constituencies were Tripura East and Begusarai (Bihar). Fig 5.5 reveals that in Andhra Pradesh, the constituencies of high positive swings were in Telangana region. This was the result of the merger of Telangan Praja Samiti into the Congress Party.[22] In the entire Hindi speaking belt there were only 4 constituencies, 3 in Madhya Pradesh and one in Bihar in which the party improved its position. In Madhya Pradesh they formed a single pocket comprised by Sidhi, Shahdol and Bilaspur constituencies.

TABLE 5.4 : SWINGS IN PERCENTAGE VOTES, CONGRESS PARTY

Percentage change	No. of constituencies with negative swings		No. of constituences with positive swings	
	1971-77	1977-80	1971-77	1977-80
Above 30 per cent	80	3	3	4
20 to 30 per cent	85	4	6	53
10 to 20 per cent	89	9	22	141
Below 10 per cent	95	84	37	156
Total	349	100	68	354

Fig. 5.5
India: Swings in Party Votes: 1971-1977-Congress Party

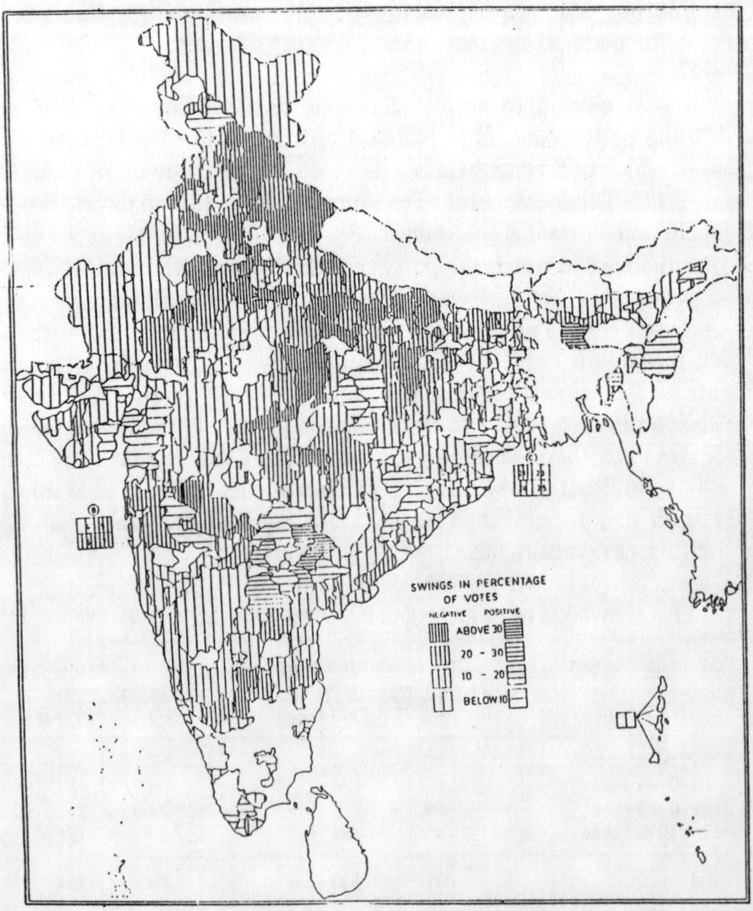

The Congress Party registered negative swings in as many as 349 constituencies. In 80 constituencies its votes declined by more than 30 per cent. The distribution of these constituencies (Fig. 5.5) reveals that except for 5 constituencies-two in Karnataka (Chikballapur and Kannakapura), two in Maharashtra (Bandara and Nanded) and one in Andhra Pradesh (Bobbili)-all were in Hindi speaking region of the north. In the areas with a considerable proportion of tribal population, the negative swings were of low magnitude.

The analysis of swings between 1977 and 1980 elections reveals that the party increased its votes by more than 30 per cent in only 4 constituencies (one each in Punjab, Uttar Pradesh, Bihar and Orissa). In one of the constituencies of the southern states of Karnataka, Andhra Pradesh, Tamil Nadu and Kerala, the party registered positive swings of more than 20 per cent (Fig. 5.6). This implies that in the areas where the party had considerable following, there was very little scope for further increase in its mass base. The most significant point to observe is that although it registered negative swings in 9 constituencies of West Bengal during 1971-1977, percentage votes increased in all the constituencies during 1977-1980. This shows that the party made considerable inroads into the Marxist stronghold during 1977-1980.[23]

Only in 100 constituencies, the Congress registered a negative swing. In 3 constituencies - Lakshadweep, Satara and Tripura East - the loss was more than 30 per cent. In the north, the party registered negative swings only in 14 constituencies lying in Rajasthan, Uttar Pradesh and Bihar. Remaining constituencies with negative swings were in Gujarat, Maharashtra, West Bengal, Orissa, Tripura, Assam, Manipur, Karnataka, Andhra Pradesh, Tamil Nadu, Kerala, Goa, Daman and Diu and Andaman and Nicobar Island.

The analysis of swings in the Congress votes reveals that they are characterized by a high degree of variation. It is evident that the areas with considerable mass following of the Congress party registered low swings. On the other hand, in the areas where other political parties posed a threat to the Congress base, the swings were of high magnitude. The analysis suggests that the party programme and appeals do not have a uniform impact on the electorate in different parts of the country because the factors of local importance command an edge over the factors of national importance.

Fig. 5.6
India: Swings in Party Votes: 1977-1980-Congress Party

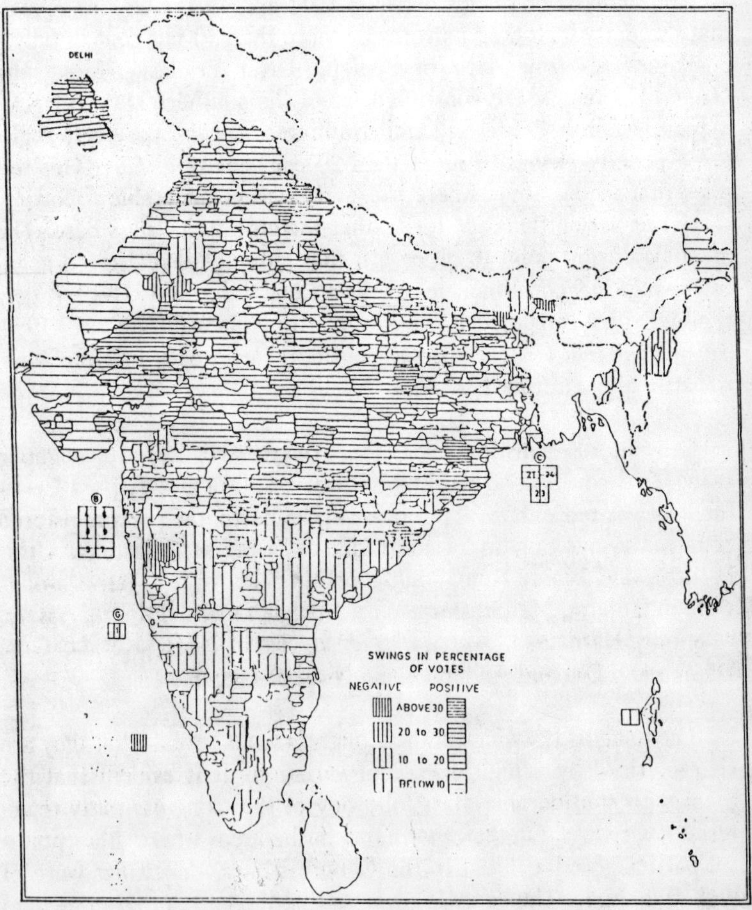

Janata Party

The Janata Party which came into existence as a result of the merger of four political parties in January 1977 had no mass base of its own at the time of 1977 elections. Even in the latter period the party could not develop its mass base and for all practical purposes operated through the organisational network of its constituents. However, the party took advantage of the anti-Congress atmosphere through capitalizing the Emergency issue and thus managed to achieve a great success. Table 5.5 shows the pattern of swings in its mass following during 1971-1977[24] and 1977-1980 elections.

TABLE 5.5: SWINGS IN PERCENTAGE VOTES, JANATA PARTY

Percentage change	No. of constituencies with negative swing		No. of constituencies with positive swing	
	1971-77	1977-80	1971-77	1977-80
Above 30 per cent	2	209	140	-
20 to 30 per cent	1	70	76	1
10 to 20 per cent	13	55	75	5
Below 10 per cent	25	40	39	3
Total	41	374	330	9

Despite a conducive climate for the Janata Party in 1977, its votes declined from combined strength of its constituents in 41 constituencies. In two constituencies (Baroda and Kalahandi), the loss was of more than 30 per cent. The distribution of these constituencies in various categories of swings indicates that the constituencies with negative swings were in Andhra Pradesh (1), Bihar (2), Gujarat (11), Jammu and Kashmir (1), Kerala (2), Madhya Pradesh (2), Manipur (2), Orissa (9), Tamil Nadu (10) and Dadra and Nagar Haveli (1).

The party registered positive swings in as many as 330 constituencies. In 140 constituencies, the gain was more than 30 per cent. Out of these 140 constituencies, only 2 constituencies were in the south (Andhra Pradesh). Similarly, of the 76 constituencies with a positive swing of 20 to 30 per cent, 17 were in Andhra Pradesh. Karnataka, Tamil Nadu and Kerala did not register positive swing of more than 20 per cent in any of the constituency.

Fig. 5.7
India: Swings in Party Votes: 1971-1977-Janata Party

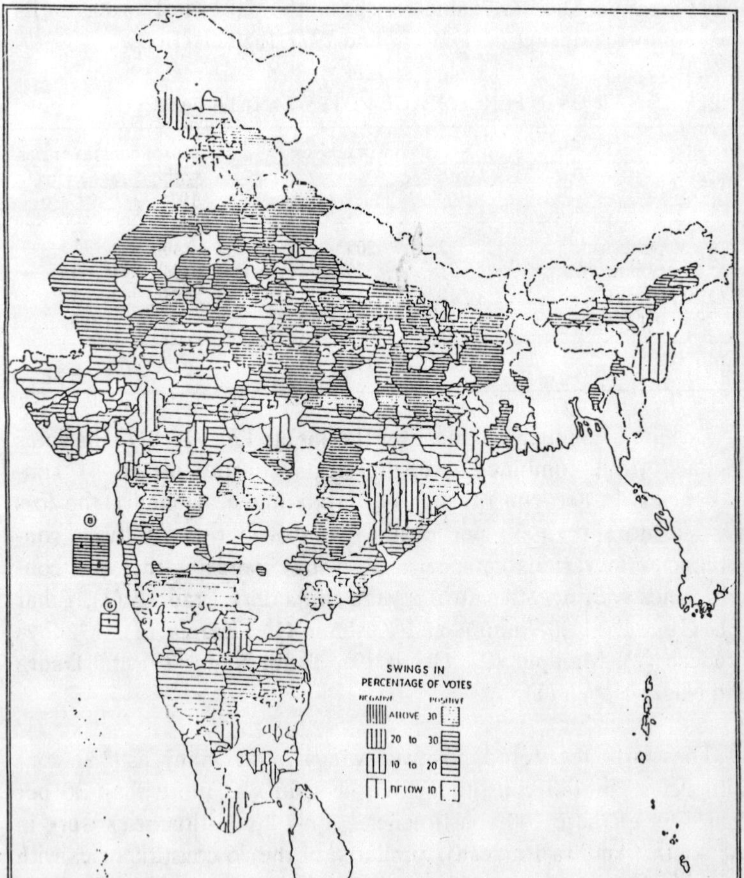

Fig. 5.8
India: Swings in Party Votes: 1977-1980-Janata Party

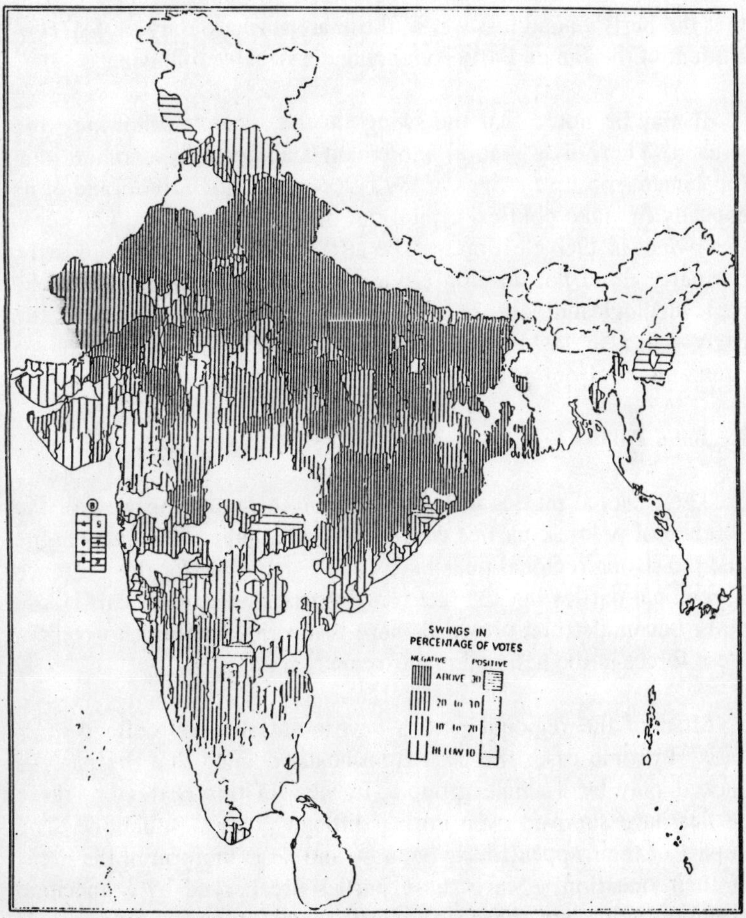

The pendulum swung the other way in 1980 elections. In this election the party registered negative swings in as many as 373 constituencies. The positive swings were confined to 9 constituencies only (Andhra Pradesh 2, Jammu and Kashmir 1, Manipur 1, Maharashtra 2, Orissa 1, and Tamil Nadu 2) The spatial distribution of constituencies (Fig. 5.8) with negative swings reveals that the loss was maximum in the States of Haryana, Rajasthan, Uttar Pradesh, West Bengal and Orissa which accounted for 187 constituencies out of 209 with negative swings of more than 30 per cent. This reveals that the party's main loss was in those areas where the Lok Dal constituent of the Janata Party commanded a sizeable following.

It may be noted that the swings in the Janata's following were uneven. There is a general agreement among the researchers that the Janata's positive swings in 1977 elections came in the wake of its capacity to make political capital out of emergency issue. The negative swings in 1980 election may be attributed to two reasons. Firstly, the party could not develop a mass base of its own because of the basic ideological differences among its constituents and secondly, the party failed in tackling the various problems, social as well as economic, confronting the Nation.

Regional Parties

The regional parties in India continue to flourish in view of the absence of political parties with an all-India image. One may argue that the strong regional pulls have been responsible for the existence of regional parties but the fact remains that the regional parties can never become strong provided there is a serious attempt to contain these forces in the national mainstream.[25]

Most of the regional parties have a socially well defined mass base. In some cases the base is so neatly defined that the party is backed only by a single group. In view of this character, these parties have survived even during difficult political situations. The impact of their appeals have been by and large uniform in the areas of their opeation. Since these parties are backed by a specified group of the society, there is very little scope for longer shifts in their mass base and therefore the magnitude of swings registered by these parties has been of a low order. Appendix VC, which shows the number of constituencies in different categories of swings, illustrates this point.

Spatial Variations in Swings: A Comparative View

The preceding analysis revealed that the swings in party following are characterized by a high degree of spatial variations. The following analysis attempts to assess the magnitude of variations in swings with the help of coefficient of variation. Table 5.6 gives the coefficients of variation for selected parties.

TABLE 5.6: VARIATIONS IN PARTY SWINGS, COEFFICIENT OF VARIATIONS

Party	Coefficients of Variation	
	1971-1977	1977-1980
Congress	299.59	1181.20
Janata Party	365.29	499.31
Communist Party of India	110.09	141.10
Communist Party of India (Marxist)	136.70	607.90
Shiromani Akali Dal	58.68	49.32
Dravida Munnetra Kazhagam	48.49	51.18
Anna-Dravida Munnetra Kazhagam	-	61.27

It is evident from Table 5.6 that the variations in swings are of higher order in case of major political parties. However, the coefficients of variation are comparatively low in regard to CPI and CPI(M).[26]

It is seen that the programme and appeals of Communist Parties have, by and large, a uniform impact on the masses. This is understandable in view of the nature of mass following of these political parties.[27] It is significant to note that the coefficients of variation are lowest in case of 3 selected regional parties. It implies that the appeals of regional parties cause more or less uniform swings between two elections. This may be explained by the nature of appeals of these parties. The programme and appeals of these parties are generally sectarian and parochial and find a strong foothold in their regional polities.

AN OVERVIEW

The above analysis is an interesting example of the electoral behaviour of the masses in relation to political parties. While in 1977 elections the internal emergency was the main issue, the Janata's in-fightings and non-performance became the main issue in 1980 elections. Although, the Janata tried to drag the issue of internal emergency once again in 1980, for all purposes it remained a non-issue. However, the local issues were important in different regions of the country.

The analysis reveals that the party swings in a single election are not uniform over space because a highly fragmented society does not respond uniformly. Since these fragments have a well defined geography and form separate enclaves in the country, the local issues discernable in their polities have an edge over the national issues. This implies that the elections in India are not truly national. The elections may be termed national if the issues involved in the elections have a national appeal and the response of the masses to these appeals is more or less homogeneous. However, the organization of Indian society, the nature of mass base of political parties, and the issues raised by political parties do not allow the electoral process to acquire a national character.

It is noted that not only the constituencies have variegated pattern of swings but even the states are characterized by marked differences. However, the spatial analysis of swings indicates that they have a regional patterning. The magnitude of swings is enough testimony to the hollowness of the mass following of political parties. The geographic patterning of party swings endorses the fact that the political opinion in the country remains, by and large fragmented.

NOTES AND REFERENCES

1. Biplab Dasgupta, *Patterns and Trends in Indian Politics: An Ecological Analysis of Aggregate Data on Society and Election* (New Delhi: Allied Publishers Private Limited, 1973), pp. 176-92.
2. D.E. Stokes, "A Variance Components Model of Political Effects," in J.M. Clauch (ed), *Mathematical Applications* in Political Science (Dallas : Southern Methodist University Press, 1965).
3. D.E. Stokes, "Parties and the Nationalization of Electoral Forces," in W.N. Chambers and W.D. Burnham (ed.), *The American Party Systems*, (New York:

Oxford University Press, 1967), pp. 182-202.

4. G. Green, "National City and Ward Components of Local Voting, "*Policy and Politics*, 1, 1972, pp. 45-54.
5. W.H. Morris-Jones, "India Discards Dictatorship," *World Today*, Vol. 33, No. 5, May 1977, pp. 161-4.
6. C.P. Bhambhari *The Janata Party* (New Delhi, 1980), p. 1.
7. "Mixture as Before," *Hindustan Times* (New Delhi), November 7, 1979.
8. The CPI contested only 48 seats in 1980 against 87 in 1971 and 91 in 1977.
9. This is significant to note that while the CPI suffered a lot due to its cooperation with the Congress, the party gained in Kerala. This happened in the wake of good performance of the coalition ministry headed by Achuta Menon.
10. "The left democratic front has done two good things for the democratic rivals. By forcing the resignation of the Koya Ministry, they have virtually lost the support of the Muslim community. They have also improved the image of Mrs. Gandhi considerably. People now say that Mrs. Gandhi alone can ensure a strong government against indiscipline and chaos in public life.*Times of India* (Bombay), December 24, 1979.
11. The Congress' highest gain in Meghalaya came in the wake of the atmosphere of uncertainity of elections in the state in the background of communal problems. Therefore, this should not be judged as the party's great sccesses.
12. This can be seen from a leaflet issued by the party which reads as "Beware that the hand that comes to you open for votes tod:. should not become a fist to strike at you tomorrow." Vote Janata: Not Dictator, Not Defectors, you can trust us."
13. Another leaflet says: "Priceless Lies," "Onions in her time sold for Rs. 4.50 per kilo, she claims the price was only Rs.1.50 per kolo. No one can beat Mrs.Gandhi in lies. In Hyderabad, where Mrs. GAndhi's government is ruling, onions are selling at Rs. 10.00 per kilo gram.".
14. *The Statesman* (New Delhi), March 24, 1977.
15. The Akali Dal's image has become blurred because of internal bickering and frequent change of stand by its leaders. The drama of referring political matters either to the Ákal Takht or religious leaders has made Akali leaders objects of ridicule. And as expected, the religious leaders too have been divided. *The Times of India* (Bombay), December 24, 1979.
16. Mr. Karunanidhi and his lieutenants had been at work building up the party afresh from the grassroots. *The Times of India* (New Delhi), January 12, 1980.
17. "Mr. Narayanaswami Naidu credits the defeat of the ADMK at the polls to his association's call to farmers to teach lesson to MGR Government for its harsh coercive measures in recovering dues, infuriating the dignity and self respect of farmers and for launching cases against them, among other things.*The Times of India* (New Delhi), January 12, 1980.
18. "Her (Mrs. Kakodkar) iron control over party .... her coolness on statehood for Goa, Daman and Diu and the promotion of Konkani, two matters dear to every Goan's heart ... and finally the growing dissidence within the MGP, collectively eroded her support.*The Times of India* (New Delhi), January 10, 1980.
19. For the purpose of this analysis, the swings have been computed only for those constituencies where the parties contested in two consecutive elections. If the party contested in one of the two elections, swings in these constituencies have not been computed.
20. *The Times of India*, (New Delhi), January 19, 1980.
21. *The Statesman* (New Delhi), January 12, 1980.
22. The Telangana Praja Samiti which was spearheading the movement for separate Telangana state had a strong base in Telangana. However, this party

merged into the Congress on September 18, 1971.

23. The another interpretation of this phenomenon may be that the party lost the support of a sizeable electorate in 1977 elections in the wake of anti-Congress wave. However, this loss was temporary and thus the party was capable to regain its lost mass following by the time of 1980 elections.
24. Since there was no Janata Party in 1971, the votes polled by its constituents have been added together to derive the votes for the Janata Party in 1971.
25. As long as the Congress Party had an all India perspective under the leadership of Nehru, the regional parties could never attain a great sucess. After the death of Nehru when the country went to polls in 1967, the regional parties emerged on political scene with their full zeal.
26. The coefficient of variation for CPI(M) during 1977-1980 is comparatively higher. This is attributed to the fact that the party entered into electoral alliance with the Janata and other likeminded parties in 1977. This significantly affected the party's performance. However, this alliance could not be repeated in 1980 elections and thus the party suffered a setback in some of the Constituencies. This contributed to a high degree of spatial variations in swings.
27. This may be attributed to two factors. Firstly, the party has a well defined economic programme and secondly, the masses having allegiance to Communist Parties have a higher degree of political consciousness.

SIX

INSTITUTIONALIZATION AND CHANGING PATTERN OF PARTY FOLLOWING

The degree of political stability reflects the relationship between the political institutions and the social forces. The Indian society is composed of various ethno-lingual groups, which are further divided into religious communities and caste groupings. With the process of modernization, the rigid boundaries defining the extent of social groupings tend to loose their rigidity and in due course are supplemented by secondary groupings. But this new line of organization does not altogether eliminate the impact of primary associations based on social variables. It is here that the political institutions become important agencies for maintaining order, resolving differences and disputes, selecting leaders and promoting unity among the heterogeneous social groups. In a simple society where the masses are organized along a simple social variable, there is little need for advanced political institutions in view of the stability of political system. However in complex societies where the social forces are divided along a number of primiary associations, the stability of the political system largely depends on the nature of political institutions. It is through the latter that the social forces attain a working equation in which different social groups can exist together.

The political parties are the most important political institutions in a complex social system. Therefore, the stability of the political system will depend upon the stability of the mass following. This, however is a function of institutionalization which may be defined as "the process by which organizations and procedures acquire value and stability."[1] Institutionalization can be defined in terms of its adaptability, complexity, unity and autonomy.[2]

The primary concern in this analysis is with only one aspect of the total political process - the voting behaviour. The emphasis is on the analysis of the differences in levels of institutionalization in India as indicated by the regularity in the patterns of party support. This is attempted here by an analysis of the nature of consistency in party support over a period of time. A low level of consistency would imply a transitory and indeterminate situation where a party does not have a well-defined territorial base. On the other hand, a high level of consistency would indicate that the extent of mass following of the political party is steady over a long period. It may be stated that since the analysis pertains to the level of constituencies, consistency relates to territorial distrubution of strength and not to the overall strength at national or state level.

There is a general tendency among researchers to base the analysis of consistency in party votes either on the criterion of seats won[3] or percentage votes polled.[4] However, this researcher feels that considering the complexity of situation in India any analysis of party consistency should take into account different aspects of party strength in constituencies. The percentage share of votes polled by a party in a constituency is only one of them. The others include the share of a party in a constituency in its all India votes and its position in relation to the winning/nearest rival candidate. It is felt that the comparison of overall strength on the basis of these indicators in the successive elections will yield a more meaningful pattern of party consistency. Therefore, the following three indicators have been chosen to construct a composite index of party strength in each of the constituencies for analysing the results of three elections of 1971, 1977 and 1980. These indicators are :

1. Votes polled by a party in a constituency as percentage of the total valid votes polled.
2. Votes polled by a party in a constituency as percentage to the total votes polled by the party in the country (Index of concentration).
3. The ratio of victory/loss.

The detailed statistical procedure involved in the analysis has been explained in the introductory chapter. The relative strength and the consistency or inconsistency have been tested in the case of 27 political parties.

CONCEPTUAL FRAMEWORK

The consistency in party support, by and large, remains a function of the nature of its mass following. Generally, parties with well defined socio-economic base will show a high degree of consistency in their territorial support. For example, the Jammu and Kashmir National Conference is neither easily displaced in Kashmir valley, nor able to expand elsewhere[5], and thus its performance will tend to be consistent. On the other hand, parties like the Jharkhand which is a champion of the tribal cause in the Chotanagpur region will tend to emerge with less consistency. AlthoughIt, it has been able to capture some support in the neighbourhood of its area of influence, its original base has been eroded considerably for various reasons.[6] Similarly, the umbrella character of the Congress Party, despite its good organizational ability, will not allow it to show consistency in its party following from election to election.

However, this phenomenon need not be universal. The voting marks the culmination of a continuous process of interaction between the social forces and political institutions. Therefore, the stability or instability in party following has to be viewed in this larger context. Generally speaking two processes govern the nature of party stability - social mobilization and economic development. The Indian experience after Independence reveals that her polity has registered both these processes with varying magnitudes in different regions.

The relationship between social mobility and party consistency is a distinct one. Social mobility results in increasing social awareness as a consequence of rapid increase in literacy and other related variables. This disrupts the traditional and social groupings and undermines the loyalty to traditional authority. The disruption of the traditional organization thus creates a need for new identification and loyalties and thus results in realignment of social forces.

Economic development may have positive or negative impact on party stability[7] depending upon the region. Its positive impact on party stability may be visualized in an area where the party is able to satisfy growing expectations It certainly reduces the degree of social frustration and thus resulting in stable (consistent) party following.

Indian electoral data provide enough testimony of this phenomenon. When the country became Independent, it was characterized by a highly feudal order and deep economic stagnation in the countryside. The first major task of the government was to bring the national economy back to the normal. The process started under the dominating influence of Nehru. The seeds were sown in First Five Year Plan. Although, the country continued to make rapid progress on economic as well as social fronts, the gains were not distributed uniformly. In the latter years the ruling Congress could not satisfy people's expectations mainly because the party did not have a leadership with a national standing after Nehru and Shastri. These events disturbed the cohesive character of the party. This helped a number of parties to emerge on the Indian political scene. Notable among these were Jana Sangh in Madhya Pradesh, Akali Dal in Punjab, Dravida Munnetra Kazhagam in Tamil Nadu, and Jharkhand Party in Bihar. The reasons are obvious. These parties represented the interests of the regional communities and therefore, they saw a new hope of getting their demands satisfied. Although, some expectations were not in national interest, some grievances were really genuine and required immediate redressal. The regional parties with their roots in traditional values found a following in the regions where people subscribed to regional demands. But with growing awareness of the masses, perception of policies and programmes of parties changed, and therefore, some of the parties suffered in their mass following.[8] The major parties were likely to gain. However, in the areas where the existing strong parties could meet the people's rising expectations in changed socio-economic conditions, the chances of change in party support were meagre. In this perspective it may be suggested that the party consistency may be explained in terms of changing socio-economic environment. The party which can contain the emergent social and economic pulls is likely to have stable party following. On the contrary, the failure of the parties to accommodate a changed environment will lead to inconsistent party following. The phenomenon may be expressed in the following model.

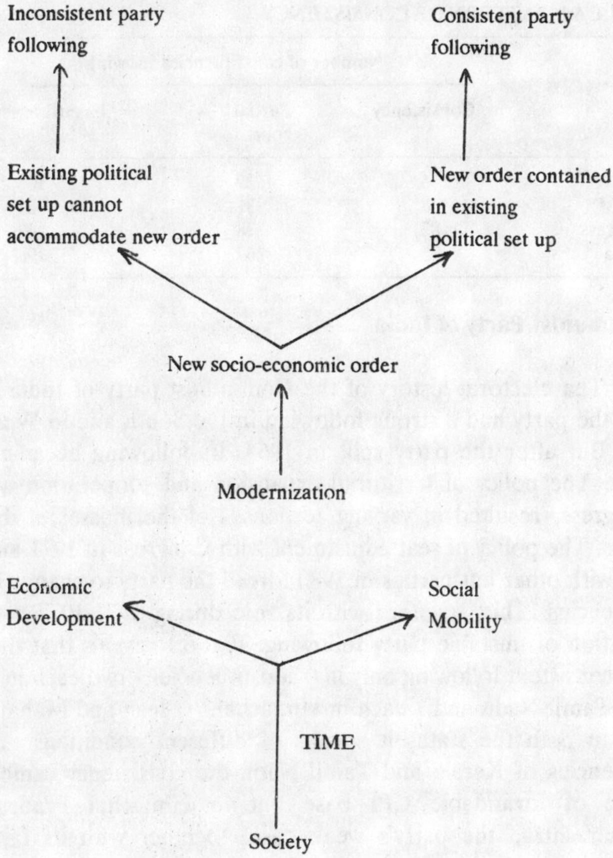

SPATIAL PATTERN OF PARTY CONSISTENCY

The Indian political scene, by its very nature is characterized by a high degree of political fluidity (Table 6.1). None of the major political parties show a stable party following during the period 1971-1980. Barring a few, even the regional parties, have failed to command a consistent party following. The following paragraphs attempt to identify the areas of consistency in the mass support of political parties.

TABLE 6.1: PATTERN OF CONSISTENCY

Party	Number of constituencies showing		
	Consistency	Partial consistency	Inconsistency
CPI	6	29	108
CPI(M)	8	31	63
Congress	82	278	149
Janata	38	267	198

Communist Party of India

The electoral history of the Communist party of India reveals that the party had a strong following in the South and in West Bengal. But after the party split in 1964, its following became highly fluid. The policy of territorial expansion and cooperation with the Congress, resulted in varying responses of the masses at different times. The policy of seat adjustment with Congress in 1971 and 1977 and with other left parties in 1980 forced the party to change its constituencies. This, together with its role during 1971-1977 created a situation of unstable party following. Fig. 6.1 reveals that the party had consistent following only in 6 constituencies - two each in Kerala and Tamil Nadu and 1 each in Himachal Pradesh and Maharashtra. But in both the states it speaks of different conditions. In constituencies of Kerala and Tamil Nadu the consistency came in the wake of formidable CPI base but in Himachal Pradesh and Maharashtra, the party's weak base[9] together with its failure to widen it, resulted in consistent following. The party had inconsistent following in 108 constituencies (Table 6.2). It is evident from Table 6.2 that all constituencies in Gujarat, Haryana, Karnataka, Meghalaya, Punjab, Rajasthan and Chandigarh show inconsistent following. It is significant to note that except Punjab, in all these states the party commands very little following. Inconsistency in these states results mainly from undefined party base. It is seen that the party contests a seat in one election but fails to do so in another election and thus contributes to inconsistency. However, the shifts in mass following is an obvious factor contributing to the phenomenon of inconsistency. The distribution of these constituencies reveals that they were in the areas where the party had a sizeable following (Fig. 6.1).

Fig. 6.1
India: Spatial Pattern of Party Consistency - Communist Party of India (Marxist)

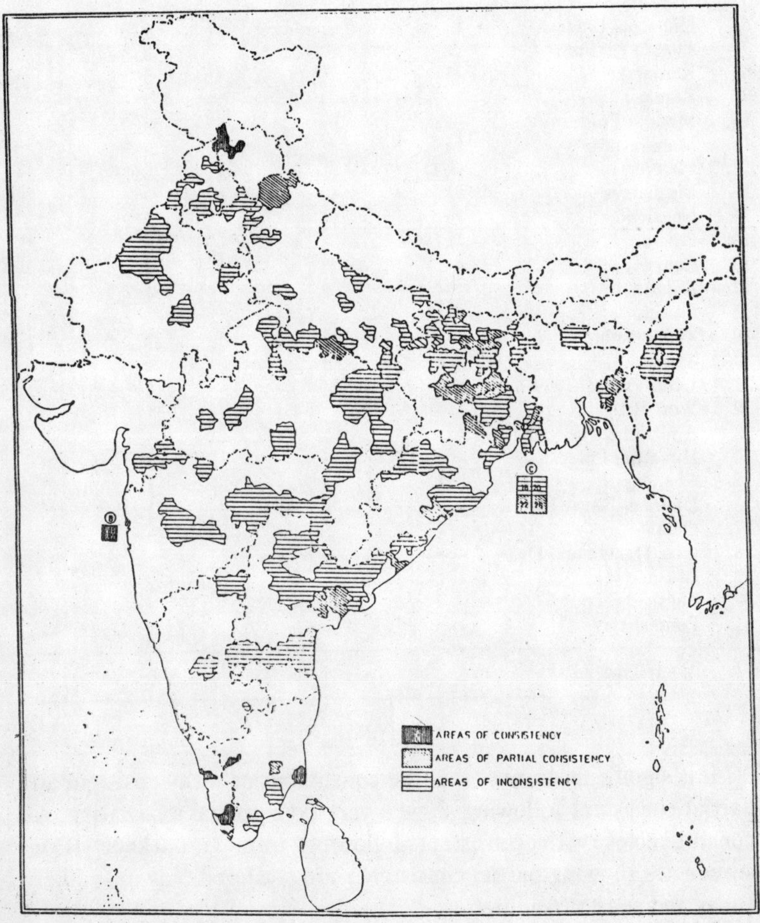

TABLE 6.2: PATTERN OF CONSISTENCY, COMMUNIST PARTY OF INDIA

S.No.	State/Union Territory	Number of Constituencies showing		
		Consistency	Partial Consistency	Inconsistency
1.	Andhra Pradesh	-	2	16
2.	Assam	-	-	-
3.	Bihar	-	11	18
4.	Gujarat	-	-	1
5.	Haryana	-	-	2
6.	Himachal Pradesh	1	-	-
7.	Jammu Kashmir	-	-	3
8.	Karnataka	-	-	3
9.	Kerala	2	2	-
10.	Madhya Pradesh	-	1	8
11.	Maharashtra	1	1	9
12.	Manipur	-	1	1
13.	Meghalaya	-	-	-
14.	Nagaland	-	-	-
15.	Orissa	-	1	6
16.	Punjab	-	-	4
17.	Rajasthan	-	-	4
18.	Sikkim	-	-	-
19.	Tamil Nadu	2	1	2
20.	Tripura	-	1	1
21.	Uttar Pradesh	-	3	14
22.	West Bengal	-	4	14
23.	Andman & Nicobar Is.	-	-	-
24.	Himachal Pradesh	-	-	-
25.	Chandigarh	-	-	1
26.	Dadra & Nagar Haveli	-	-	1
27.	Delhi	-	1	-
28.	Goa, Daman and Diu	-	-	-
29.	Lakshadweep	-	-	-
30.	Lakshadweep	-	-	-
31.	Pondicherry	-	-	-
	INDIA	6	29	108

It is significant to note that the constituencies with consistent and partial consistent following show a very poor spatial association. All constituencies with consistent following form 6 pockets. Constituencies showing partial consistency are clustered only in southern Bihar and coastal Andhra.

Communist Party of India (Marxist)

The Communist Party of India (Marxist) has, since its inception, been operating mainly in West Bengal and Kerala.[10] This concentration was the result of party organization which was dominated by the leaders belonging to these two states at the time of split. The policy of concentration has benefited the party significantly in maintaining a speedy growth in its mass base. However, it is significant to note that despite the tactics of concentration the party has not been able to command a stable following. This is evident from the fact that the party had consistent following only a 8 constituencies of which 4 were in West Bengal and 2 each in Andhra Pradesh and Kerala (Fig. 6.2, Table 6.3). This shows that despite its well-defined mass base its following is characterized by a high degree of fluidity.

This is further illustrated by the fact that only in 31 constituencies, the party had partial consistency. The distribution of these constituencies reveals that out of 31 constituencies, West Bengal and Kerala accounted for 26 constituencies (West Bengal 18 and Kerala 8). It is significant to note that constituencies in West Bengal were in industrial complexes. This is a reflection of the nature of party's mass following in the state. In Kerala these constituencies form a cluster in Palghat region.

Inconsistency in party following is associated with the areas where the party commands insignificant mass following. In all there were 63 constituencies in this category. It is significant to note that despite its strong base in West Bengal, the party's following remains inconsistent in as many as 18 constituencies. The spatial pattern of these constituencies reveals that they are located around the zone of consistency and partial consistency. It is further observed that the areas of inconsistency in the state more or less correspond with the areas where agriculture continues to be the main economic activity. This indicates that among the agricultural population the party does not have a stable following. Probably expansion of the party's base among the rural population has contributed to this phenomenon.

The pattern of inconsistency in other states does not reveal any geographic pattern. However, it is important to note that the inconsistency was perfect in states like Haryana, Himachal Pradesh,

Madhya Pradesh, Maharashtra, Orissa, Punjab, Tamil Nadu, Uttar Pradesh and in the Union Territories of Andaman and Nicobar Islands and Dadra and Nagar Haveli. It reveals that inconsistency is associated mainly with the areas of weak party base.[11] However, a weak organisational network further contributes to the process of inconsistency.

TABLE 6.3: PATTERN OF CONSISTENCY, COMMUNIST PARTY OF INDIA (MARXIST)

S.No.	State/Union Territory	Number of Constituencies showing		
		Consistency	Partial Consistency	Inconsistency
1.	Andhra Pradesh	2	1	3
2.	Assam	-	-	-
3.	Bihar	-	1	5
4.	Gujarat	-	-	-
5.	Haryana	-	-	2
6.	Himachal Pradesh	-	-	1
7.	Jammu & Kashmir	-	-	-
8.	Karnataka	-	1	1
9.	Kerala	2	8	4
10.	Madhya Pradesh	-	-	2
11.	Maharashtra	-	-	5
12.	Manipur	-	-	-
13.	Meghalaya	-	-	-
14.	Nagaland	-	-	-
15.	Orissa	-	-	1
16.	Punjab	-	-	3
17.	Rajasthan	-	1	4
18.	Sikkim	-	-	-
19.	Tamil Nadu	-	-	6
20.	Tripura	-	1	1
21.	Uttar Pradesh	-	-	5
22.	West Bengal	4	18	18
23.	Andaman & Nicobar Is.	-	-	1
24.	Arunachal Pradesh	-	-	-
25.	Chandigarh	-	-	-
26.	Dadra & Nagar Haveli	-	-	1
27.	Delhi	-	-	-
28.	Goa, Daman & Diu	-	-	-
29.	Kakshadweep	-	-	-
30.	Mizoram	-	-	-
31.	Pondicherry	-	-	-
	INDIA	8	31	63

Fig. 6.2
India: Spatial Pattern of Party Consistency - Communist Party of India (Marxist)

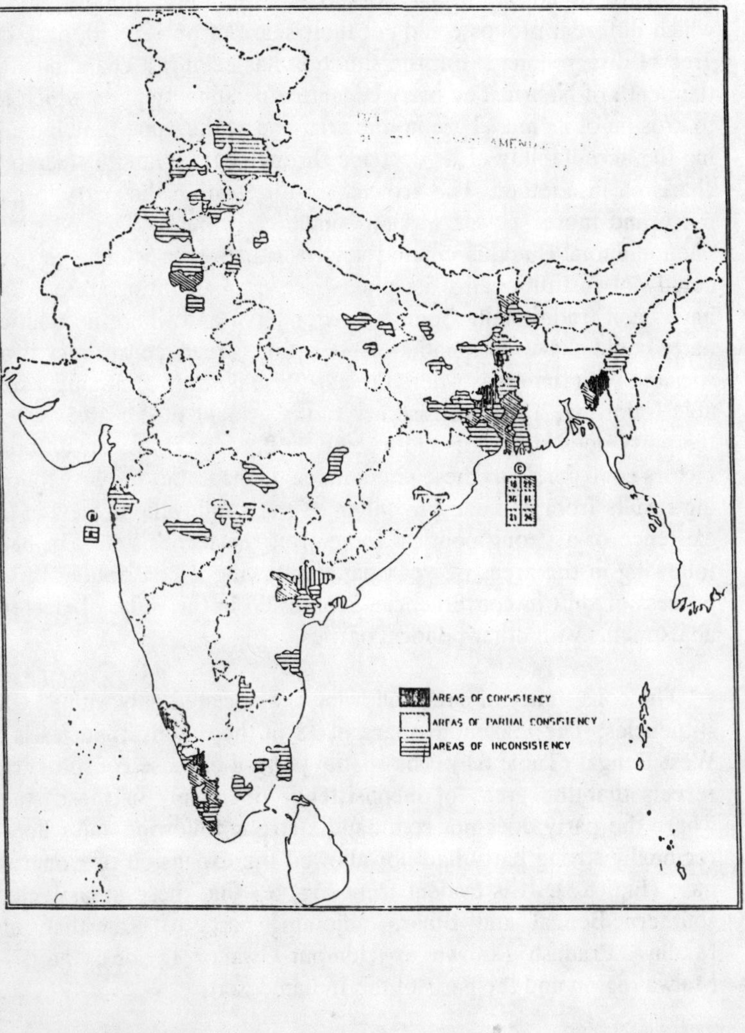

It may be noted that despite a well defined programme and party base the CPI (M) has failed to attain high degree of institutionalization. It implies that even in the areas of CPI (M) following, the process of politicization is at low key.

Congress Party

The Congress Party which started its political history as a nationalist organization, has worked as an umbrella organization in which different groups could get their share of power with little degree of disagreement. But the situation has been fast changing after the death of Nehru. The party became a personality party which led to erosion of its mass base in one area and at the same time increasing the acceptability of its doctrine through Mrs. Gandhi's personal charisma in another. The growing conflict within the party to gain more and more power was the single contributory factor for this phenomenon. But this created such a situation in which the party could not institutionalize its mass base even in those areas which have been traditionally Congress' stronghold and where no political party could shake its foundation. It is noted that consistency is associated with the areas where the party could never command a sizeable following. The inconsistency too is evident in the areas where the party does not command a strong following. However, different factors contributed to these phenomena. Consistency in party following results from its failure to widen its mass following in view of the existence of a strong political force. But the inconsistency in party following in the areas of weak party following is contributed by the process of shift in constituencies contested in the wake of electoral adjustments with other political parties.

The consistency in party following is associated only with 82 constituencies. The maximum share of 18 in these constituencies is of West Bengal (Table 6.4). The spatial pattern of these constituencies reveals that the areas of inconsistency lie mainly in those states where the party does not command a strong following and where a regionally strong party had not allowed the expansion of Congress' base (Fig. 6.3). It is evident from Fig. 6.3 that these areas include southern Bengal and Bihar, adjoining parts of Rajasthan and Madhya Pradesh (known as Udaipur-Gwalior region), parts of Malwa region and the parts of the Indian desert.

Fig. 6.3
India: Spatial Pattern of Party Consistency - Congress Party

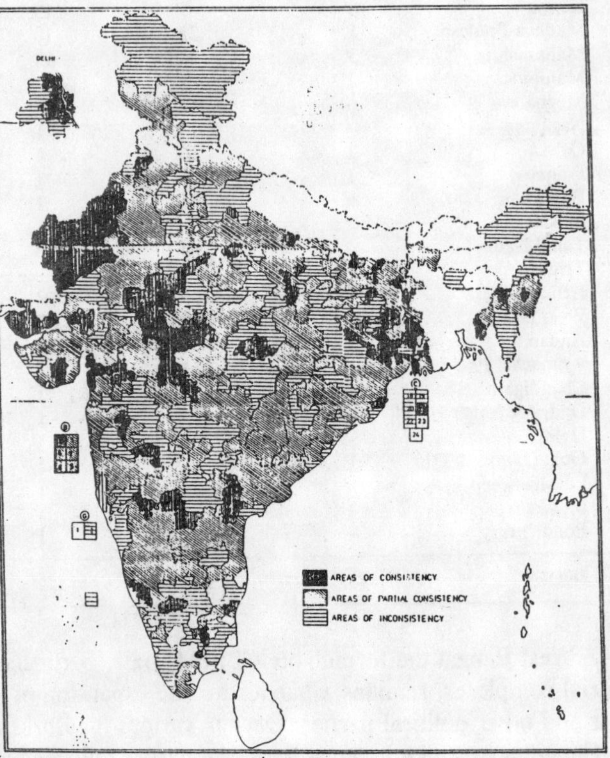

TABLF 6.4: PATTERN OF CONSISTENCY, CONGRESS PARTY

S.No.	State/Union Territory	Number of Constituencies showing		
		Consistency	Partial Consistency	Inconsistency
1.	Andhra Pradesh	4	26	12
2.	Assam	-	-	-
3.	Bihar	10	28	16
4.	Gujarat	6	18	2
5.	Haryana	-	6	4
6.	Himachal Pradesh	-	1	3
7.	Jammu & Kashmir	-	2	4
8.	Karnataka	4	19	5
9.	Kerala	1	5	13
10.	Madhya Pradesh	8	22	10
11.	Maharashtra	7	28	13
12.	Manipur	1	1	-
13.	Meghalaya	-	-	-
14.	Nagaland	-	-	1
15.	Orissa	1	16	4
16.	Punjab	1	11	1
17.	Rajasthan	6	15	4
18.	Sikkim	-	-	1
19.	Tamil Nadu	4	6	13
20.	Tripura	1	1	-
21.	Uttar Pradesh	9	48	28
22.	West Bengal	18	17	7
23.	Andaman & Nicobar Is.	-	1	-
24.	Arunachal Pradesh	-	1	1
25.	Chandigarh	-	-	1
26.	Dadra & Nagar Haveli	-	-	1
27.	Delhi	-	6	1
28.	Goa, Daman & Diu	1	-	1
29.	Lakshadweep	-	-	1
30.	Mizoram	-	-	1
31.	Pondicherry	-	-	1
	INDIA	82	278	149

In West Bengal the formidable CPI (M) base, particularly in industrial complexes, remains a barrier for the expansion of the Congress and other political parties. Despite various measures taken by the Congress to widen its mass base, the party's following remained static. Similarly in southern Bihar, the party had failed miserably to make significant inroads into the tribal communities of these areas. By virtue of their primitive social order, the political opinion in the tribal areas continues to be shaped by the local issues. The failure of the Congress Party to meet the persistent demand for the creation of Jharkhand state did not allow it to widen its base. Thus the party continues to satisfy itself with a 'stable low mass following'. The situation in Madhya Pradesh and Rajasthan is created by the existing feudal order where the ex-princely *gharanas* still enjoy their status among the illiterate rural folk. This helped the Jana Sangh to gain a foothold in this region which in subsequent period became so strong that it emerged as a formidable force. The composite scores of other constitutencies with stable party following reveals that they do not have strong party following. There are only a few exceptions to this general phenomenon.

The partial consistency is a phenomenon in a large part of the country. In all 278 constituencies show partial consistency with respect to Congress following. Distribution of these constituencies in different states is presented in Table 6.4 However, it is evident from Fig. 6.3 that these areas show a high degree of spatial association. It is significant to note that the areas of partial consistency are associated with the areas where the party commands a strong following.

Inconsistency in Congress followership is again a phenomenon in the areas of weak base. There are as many as 149 constituencies which reveal inconsistent party following. Fig. 6.3 shows that inconsistency is a general phenomenon in Jammu and Kashmir, Kerala, Tamil Nadu, Western Uttar Pradesh, southern Bihar, Mizoram and Nagaland. Besides, parts of Madhya Pradesh (adjoining areas of Vindhyachal and Chhatisgarh), Maharashtra and Telangana too reveal inconsistency in party following. However, it is important to point out that the inconsistency in Jammu and Kashmir, Kerala, Tamil Nadu, Mizoram and Nagaland is different from that of other parts. In these states this phenomenon is attributed to the existence of strong regional parties with whom the Congress has forged alliance at different occasions. Sometimes it did not even field its candidates in view of the lack of popular support. In other parts the inconsistency is a function of the change in its popular support in view of existing political context.

This leads one to conclude that despite remaining in power since the Independence, with a break of just about 33 months, the party has not been able to command a stable party following in the country. This is a manifestation of the fluidity of its mass base.

Janata Party

Since, the constituents of the Janata party never commanded a well defined social base, the Janata Party too, could not achieve a significant degree of stability in its mass following. Infighting in the Janata's constituents resulted in the breakdown of the party which created a situation in which stability was a far cry. It is significant to note that the major factor which contributed to this process was a desire by individual constituent groups to widen their base which was fluid in character with a few exceptions. The result of this process proved disastrous to the Janata Party which lost much of its glory achieved in 1977. Therefore, the lack of cohesion among the constituent groups and the ill-defined party base did not allow the party to have a regular pattern of territorial support. Table 6.5 shows the pattern of consistency in different states. It is evident from Table 6.5 that the party emerged consistent only in 38 constituencies. The spatial pattern of these constituencies (Fig. 6.4) reveals that the majority of them were in those areas where the party had no following at all. Its failure to widen its base in these areas resulted in consistent party support. It is evident from Fig. 6.4 that in the north Indian states the party had consistent following in 4 constituencies - 3 in western Madhya Pradesh and 1 in Jammu and Kashmir. It is significant to note that among the constituencies of consistent party following, only these 3 constituencies of Madhya Pradesh are characterized by the strong party base.[12] Although, the constituencies of consistency are scattered, all the 17 constituencies of this category in Karnataka form a single cluster. Probably the formidable Congress base in Karnataka explain this situation.

The partial consistency is a phenomenon in nearly half of the constituencies. A comparative view of the derived composite scores of these constituencies reveals that they fall in the same category in 1971 and 1980. This shows that the Janata's support in 1980 was broadly same as that of 1971. It is significant to note that even the constituencies of partial consistency do not reveal geographical contiguity. However, the constituencies are clustered. The spatial

Fig. 6.4
India: Spatial Pattern of Party Consistency - Janata Party

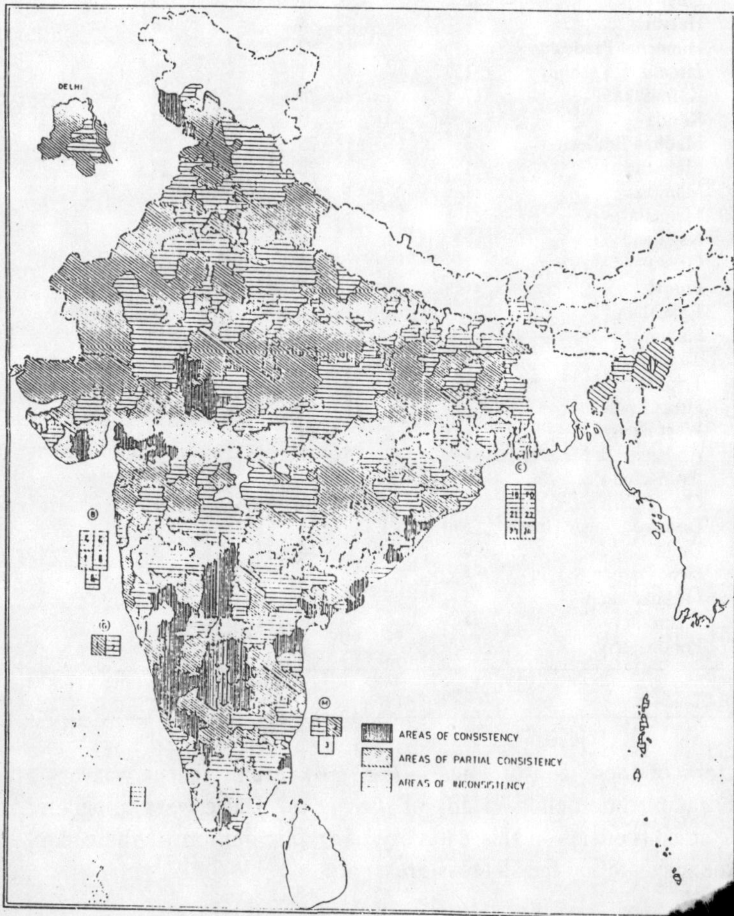

TABLE 6.5: PATTERN OF CONSISTENCY, JANATA PARTY

S.No.	State/Union Territory	Number of Constituencies showing		
		Consistency	Partial Consistency	Inconsistency
1.	Andhra Pradesh	8	22	12
2.	Assam	-	-	-
3.	Bihar	-	34	20
4.	Gujarat	2	21	3
5.	Haryana	-	4	6
6.	Himachal Pradesh	-	2	2
7.	Jammu & Kashmir	1	1	1
8.	Karnataka	17	10	1
9.	Kerala	-	3	9
10.	Madhya Pradesh	3	25	12
11.	Maharashtra	1	20	24
12.	Manipur	1	1	-
13.	Meghalaya	-	-	-
14.	Nagaland	-	-	-
15.	Orissa	1	15	4
16.	Punjab	-	5	7
17.	Rajasthan	-	16	9
18.	Sikkim	-	-	-
19.	Tamil Nadu	3	12	23
20.	Tripura	-	1	1
21.	Uttar Pradesh	-	55	30
22.	West Bengal	-	14	27
23.	Andaman & Nicobar Is.	-	-1	
24.	Arunachal Pradesh	-		-
25.	Chandigarh	-	-	1
26.	Dadra & Nagar Haveli	1	-	-
27.	Delhi	-	4	3
28.	Goa, Daman & Diu	-	1	1
29.	Lakshadweep	-	-	1
30.	Mizoram	-	-	-
31.	Pondicherry	-	1	-
	INDIA	38	267	198

pattern of these constituencies (Fig. 6.4) reveals that it was not a general phenonmenon in any of the states. There were altogether 267 constituencies in this category. The distribution of these constituencies among the states is presented in Table 6.5.

id mass following of the Janata party is indicated by a f constituencies. Altogether, 198 constituencies fall in this category. The spatial pattern of the constituencies of inconsistency reveals that their major concentration is in the states of Punjab, Kerala, Tamil Nadu and West Bengal. This reveals that in the areas characterized by the existence of a strong regional party, the Janata's following has varied over time considerably. In all these states the Janata's constituents had no mass following at all. However, the party was benefited in 1977 by the support it received from selected regional parties. But this support for the Janata Party was highly superficial and did not help it to generate positive response among the masses because of its failure to absorb regional sentiments to its fold. In fact during its tenure in power the social harmony reached its worst phase. Its implications were reflected in 1980 elections when not only the regional parties withdrew their support but the party's base was also considerably eroded. Other areas where inconsistency is a phenomenon includes southern Haryana, parts of Rajasthan, western Uttar Pradesh, Baghelkhand (Madhya Pradesh), Vidarbha and western Maharashtra. The inconsistency in Rajasthan, Haryana and Uttar Pradesh was the result of the Janata's split in which the Lok Dal constituent of the party parted the company. The strong following of the Lok Dal constituent in these areas proved fatal to the Janata party in these areas. The party could not achieve the amout of support it enjoyed even in 1971.

The analysis is a manifestation of the fluid party base of the Janata. The major factor which contributed to this process was the absence of its own mass following. Even after assuming power at the centre and in a number of states, the party could not develop the mass base of its own. During its tenure in power, it had to operate through the network of its constituents. In fact the mass base of its constituents too was not well defined. The nature of mass following of the Janata, did not permit the process of institutionalization and therefore the unstable party following remained a general phenomenon.

Regional Parties

Broadly speaking a majority of regional parties in India are organized along caste/community/religion/linguistic basis. This provides them a well defined party base. In such a situation a party is likely to have a stable following by the virtue of the nature of its

TABLE 6.6: PATTERN OF CONSISTENCY, OTHER PARTIES

S.No.	Party	Number of Constituencies showing		
		Consistency	Partial Consistency	Inconsistency
1.	Anna Dravida Munnetra Kazhagam	4	-	24
2.	Dravida Munnetra Kazhagam	-	9	25
3.	Forward Bloc	-	8	30
4.	National Conference	2	-	4
5.	Kerala Congress	-	1	2
6.	Maharashtrawadi Gomantak Party	-	2	-
7.	Manipur People's Party	-	1	1
8.	Muslim League	1	1	10
9.	Peasants & Workers Party	1	2	10
10.	Revolutionary Socialist Party	-	3	10
11.	Shiromani Akali Dal	1	8	3
12.	Tripura Upjati Juja Samiti	-	-	2
13.	United Democratic Front	-	-	1
14.	Ram Rajya Parishad	-	-	27
15.	Indian Labour Party	-	-	7
16.	Bihar Prant Hull Jharkhand	-	1	5
17.	Jharkhand Party	2	10	16
18.	Muslim Majlis of U.P.	-	-	11
19.	Republican Party of India	-	1	34
20.	Republican Party of India (K)	-	7	50
21.	Shiv Sena	-	-	6
22.	Soshit Dal	-	1	12

mass base. But interestingly, the analysis of consistency do not confirm this point. It is noted that a large number of regional parties too do not command a consistent party following. However, the degree of consistency is more in case of those parties which are region specific and have strong roots in their polities. It is evident from Table 6.6 that Anna Dravida Munnetra Kazhagam, National Conference, Muslim League, Peasant's and Worker's Party, Akali Dal and Jharkhand party show consistency in certain constituencies. Considering the limited areas of their operation, the degree of consistency revealed by these parties is greater than the major parties.

But a large number of constituencies characterized by inconsistency (Table 6.6) illustrate that even the strong regional parties cannot take the voters for granted. The allegiance of the masses to political parties do not remain static. The process of polarization and repolarization takes place in such a way that the fluid party following becomes a general scene.

AN OVERVIEW

The pattern of consistency highlighted by this analysis shows that the process of institutionalization which results in stable party following continues to be at a low key in India. This is evident from the fact that the following of major political parties is characterized by a high degree of fluidity. Even parties like CPI and CPI (M) which have a well defined mass following in politically conscious strata of society do not have consistency in party following. While the CPI has consistent following only in 6 constituencies, the CPI(M) emerges consistent in 8 constituencies. It is significant to note that even in West Bengal and Kerala the communist parties could not achieve institutionalization in their mass base. That the Congress Party commands stable party following in only 83 constituencies supports the view that the party does not have a nation wide mass base. The degree of inconsistency revealed by the Janata Party illustrates that the party had a weak and ephemeral mass following. However, a certain degree of consistency in the mass following of some of the regional parties reveals that their polities are influenced uniformly by the factors operating on the eve of elections. It also indicates a well defined mass following of these parties. The results of this analysis lead to the conclusion that the party system is weak in its organisation and functioning and needs to be made better if it has to serve Indian Democracy.

NOTES AND REFERENCES

1. Samuel P. Huntington, *Political order in Changing Societies* (Bombay: Vakils, Fetter and Simons Pvt. Ltd., 1968), p. 13.
2. *Adaptability* refers to the process by which the organizations acquire the capacity to adjust in changing socio-economic environment. Higher degree of adaptability will lead to higher level of institutionalization. *Complexity* implies that in order to have a higher level of institutionalization an organization should have a variety and number of sub-units. The organizations which perform many functions have a higher degree of complexity. *Unity* means that the

members of organizations should agree on the basic functions of the organization. A higher level of institutionalization. *Autonomy* means that an organization should be able to exist and develop without control of others. *Ibid.*, pp. 13-23.

3. See, Paul R. Brass, "Ethnic Cleavage and the Punjab Party System, 1952-1972," in Myron Weiner and John Osgoodfield, eds., *Electoral Politics in the IndianStates* (Manohar Book Service, 1975), Vol. IV, p. 37.
4. Biplab Dasgupta and W.H. Morris-Jones,*op.cit.,* pp. 138-63.
5. Although, the National Conference has a strong organizational network in Jammu region, the party's main following lay in the Kashmir valley.
6. The most significant factor for the loss of credibility of the Jharkhand Party is the personal interests of its leaders. This is evident from the fact that the party was merged into the Congress Party in 1963 on the insistence of late Jaipal Singh. However, the party had to be revived in the same year. In 1972 the party was split because of the personality clash between Bagun Sumbrui and Horo. Horo left the parent organization and formed another Jharkhand Party. Subsequently, the parent organization, led by Bagun Sumbrui, merged into the Janata Party in November 1979. Presently, another group - Jharkhand Mukti Morcha - is spearheading the movement for separate Jharkhand state.
7. Lucian W. Pye, *Aspects of Political Development* (New Delhi : Amerind Publishing Co. Pvt. Ltd., 1972) pp. 72-74.
8. The rise and fall of Shiv Sena in urban areas of Maharashtra illustrate this point.
9. The weak base of the CPI in these constituencies is reflected in the composite scores which are below mean in all the three elections.
10. This is evident from the fact that in 1971 the party contested 85 seats out of which 49 were in West Bengal and Kerala. Similarly in 1977, 29 seats out of 53 and in 1980, 38 seats out of 63 were in West Bengal and Kerala.
11. It may be pointed out here that although, the united Communist Party had a strong base in Tamil Nadu (then Madras),after the split much of its mass following was captured by the CPI. This was due to the fact that the leading personalities of the party in the state opted for the CPI camp.
12. Composite scores for these three constituencies are above mean level.

SEVEN

FRAGMENTATION OF POLITICAL BEHAVIOUR : FRAGMENTED NATURE OF PARTY DOMAINS

It is customary in voting behaviour research to call a party dominant if it secures majority of seats. This, however, is a disputable assumption as it is often seen that though the parties secure majorities in terms of seats won, their share of votes seldom goes beyond fifty per cent. It may be assumed that if a party polls majority votes in a certain constituency it can be regarded as a dominant party in that particular area. A more rational way for determining the dominance of a party would be to consider all the factors which contribute towards this dominance. Whether, a particular seat has been won or lost is one such consideration. Others include its share in the all-India support, the votes polled by it as share of the total votes in a constituency and the ratio of victory or loss. It is in due regard to these multiple factors that a procedure has been developed in this study which attempts at delineating the areas of dominance of political parties in India.

Political parties in India acquired their present character through their development during the freedom struggle. Their evolution in the post-Independence period reveals continuity of pre-Independence norms and behaviour. Subsequently, the emergent socio-political order has significantly influenced the nature of political parties. Spread of education, industrialization and emergence of new political institutions played significant roles in determining the organisation and functioning of political parties in India. In the Indian situation which is characterized by a low level of social integration and where primary associations based on caste and community continue to have an edge over secondary associations, political opinion continues to get polarized along the primary social attributes. This has been a significant factor contributing to the emergence of sectarian and parochical parties. Both these phenomenon have contributed to a situation in which the mass following of political parties remains fragmented.

Fragmentation refers to the process in which the mass following of political parties is so restricted that it forms a spatial pattern of enclaves. Further the process of fragmentation may also be seen in the nature of political landscape which remains dominated by a number of political parties. The following analysis attempts to analyse the nature of party domains in the country based on data of 1971, 1977 and 1980 Parliamentary elections.

The areas of dominance of political parties have been identified by means of a composite index of party strength in different constituencies. The following indicators of party strength have been considered in developing such a composite index:

- Ia. Percentage of votes polled by a party in a constituency in 1971
- Ib. Percentage of votes polled by a party in a constituency in 1977
- Ic. Percentage of votes polled by a party in a constituency in 1980
- IIa. Index of concentration, 1971
- IIb. Index of concentration, 1977
- IIc. Index of concentration, 1980
- IIIa. Ratio of victory/loss, 1971
- IIIb. Ratio of victory/loss, 1977
- IIIc. Ratio of victory/loss, 1980.

The detailed procedure involved in the analysis has been explained in the introductory chapter.

PROCESS AT WORK

The role of political parties as instruments of power has provoked a lively discussion in academic circles. Much has been said about the degree of competition among parties[1] and the interrelationship between the government and its organizational wing.[2] It is said that democratic system gets expressed in the plurality of parties because it can accommodate divergent opinion.[3] The concept of freedom and competition for a stable democratic system reveals that the two party system is best suited to democracy because a plethora of political parties cannot command a full authority without indulging in unprincipled means.

However, in developing societies this process acquires a great complexity. In developed societies the competition for power within an institutional framework is an important component of check on authority. However, in developing societies this imposes constraints on the structure of democracy. This results from the fact that in such societies not only do the masses have a low level of political consciousness but also the political institutions are far from developed. In this situation what is important is that political parties should compete for power without disturbing the process of national integration.

The overwhelming success of the Congress since the first general elections and a weak opposition have been a matter of great concern to all those interested in the democratic institutions in India, Students of Indian party system have described this process as of "one party dominance system."[4] However, this characterisation of Indian party system is based on numerical strength of parties in parliament which seems to be a disputable proposition. In a complex situation where a large number of candidates are elected by strikingly low proportion of votes; where there is no consistency in party support, such assumptions have to take note of the various facets of voting preferences. This point is clearly brought out by this analysis which reveals that the Indian political landscape is characterized by a high degree of political fragmentation. This is evident from the enclaved nature of party following. It is interesting to note that this phenomenon is evident despite landslide victories of political parties at different elections.

The explanation for the process of fragmentation lies in the evolution of Indian polity and the existing socio-cultural and ethnic diversity. In the process of electioneering the political parties try to get support of various sections of population and the basic objective of a party becomes mass support rather than strengthening organization. In this process the parties become an agglomeration of groups having some influence in various strata of society. However, it is at this juncture that the elections start a process of interaction between political parties, on the one hand, and society, on the other. The Indian society is characterized by a low degree of social integration and primarily agglomerative character.[5] This has resulted from the fact that the caste and community have been the essence of Indian politics despite great reform movements.[6] In a struggle for power and influence, the political parties indulged in exploitation of group sentiments and thus solidified already disintegrative and parochial tendencies.[7] It is significant to note that this process was so deeply rooted that even the political parties were formed on these lines.This can be traced back to the beginning of this century when the all-India Muslim League and Akhil Bharatiya Hindu Mahasabha followed by the Justice Party were formed. The worst aspect of this development has been that parties representing organized class interests have been very few- the only significant exception was Unionist party representing the interests of the Hindu, Muslim and Sikh landlords in Punjab.[8] In the wake of the freedom movement, political ideas percolated Indian society promoting increased political awakening among the masses. However, this was not accompanied by the forces of national integration. The cumulative effect of this was felt in hardening group identities. Although attempts have been made to make the masses political conscious and thereby loosen social rigidities, success has been unimpressive and the masses continue to be guided largely by group affinities. The major responsibility for this development has been that of the political parties themselves who raised and emphasised parochial issues exploiting the sentiments of the people. For the majority of voters, caste and community are of importance and the parochial identities and loyalities become the main factors determining the choice of the candidate. In this background the choice continues to be guided by, what has been termed as, modern idioms.[9] It is significant to note that even the Congress party which has progressively descended from its national stance has been indulging in exploiting group loyalities by not only chosing the candidates of numerically dominant caste groups, but also by giving concessions to particular caste groups on the eve of elections. This provided a chance for other politial parties to counter this by exploiting regional sentiments. The net result of this phenomenon has been that every political party finds an expression in certain section/region. Since social groups in India have regional patterning, the political opinion in the country remains by and large unorganised.

SPATIAL PATTERN OF PARTY DOMAINS

It is seen from Fig.7 that the mass following of political parties is characterized by a high degree of spatial fragmentation. The Congress Party acquired a strong position since the very beginning and has managed to achieve a semblance of national unity on the basis of a broad policy framework having an all-India appeal. The death of Nehru dismantled this superstructure and created a political vaccum. The Janata Party tried to fill this vaccum in 1977 but was constrained by a number of factors, the foremost among these factors was its fragmented mass base. In fact, the party did not have a mass base of its own - it operated through the network of its constituent parties. This network in itself was highly fragmented and was largely confined to the north. Secondly, the components of the Janata Party had drawn their political strength from highly localized, parochial or sectional issues. They consisted of groups which were either the relics of the Congress - Congress(O) and CFD - denuded of their political power, and having no mass base at all, or groups whose programme was specific to certain class or sectional interests. The Jana Sangh sustained itself on the support of the Hindu trading classes in urban areas of Hindi speaking north and the Bhartiya Lok Dal represented and worked to preserve the interests of the middle ranking land-owning castes in the north. The Socialists had enclaves of influence with a wider regional spread, but commanded little political hold on the masses. Thirdly, after emergence of the Janata as a unified party, definitionally, the component groups failed to shed off their former identities and the group loyalities continued to be fragmented. This thwarted the very process of political assimilation of forces within the Janata Party and did not permit it to emerge as a cohesive all-India force. Fourthly, lack of cohesion within the Janata Party, its major accent on north-centric caste and Kulak-biased politics and social approval of explicitly communal and obscurantist tendencies, gave new lease of life to these forces and accelerated the process of social and political disintengration. Fifthly, the absence of a political force with a national perspective at the centre which could command wider control and carry with it Indian polity led to the rise of

Fig. 7.1
India: Spatial Pattern of Party Diminance

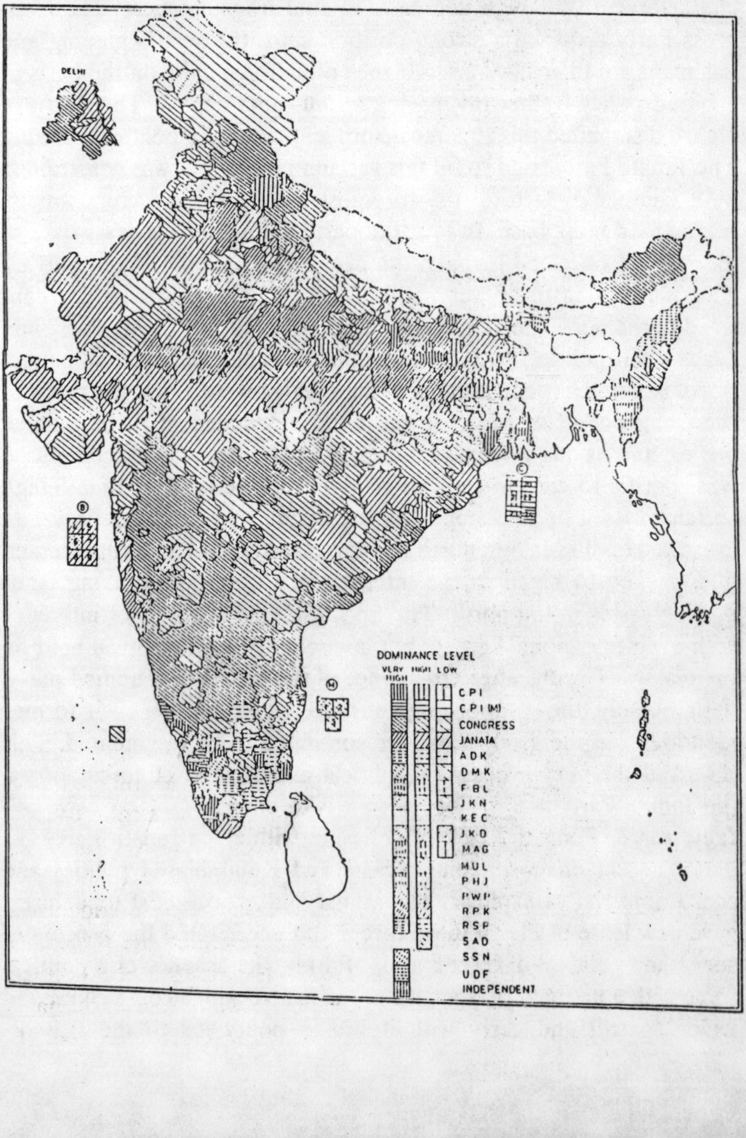

centrifugal forces which were particularly noted for their vigour on the periphery of the union.

The fragmented nature of mass following is highlighted by Fig.7. It is evident that the scene in the north is dominated by the Janata Party. However, the level of dominance is characterized by a high degree of variation further accentuating the process of fragmentation. The scene in the states of Maharashtra, Andhra Pradesh and Karnataka is dominated by the Congress. West Bengal remains under the domain of the CPI(M). Table 7.1 presents the all-India picture in regard to party dominance.

TABLE 7.1: CONSTITUENCIES CLASSIFIED BY PARTY DOMINANCE

Party	Dominance Level			Total
	Very High	High	Low	
Communist Party of India	17	9	-	26
Communist Party of India (Marxist)	21	18	2	41
Congress Party	83	115	21	219
Janata Party	76	93	4	173
Others	32	7	28	67
Total	229	242	55	526*

* Excluding 14 constituencies of Assam and 2 constituencies of Meghalaya.

It is evident from Table 7.1 that the political landscape remains dominated by different parties. It is also seen that the level of dominance of political parties varies considerably. The party-wise analysis is presented in the following paragraphs.

Communist Party of India

The Communist Party of India emerged as the dominant party in 26 constituencies. In 17 constituencies out of 26 the dominance level was very high. Distribution of these consttuencies among the states is presented in Table 7.2. Fig.7 read along with Table 7.2 reveals that the party's areas of following lay mainly in Bihar, Kerala, Tamil Nadu, Uttar Pradesh and West Bengal. The location of these constituencies in Punjab, Uttar Pradesh and Bihar points out the nature of its area of influence. In Punjab the party emerged dominant in

TABLE 7.2: PATTERN OF DOMINANCE, COMMUNIST PARTY OF INDIA

S.No.	State/Union Territory	No. of constituencies classified by dominance level		
		Very High	High	Low
1.	Andhra Pradesh	-	-	-
2.	Assam*	-	-	-
3.	Bihar	4	4	-
4.	Gujarat	-	-	-
5.	Haryana	-	-	-
6.	Himachal Pradesh	-	-	-
7.	Jammu & Kashmir	-	-	-
8.	Karnataka	-	-	-
9.	Kerala	4	-	-
10.	Madhya Pradesh	-	-	-
11.	Maharashtra	-	-	-
12.	Manipur	-	1	-
13.	Meghalaya	-	-	-
14.	Nagaland	-	-	-
15.	Orissa	-	1	-
16.	Punjab	1	-	-
17.	Rajasthan	-	-	-
18.	Sikkim	-	-	-
19.	Tamil Nadu	3	-	-
20.	Tripura	-	-	-
21.	Uttar Pradesh	2	3	-
22.	West Bengal	3	-	-
23.	Andaman & Nicobar Is.	-	-	-
24.	Arunachal Pradesh	-	-	-
25.	Chandigarh	-	-	-
26.	Dadra & Nagar Haveli	-	-	-
27.	Delhi	-	-	-
28.	Goa, Daman and Diu	-	-	-
29.	Lakshadweep	-	-	-
30.	Mizoram	-	-	-
31.	Pondicherry	-	-	-
	INDIA	17	9	-

* Excluded from analysis.

Bhatinda constituency. This area of Punjab has been a scene of organized peasant's struggle.[10] The party has dominant position in 5 constituencies of Uttar Pradesh of which 2 lie in hill areas and 3 in eastern Uttar Pradesh. Altogether it has dominant position in 8 constituencies of Bihar of which 5 constituencies form a cluster in Central Bihar - south of the Ganga. Two constituencies lie in Tarai belt and one in Rajmahal hills. It is significant to note that the party's strong base in West Bengal is not in industrial areas but in areas where the agriculture is the main economic activity.

The spatial patterning of the areas of CPI's dominance reveals that the party's influence lies in areas where organized peasant movement have been quite strong in the recent past.

TABLE 7.3: PATTERN OF DOMINANCE, COMMUNIST PARTY OF INDIA (MARXIST)

S.No.	State/Union Territory	No. of constituencies classified by dominance level		
		Very High	High	Low
1.	Andhra Pradesh	-	-	-
2.	Assam*	-	-	-
3.	Bihar	-	-	-
4.	Gujarat	-	-	-
5.	Haryana	-	-	-
6.	Himachal Pradesh	-	-	-
7.	Jammu & Kashmir	-	-	-
8.	Karnataka	-	-	-
9.	Kerala	2	5	1
10.	Madhya Pradesh	-	-	-
11.	Maharashtra	-	-	-
12.	Manipur	-	-	-
13.	Meghalaya	-	-	-
14.	Nagaland	-	-	-
15.	Orissa	-	-	-
16.	Punjab	-	1	-
17.	Rajasthan	-	-	-
18.	Sikkim	-	-	-
19.	Tamil Nadu	-	1	-
20.	Tripura	1	1	-
21.	Uttar Pradesh	-	-	-
22.	West Bengal	18	10	1
23.	Andaman & Nicobar Is.	-	-	-
24.	Arunachal Pradesh	-	-	-
25.	Chandigarh	-	-	-
26.	Dadra and Nagar Haveli	-	-	-
27.	Delhi	-	-	-
28.	Goa, Daman and Diu	-	-	-
29.	Lakshadweep	-	-	-
30.	Mizoram	-	-	-
31.	Pondicherry	-	-	-
	INDIA	21	18	2

* Excluded from analysis.

Communist Party of India (Marxist)

The CPI(M) for all practical purposes has been operating in West Bengal, Tripura and Kerala. The tactics of concentration has helped it a lot in maintaining its areas of influence. This point is brought out by this analysis which shows that out of 41 constituencies in which the party emerged as dominant, 39 constituencies lie in these states. The other two constituencies are Phillaur of Punjab and Madurai of Tamil Nadu.

The party emerged dominant in 29 constituencies of West Bengal of which 18 constituencies are characterized by very high levels of dominance (Table 7.3). All these constituencies form a single cluster in southern Bengal. However, it is significant to note that in Calcutta urban agglomaration, only in two constituencies the party has very high dominant position. Both constituencies of Tripura has CPI(M) as the dominant party. However, only in one constituency its dominance level is very high. Altogether 4 constituencies of Kerala have CPI(M) as the dominant party out of which in two constituencies (Kasargode and Palghat) it has very high level of dominance.

This shows that although the party has an all India economic programme for the masses in the country, it has an appeal in a few states only. In this situation whether the party should be regarded as a national party is an open question.

Congress Party

Despite landslide victories of the Congress Party in 1971 and 1980 elections, it did not emerge as an all India political force. This analysis reveals that the party has dominant position only in 219 constituencies of the Indian Union. Distribution of these constituencies is presented in Table 7.4. It is evident from Fig.7 along with Table 7.4. that the main influence of the party lay in Himachal Pradesh, Maharashtra, Karnataka and Andhra pradesh. It is significant to note that in the Hindi speaking north, the party commands little influence except in certain parts of Madhya Pradesh.

The Congress emerged as the highly dominant political force

only in 82 constituencies of which 65 were in the states of Andhra Pradesh (21 constituencies), Karnataka (22 constituencies) and Maharashtra (22 constituencies). Constituencies of very high dominance in Maharashtra form two clusters - one in western Maharashtra and the second in Vidarbha. It is significant to note that in the constituencies of Bombay and Konkan region the Congress does not emerge as dominant. In Karnataka all the constituencies form a single bloc. Constituencies of high dominance in Andhra Pradesh form 3 clusters, the biggest one lies in the southern half of the state. This pattern of Congress dominance may be explained by the history of political parties in these areas. The Konkan region of Maharashtra is entirely different from rest of the state. This area has always been under the influence of the Socialist Party which has led to a number of peasant movements opposed to the dominating influence of the Marathas. Western Maharashtra and the Vidarbha have always been a monolith of the Congress since the dominating landowning castes in these areas have aligned themselves with the Congress. Although in 1978 split of the congress, a large section of leaders, including Y.B. Chavan, having an influence in Western Maharashtra opted for the Congress (S) (later Congress (U), they were denuded of their political strength in the subsequent period. The Vidarbha region is opposed to the political influence of the Marathas, a dominant caste in western Maharashtra, and therefore, has a tendency to oppose the dominating influence of the Marathas.

Mass sentiments in Karnataka did not allow parties other than the Congress to get a foothold in the state. This analysis reveals that the Congress is a dominant party in all 28 constituencies of the state. In 22 constituencies the party commands a very high dominant position. The factors are obvious. Both the dominating castes of Karnataka *Viz.*, Lingayata and Vokkaliga have aligned with the Congress Party. Although, Dev Raj Urs parted company with the parent organization, he was completely isolated by the masses.[11] In fact he himself was the architect of this isolation. During the time when he was with Mrs. Indira Gandhi, he and his supporters lost no opportunity to tell the people that the successful implementation of socio-economic programmes in the state was mainly due to Mrs. Gandhi's leadership and the credit should go to her.[12]

TABLE 7.4: PATTERN OF DOMINANCE, CONGRESS PARTY

S.No.	State/Union Territory	No. of constituencies classified by dominance level		
		Very High	High	Low
1.	Andhra Pradesh	21	18	3
2.	Assam	-	-	-
3.	Bihar	2	5	-
4.	Gujarat	-	12	-
5.	Haryana	-	2	2
6.	Himachal Pradesh	3	1	-
7.	Jammu & Kashmir	-	1	2
8.	Karnataka	22	5	1
9.	Kerala	-	-	1
10.	Madhya Pradesh	2	13	2
11.	Mahaharashtra	22	9	3
12.	Manipur*	-	1	-
13.	Meghalaya	-	-	-
14.	Nagaland	-	-	-
15.	Orissa	2	10	1
16.	Punjab	-	5	-
17.	Rajasthan	-	5	2
18.	Sikkim	1	-	-
19.	Tamil Nadu	-	5	3
20.	Tripura	-	-	-
21.	Uttar Pradesh	5	18	1
22.	West Bengal	-	-	-
23.	Andaman & Nicobar Is.	1	-	-
24.	Arunachal Pradesh	1	-	-
25.	Chandigarh	-	1	-
26.	Dadra and Nagar Haveli	-	1	-
27.	Delhi	1	1	-
28.	Goa, Daman and Diu	-	-	-
29.	Lakshadweep	-	1	-
30.	Mizoram	-	-	-
31.	Pondicherry	-	1	-
	INDIA	83	115	21

* Excluded from analysis.

The pattern in Andhra Pradesh is similar to that of Karnataka - the Congress Party emerging dominant in all 42 constituencies. However, only in half of the constituencies the dominance level is very high. Majority of these constituencies are in the Rayalseema region where the Reddy community is a dominant social force. In Telangana area the party could not emerge as highly dominant because of the fact that in this region the forces opposed to the Congress have been very active till recently. It was only after the merger of the Telangana Praja Samiti into the Congress,that the party could command a sizeable following in this region.

Outside these three states the Congress emerged dominant in 7 constituencies of Bihar, 12 constituencies of Gujarat, 4 constituencies each of Haryana and Himachal Pradesh, 3 constituencies of Jammu and Kashmir, 17 constituencies of Madhya Pradesh, 12 constituencies of Orissa, 5 constituencies of Punjab, 7 constituencies of Rajasthan, 8 constituencies of Tamil Nadu, 24 constituencies of Uttar Pradesh, 2 constituencies of Delhi and 1 constituency each in Kerala, Manipur, Meghalaya, Sikkim, Andaman and Nicobar Islands, Arunachal Pradesh, Chandigarh, Dadra and Nagar Haveli, Lakshadweep and Pondichery.The following points are noteworthy.

1. In Uttar Pradesh the party commands dominant position mainly in hill areas and in the Terai belt.

2. The constituencies having party dominance in Rajasthan are clustered in Luni Basin.

3. In Madhya Pradesh all constituencies, but one, of party dominance form a single cluster in the south and south-eastern part of the state. It is significant to note that this covers most of the tribal belt of the state except Bhil territory in the west and Bastar district in the south-east. However, the constituencies are of different dominance level.

It is evident from the preceding analysis that the Congress Party may be characterized as a dominant political force only in Himachal Pradesh, Maharashtra, Karnataka and Andhra Pradesh. In West Bengal, Tripura and Kerala the party commands very little political base. The party's position is very weak in the Hindi speaking north except in a part of Madhya Pradesh.

Janata Party

The Janata Party remains far from national in the true sense of the term. This is evident from the fact that the party emerged dominant only in 173 constituencies of which in 76 constituencies the

TABLE 7.5: PATTERN OF DOMINANCE, JANATA PARTY

S.No.	State/Union Territory	No. of constituencies classified by dominance level		
		Very High	High	Low
1.	Andhra Pradesh*	-	-	-
2.	Assam	-	-	-
3.	Bihar	18	15	1
4.	Gujarat	1	11	2
5.	Haryana	5	1	-
6.	Himachal Pradesh	-	-	-
7.	Jammu & Kashmir	-	-	-
8.	Karnataka	-	-	-
9.	Kerala	-	-	-
10.	Madhya Pradesh	4	18	1
11.	Maharashtra	1	6	-
12.	Manipur*	-	-	-
13.	Meghalaya	-	-	-
14.	Nagaland	-	-	-
15.	Orissa	-	6	-
16.	Punjab	-	-	-
17.	Rajasthan	9	9	-
18.	Sikkim	-	-	-
19.	Tamil Nadu	-	2	-
20.	Tripura	-	-	-
21.	Uttar Pradesh	36	20	-
22.	West Bengal	2	-	-
23.	Andaman & Nicobar Is.	-	-	-
24	Arunachal Pradesh	-	-	-
25.	Chandigarh	-	-	-
26.	Dadra and Nagar Haveli	-	-	-
27.	Delhi	-	5	-
28.	Goa, Daman and Diu	-	-	-
29.	Lakshadweep	-	-	-
30.	Mizoram	-	-	-
31.	Pondicherry	-	-	-
	INDIA	76	93	4

* Excluded from analysis.

dominance level is very high. It is significant to note that out of 173 constituencies 142 are in the Hindi-speaking north. The distribution pattern in other states is as follows : Gujarat-14, Maharashtra-7, Orissa-6, Tamil Nadu and West Bengal-2 each. This pattern of Janata dominance is in conformity with the operation of political forces in Indian polity in the past. As explained earlier, the constituent groups of the Janata Party have been operating with their full vigour in the north only. However, some of its constituents were influential in other parts of the country such as socialists in Konkan region, Swatantra and Congress(O) in Gujarat, Swatantra and Bhartiya Lok Dal in Orissa,[13] and Congress(O) in Tamil Nadu.

It is evident from Table 7.5 (Fig. 7) that the Janata commanded the strongest position in Uttar Pradesh where, in 36 constituencies the party emerged as highly dominant. The state of Bihar follows Uttar Pradesh with 18 constituencies of very high dominance and is followed by Rajasthan where in 9 constituencies the party commanded very high dominant position. All these constituencies are clustered in south-western part of the state. It is significant to mention here that this area of the state has traditionally been under the influence of ex-princely houses which have supported the Jana Sangh constituent of the Janata Party.

Another 93 constituencies are characterized by high level of dominance. The state of Madhya Pradesh ranks first in this category by contributing 18 constituencies. Except 3 constituencies, all constituencies form a single cluster in western part of the state. It is evident from Fig. 7 that in other states these constituencies form enclaves in different parts.

It is significant to note that in South India, the Janata emerged as a dominant party only in 2 constituencies of Tamil Nadu. Both these constituencies (Tiruchendur and Nagercoil) lie in the extreme south. In this area the influence of Janata is attributed to the mass base of Congress(O) constituent because of the personal influence of Late Shri Kamaraj who hailed from this area.

The preceding analysis shows that the states of Andhra Pradesh, Himachal Pradesh, Jammu and Kashmir, Karnataka, Kerala, Manipur, Nagaland, Punjab, Sikkim and Tripura and all the Union Territories except Delhi are outside the Janata domain. Its area of operation lies within the limits of the Hindi region. Even in this area the level of dominance varies from very high to low.

Other Parties

The other parties (State and Registered) have been noted for their vigour mainly on the periphery of the Indian Union. Altogether

15 parties emerged dominant in 67 constituencies (Fig. 7, Table 7.6). Fig. 7 reveals that the National Conference commands very high dominant position in 2 constituencies and high dominant position in one constituency of Kashmir valley. The Akali Dal emerged dominant in 6 constituencies of Punjab. However, in none of the constituencies it could attain very high level of dominance. The Jharkhand Party commands dominant position in 4 constituencies of Bihar and one constituency of Orissa. It is significant to note that the existence of Jharkhand Party flows from the general resentment among the local tribal people. The continued exploitation of the tribal people and low pace of development in this region of rich natural resources have forced the tribal people to organize themselves under the banner of Jharkhand movement. In the northeast, Nagaland falls under the domain of the United Democratic front, Mizoram and Arunachal west constituencies fall under the domain of Independents. Maharashtrawadi Gamantak Party emerged dominant in both constituencies of Goa, Daman and Diu and Peasant and Workers Party in 3 constituencies of Maharashtra.

In Tamil Nadu, the scene is dominated by Dravida Munnetra Kazhagam and Anna Dravida Munnetra Kazhagam. The former emerged dominant in 11 constituencies and latter in 13 constituencies. Following is the position in regard to other parties (see also Table 7.6). Forward Bloc: West Bengal-4, Tamil Nadu-1; Muslim League: Kerala-3; Kerala Congress: Kerala-2; Revolutionary Socialist Party: Kerala-2, West Bengal-4; RPI(K): Maharashtra-3; and Shiv Sena: Maharashtra-1.

AN OVERVIEW

The above study of party domains reveals that the mass base of political parties is characterized by a high degree of fragmentation. None of the major parties such as the CPI, CPI(M), Congress and Janata command extensive bases. Their areas of dominance are in the form of enclaves.

It is seen that the Congress Party commands a dominant position only in 219 constituencies. The spatial patterning of these constituencies shows that the areas of its main influence lie in Andhra Pradesh, Himachal Pradesh, Karnataka and Maharashtra. The Janata Party emerges dominant in 173 constituencies which lay mainly in the Hindi Heartland. The CPI and CPI(M) command dominant position in 26 and 41 constituencies respectively. It is significant to note that although the CPI(M) has a concentric mass base, the CPI commands a wider following. As many as 67 constituencies are dominated by other parties.

TABLE 7.6: PATTERN OF DOMINANCE, OTHER PARTIES

S.No.	State/Union Territory/Party	No. of constituencies classified by dominance level		
		Very High	High	Low
1.	Bihar			
	PJH	-	-	-
	JKD	2	2	-
2.	Jammu & Kashmir			
	JKN	2	1	-
3.	Kerala			
	KEC	1	1	-
	MUL	2	1	-
	RSP	1	1	-
4.	Maharashtra			
	PWP	3	-	-
	RPK	3	-	-
	SSN	-	2	-
5.	Nagaland			
	UDF	1	-	-
6.	Orissa			
	JKD	1	-	-
7.	Punjab			
	SAD	-	4	2
8.	Tamil Nadu			
	ADMK	6	5	2
	DMK	5	3	3
9.	West Bengal			
	FBL	3	1	-
	RSP	2	2	-
10.	Aruchal Pradesh			
	IND	-	1	-
11.	Goa, Daman and Diu			
	MAG	-	2	-
12.	Mizoram			
	IND	1	-	-

The pattern of dominance of other parties clearly indicates their operation in the peripheral areas of the Indian Union. It is important to note that despite various attempts to liquidate the regional parties, these parties continue to command a strong hold on the masses.

NOTES AND REFERENCES

1. Maurice Duverger, *Political Parties* (London : Methuen, 1954), pp. 206-80.
2. R.T. McKenzie, *British Political Parties* (London : Heinemann, 1955).
3. S. Neumann, "Towards a Comparative Study of Political Parties," in S. Neumann (ed.), *Modern Political Parties* (Chicago: 1956), p. 397.
4. Rajni Kothari, "The Congress System in India," *Asian Survey*, Vol.IV, No.12, December 1964, pp. 1161-73. And also, W.H. Morris Jones, "Parliament and Dominant Party," *Parliamentary Affairs*, Vol. XVII, No.3, Summer 1964, pp. 296-307.
5. Irawati Karve,*Hindu Society - An Interpretation* (Poona : 1961), p. 111.
6. J.N. Farquhar, *Modern Religious Movement in India* (London : 1915).
7. M.N. Srinivas, *Caste in Modern India and Other Essays* (Bombay : Asia Publishing House, 1962), pp. 15-41.
8. Azim Husain, *Fazl-I-Hussain- A Political Biography* (Bombay : Longmans Green, 1946), p. 305.
9. W.H. Morris-Jones, "India's Political Idiom," in C.H. Philips (ed.), *Politics and Society in India* (London : 1963), pp. 133-154.
10. Poor agricultural potentials and exploitative tendencies of dominant Jat peasantry have provided favourable conditions for the organized peasants struggle in this region.
11. "Unconvincing Rhetoric in Karnataka Elections," *Times of India* (New Delhi), January 17, 1980.
12. "Janata and Congress(I) Main Contenders in Karnataka," *The Statesman* (New Delhi), January 1, 1980.
13. This is important to mention here that only Utkal Congress constituent of the Bhartiya Lok Dal was influential in Orissa.

EIGHT

FRAGMENTATION OF POLITICAL BEHAVIOUR: OPERATION OF CENTRIFUGAL FORCES IN THE POLITY

The spatial fragmentation of political behaviour in India has also been accentuated through the operation of centrifugal forces in the Indian polity. In this chapter an attempt has been made to identify and measure with the help of a statistical method, the operation or otherwise of the centrifugal tendencies in India as evident in electoral behaviour.

The centrifugal forces within the polity are very much evident in India today. They are quite vigorous in the peripheral regions of the country - Nagaland, Manipur and Mizoram in the northeast; West Bengal in the east; Tamil Nadu and Kerala in the south; and Punjab and Jammu and Kashmir in the north west - where they operate through tribal, religious or linguistic identities in contradistinction to the characteristic traits of the core. The political parties in these regions have emerged and managed to survive by arousing the public sentiments on issues, such as regional or sub-national autonomy which an all-powerful centre has supposedly denied to the people in these regions. That these strategies have succeeded is evident from the fact that the centralist parties, such as the Congress or the Janata, have gradually lost ground in these regions. In fact, the Janata was not capable of gaining any ground in the north-east and the deep south whatsoever. Electoral data thus contain important clues to the extent and magnitude of operation of centrifugal forces in the Indian polity.

In the preceding chapter the spatial fragmentation in political behaviour has been evaluated with the help of the fragmented domains of the political parties both in space and time. It has been noticed that the political landscape is dominated by different political parties in different parts of India. Their areas of dominance, or domains, are in the form of enclaves. A striking feature of this phenomenon is that as one moves away from the core region of the North, regional parties emerge on the scene holding a dominant position and thriving on regional, parochial or sectarian sentiments in peripheral regions of the country. This emergent pattern is understandable in the context of the working of Indian federalism during the last three decades or so.

With the end of the British rule in 1947, the powers of political freedom culminated in the establishment of democratic system of government, and the Indian Constitution adopted in 1950 provided for a Union of federating states.

> The Indian leadership which fou ,at for national Independence saw in federation a needed device to achieve their twin objectives of national integration and economic development. The framers of the Constitution devised a system in which the Central Government was expected to provide leadership to the constituent or state units in matters of national importance.[1]

The Centre-State relations as they developed in the early formative years were highly flexible and ad-hoc in nature. The states, which were the consitituent units in this federation, were being ruled by the Congress Party under the imposing leadership of Jawaharlal Nehru. The centre-state problems were thus subsumed within the functioning of the Congress Party at the central level and its state units. Very often, the Prime Minister was also holding the office of the party president. Such a mechanism contradicted the federal spirit of the Constitution. In the words of K. Santhanam :

> The Indian Republic started with a contradiction. While the Constitution established a federal system of government, all the political parties existing at the time it came into force were unitary and highly centralized. This was particularly the case with the Congress.[2]

The system functioned satisfactorily if there were no occasions of clash of personality or of clash of interest between the central and the state leaderships. The Constitution was under great strain when one of the constitent states (Kerala) came to be ruled by the Communists in 1957. The Congress Party resolved this problem by evolving tactics of destablising the Communist Ministry in Kerala and thus avoided facing squarely the real issue of the centre-state ties within the framework of the Constitution. A political scientist analysed the question of centre-state relations to study the working of the federal principle in the following words :

> As in every federation, however, no overarching level of government can provide effective leadership for the other levels, simply by constitutional fiat. Institutional or political devices must be created to make the constituent units accept the authority, guidance and leadership of the federal government, since a formal constitution rarely adequately reflects the operation of political forces. Apart from legal authority, the prime requisite for effective central control revolves around the degree of political support. If this support is either lacking or withdrawn, constitutional forms become politically meaningless and the central government will slide into a relatively weak position vis-a-vis the state government.[3]

The Congress leadership under Nehru managed to create a semblance of stability by tackling the overriding centre-state problems within the framework of the party constitution and its tradition. The exit of Nehru from the scene exposed the basic weakness of the system, when the political support which the party hitherto enjoyed was withdrawn to such an extent that the ruling party at the Centre became a pawn in the hands of the powerful state bosses who managed to overrule the Prime Minister in all important matters. The powers enjoyed by the "Syndicate" within the Congress Party in the post-1967 period is a case in hand.

Evidently, the centralist tendencies of the ruling Congress Party at the centre after Nehru proved a real setback to the political stability of the country. The ruling party attempted to accumulate all powers within its hands to perpetuate its authority. This naturally resulted in general discontent within the party rank and file and endless chain of intra-party factions and splits began. The Process of dismemberment of the Congress Party which was hastend by this vaccum of power at the apex level, brought new political forces on the scene and the old loyalities gave way to new equations based on political exigencies of the time. A serious outcome of these developments was seen in the rise of forces of national disintegration. In other words, as the super-structure of unity was threatened after the death of Nehru, it introduced a risk of fragmentation in Indian polity. A true federal system strikes a balance between centripetal and centrifugal forces.[4] However, the existing political fragmentation in the country has created a situation in which the centrifugal forces are dominating the centripetal forces in many parts of the country particularly in the peripheral states. This may be seen in the programmes and appeals of political parties having their base in these regions as well as in the people's allegiance to their policies. It may be assumed that a response to the policies of political parties which thrive on the regional sentiments, indicates the operation of these forces in the polity. The present analysis of the operation of centrifugal forces in India attempted with the help of data for General Elections to Lok Sabha held in 1971, 1977 and 1980 aims to explore genetic relationship between this phenomenon and the process of fragmentation.

FEDERALISM : A BALANCE BETWEEN CENTRIPETAL AND CENTRIFUGAL FORCES

The interplay of the centripetal and centrifugal forces throughout history was the basic guiding principle to the makers of the Indian Constitution. The Indian Constitution provides for enough power to the central authority to bind the diverse regional entities. However, this also required that the central authority should be able to generate a national loyality. Secondly, there should be enough autonomy with the constituent units so that the central authority does not interfere in the local matters and allows them internal freedom. These provisions were necessary in view of the existing socio-cultural diversity which has a geographic foundation. Indian polity incorporates regional units with their own distinctive social identity. These diverse units have maintained their separate cultural identity throughout history. Therefore, balance of power for the stable state was achieved by adopting a federal system of government.

Federalism has been defined as "a method of dividing powers so that the general and regional governments are each within a sphere, coordinate and independent."[5] According to Dicey :

> The distribution of powers is an essential feature of Federalism. The object for which a federal state is formed involves a division of authority between the national government and the separate States. The powers given to the nation form in effect so many limitations upon the authority of the separate States and as it is not intended that the Central Government should have the opportunity of encroaching upon the rights retained by the States, its sphere of action necessarily becomes the object of rigorous definition.[6]

Although these definitions make the distribution of power within a federal state evidently clear, its actual working in a social system is highlighted in the following words :

> Federalism is also the process of federalizing a political community, that is to say, the process by which a number of separate political communities enter into arrangements for working out solutions, adopting joint policies and making joint divisions on joint problems, and, conversely, also the process by which a unitary political community becomes differentiated into a federally organized whole.[7]

It is evident that in such an arrangement a federal society will strike a balance between centripetal and centrifugal forces together. This is possible because federalism provides a device which brings a unity in diversity by maintaining an equilibrium between these two opposing forces in order to achieve the common goal of national integration. By this very process the federal system is not a fixed and unchanging arrangement but a dynamic framework. Every society is faced with own problems and therefore they have to evolve own norms for maintaining a true federal state. Frankfurt rightly pointed out that, "Federal Governments are not the offspring of political science; they are the product of economic and social pressures."[8] The socially viable aspect of federalism is highlighted in the words of Livingston :

> The essential nature of federalism is to be sought for, not in the shadings of legal and constitutional terminology, but in the forces - economic, social, political, cultural - that have made the outward forms of federalism necessary... The essence of federalism lies not in constitutional or institutional structure but in the society itself. Federal government is a device by which the federal qualities of the society are articulated and protected.[9]

In view of the merits of federal structure India had conducive conditions for adopting such a system. Its vast ethno-lingual diversity could not have got a better expression in any other form of system. In this context the Constitutent Assembly took the right step by adopting a federal system of government in India. Its size and population further strengthened the idea of adopting a federal system. Scholars have argued that a large territory and population are favourable conditions for the evolution of a federation.[10]

The Constitution of India incorporated the basic characteristics of federalism by allocating functions and powers between States and the Union Government. All subjects of legislation have been arranged under three separate lists in the Seventh Schedule of the Constitution-the Union List, the State List and the Concurrent Jurisdiction List.

However, the Constitution made some provisions which introduced a bias in favour of the Union Government and put the States in a weaker position. These include Article 248, 249, 256, 257, 328, 356 and 360. Provisions of these Articles, to some extent, disturbed the balance of centripetal and centrifugal forces. In fact, they introduced some shades of unitary element in the federation. However, the strong position of the Congress Party and a dominant leadership was able to ensure balance and thus check the centralist tendencies of the Constitution.

Since 1967, India witnessed a critical phase in the working of federalism. The domination of the centre on the constituent units gave way to a new situation in which the centre became a weak body. Centrifugal tendencies became strong in a number of states. Basically two factors contributed to this process. Firstly, the Constitution itself tended to favour the centre and secondly, the leadership which emerged in the country did not gain a national status. The 1967 General Elections to the State Vidhan Sabhas and Lok Sabha created an unprecedent situation. The Congress Party was defeated in a number of states and even in Parliament it was returned with a considerably reduced strength. This gave a chance to a number of state governments to expose the basic weaknesses of the Constitution.

The centrifugal tendencies were expressed in two different forms. Firstly, there was an attempt to do away with those constitutional provisions which put the states in weaker position and secondly, separatist feelings were gaining ground. The feeling of separatism emerged because of the factor of negligance by the central leadership in the domains.of regional development.

It is significant to note that these centrifugal tendencies were not checked through a harmony but instead the central government tried to crush these tendencies by taking advantage of the constitutional provisions. The result was that the balance between centripetal and centrifugal forces could never be attained. The 1971 elections which came after a prolonged conflict with Pakistan and the Indian involvement in the erstwhile East Pakistan, gave a mandate to the Congress to carry forward its programme and policies. However, the 1977 elections changed the political complexion of the country. The regional forces emerged on the Indian political scene. This time the ruling party at the centre was not the Congress but the Janata Party. Once again the question of review of centre-state relations arose. The following examples will indcate that the basic element of centrifugality lies in the Constitution itself which has forced the political forces to express them time and again. After the June 1977 elections, the Finance Minister of West Bengal, while addressing a press conference in Delhi, sought a national debate on a new relationship between centre and states on fiscal matters.[11] In his opinion centre controls four-fifths of the total revenue and "we have to come to the centre, persuade it, cajole it, plead with it to help us out..... We do not want to hustle the nation but there should be a national debate on this."[12] This plea was supported by the Chief Minister of West Bengal who emphasised that "political decentralization without corresponding economic decentralization does not serve any purpose."[13] In this regard it is significant to note that the Congress

Party aimed at establishing a socialist India through peaceful and constitutional means. In order to achieve this, a planned programme of economic development was taken up. However, the planning process has been such that it not only emphasised centralization but virtually superceded the functioning of a federal system making the country work like a unitary system in many respects.[14] The formation of the Planning Commission and the working of the National Development Council illustrate the point further.

The worst aspect of the contemporary situation has been the misuse of the constitutional provisions by the central leadership. There are a number of occassions when the Union Government misused the various constitutional provisions in its favour and thus questioned the principle of state autonomy.

This indicates that the basic principle of the balance between centripetal and centrifugal forces which constitute the crux of a federal system has been ignored in the working of Indian federal system. In fact the Constitution itself does not incorporate this principle and makes the States subservient to the Union Government in many respects. This very structure which introduces unitary system, has sown the seeds of centrifugal tendencies.

THE PARTY SYSTEM

The political parties in a federal state are supposed to be an instrument of maintaining a balance between two opposite tendencies - centripetal and centrifugal forces. They create such a situation that the basic question of national unity is never at stake. A true federal system presupposes a healthy opposition, both at national as well as at state level. The regional parties help in creating awareness in their polities and help in creating a balance of power between the Centre and the States. However, the working of the federal system in India has generated a basic contradiction. The Union Government has not cared tc understand the regional feelings and regional parties care little to work for national prosperity. While the congress Party believes in highly centralised tendencies with a powerful authority at the Centre, the regional parties try to crush the centralized tendencies either by questioning the validity of the constitutional provisions or by sowing the seeds of centrifugality. A brief look to the party ideology on the question of centre-state relations will illustrate this point.

The Indian National Congress always believed in a unified India in which, "the writ of the Centre is made to run in the States"[15] so that the "matrix is strong enough to withstand the occasional squalls and tempests."[16] The Bhartiya Jana Sangh favoured a strong Centre in view of the country's political situation.[17] It emphasised that "in place of present federal Constitution with unitary characteristics, Jana Sangh would prefer a unitary Constitution with federal characteristism."[18]

The two Communist Parties want to do away with all those constitutional provisions which make the states subservient to the Union Government.[19] The Hindu Maha Sabha is in favour of a "well knit homogenous state with a strong Centre and not a loose combination of autonomous states."[20] Although, Praja Socialist Party and Samyukta Socialst Party were not against a strong Centre, they believed in decentralization at grass root level.[21]

Among the regional parties the Shiromani Akali Dal is in favour of more autonomy to the states, particularly in the field of finance and legislations. It wants the Constitution to be made federal in content.[22] The Dravida Munnetra Kazhagam stands for "State rights without infringement by the Centre" and the transferring of "unspecifield or residuary powers which are vested in the Centre,"[23] to the states. It is significant here that although both these parties have shown separatist tendencies, their manifestos do not highlight this question. The Anna Dravida Munnetra Kazhagam favour decentralization of economic resources. It believes that the present Constitution needs basic changes in order to make it federal.[24] The Jharkhand Party wants to establish State in order to "check the age old exploitation of the local tribals."[25]

The regional parties in the northeast are more vocal about autonomy to the states. This demand is more pronounced in Nagaland and Mizoram. In Nagaland, the Nagaland Nationalist Organization and in Mizoram, Mizo National Front, have been sowing the seeds of separatism. The All Party Hill Leaders Conference in Meghalaya, Manipur People's Party in Manipur and Tripura Upjati

TABLE 8.1 : SEATS NOT CONTESTED OR LEFT TO ELECTORAL ALLIES BY THE CONGRESS PARTY AT RESPECTIVE GENERAL ELECTIONS

(Figures within brackets indicate seats not contested)

S.No.	State/Union Territory	Number of seats				%Electorate Left	
		1962	1971	1977	1980	1971	1980
1.	Andhra Pradesh	43(0)	41(4)	42(0)	42(0)	9.42	-
2.	Assam	12(0)	14(1)	14(0)	14(12)*	6.67	-
3.	Bihar	53(0)	53(6)	54(0)	54(0)	11.19	-
4.	Gujarat	22(0)	24(1)	26(0)	26(0)	4.32	-
5.	Haryana	-	9(0)	10(1)	10(0)	-	11.32
6.	Himachal Pradesh	4(10)	4(0)	4(0)	4(0)	-	-
7.	Jammu & Kashmir	-	6(0)	6(3)	6(5)	-	59.30
8.	Karnataka	26(0)	27(0)	28(0)	28(0)	-	-
9.	Kerala	18(4)	19(12)	20(9)	20(9)	63.40	44.60
10.	Madhya Pradesh	36(1)	37(1)	40(2)	40(1)	2.44	5.67
11.	Maharashtra	44(0)	45(1)	48(1)	48(0)	2.09	2.01
12.	Manipur	2(0)	2(0)	2(0)	2(0)	-	-
13.	Meghalaya	-	-	2(0)	2(1)**	-	-
14.	Nagaland	-	1(1)	1(0)	1(1)	100.00	-

15.	Orissa	20(0)	20(1)	21(1)	21(0)	5.15	4.28
16.	Punjab	22(0)	13(2)	13(0)	13(0)	14.97	-
17.	Rajasthan	22(1)	23(0)	25(0)	25(0)	-	-
18.	Sikkim	-	-	1(0)	1(1)	-	-
19.	Tamil Nadu	41(0)	39(30)	39(24)	39(17)	77.15	61.70
20	Tripura	2(0)	2(0)	2(0)	2(0)	-	-
21.	Uttar Pradesh	86(0)	85(7)	85(0)	85(0)	8.27	-
22.	West Bengal	36(0)	40(9)	42(8)	42(1)	23.66	19.77
23.	A.& N. Islands	-	1(0)	1(0)	1(0)	-	-
24.	Arunachal Pradesh	-	-	2(0)	2(0)	-	-
25.	Chandigarh	-	1(0)	1(0)	1(0)	-	-
26.	D & N Haveli	-	1(0)	1(0)	1(0)	-	-
27.	Delhi	5(0)	7(0)	7(0)	7(0)	-	-
28.	Goa, Daman & Diu	-	2(1)	2(0)	2(1)	52.00	-
29.	Lakshadweep	-	1(0)	1(0)	1(0)	-	-
30.	Mizoram	-	-	1(0)	1(1)	-	100.00
31.	Pondicherry	-	1(0)	1(0)	1(0)	-	-
	INDIA	494(6)	518(77)	542(50)	542(50)	15.64	9.88

* Elections were held later in 12 constituencies

** Election was held later in 1 constituency.

Fig. 8.1
India: Seats not Contested - Congress Party, 1971, 1977 and 1980

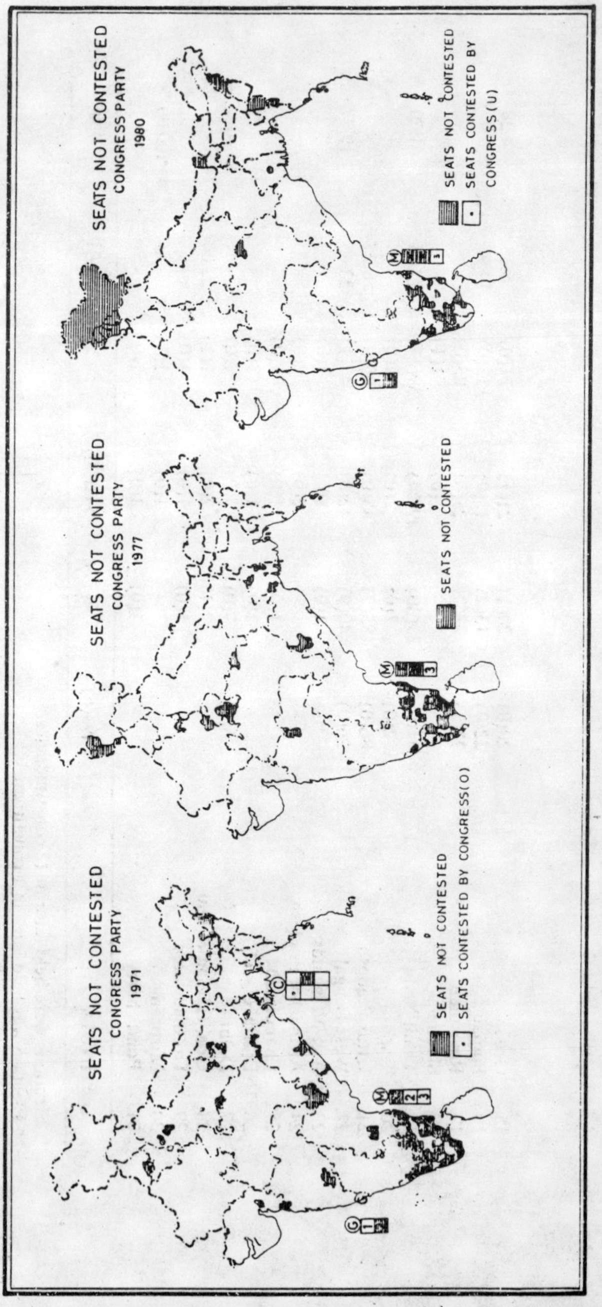

Juja Samiti in Tripura, take a milder attitude towards the question of autonomy but favour the safeguard of tribal interests.

It is evident from this brief analysis that political parties with different ideologies exist in the country. If parties like the Hindu Maha Sabha and Jana Sangh favoured a very strong Centre, the regional parties like Akali Dal, and Dravida Munnetra Kazhagam are opposed to such centralised tendencies and want states to be autonomous. The Congress Party has adopted a mid-way path and favours the existing system.

The working of the Indian federal system reveals that upto 1967 the Congress was able to give a lead to the nation by maintaining a balance between the forces of integration and forces of division. After 1967 the hegemony of the Congress Party was challenged in the wake of emergent regional forces and therefore in the 1971 elections the Congress Party had to forge electoral alliances with parties like the Dravida Munnetra Kazhagam. This is a very significant aspect of contemporary India politics. It is a significant aspect because it indicates a process in which a party opposed to centrifugal forces, cooperates with the forces of divisive nature and thus strengthens the centrifugal tendencies. It is evident from Table 8.1 that the Congress Party did not contest only in 6 constituencies in 1962 elections. However, in the changed political situation in post-1967 period the party did not field its candidates in as many as 77 constituencies in 1971 elections. The state level pattern of these uncontested constituencies reveals that the Congress left 30 seats in Tamil Nadu and 12 seats in Kerala (Fig. 8.1). The process was repeated in the 1977 elections when the party left 50 seats uncontested (Table 8.1). The maximum number of seats uncontested by Congrees Party were in Tamil Nadu where the party had an electoral alliance with the ADMK. It left 3 seats to National Conference in Jammu and Kashmir. The pattern in 1980 elections reveals that the Congress did not contest in 50 constituencies of which 17 were in Tamil Nadu, 9 in Kerala and 5 in Jammu and Kashmir.

It is significant to note that the splinter groups of the Congress, viz. Congress (O) and Congress(U), although claiming themselves as national parties, at the very beginning of electoral process, cease to be national Parties. The Congress(O) in 1971 left 280 seats

Fig. 8.2
India: Seats not Contested - Janata Party 1971, 1977 and 1980

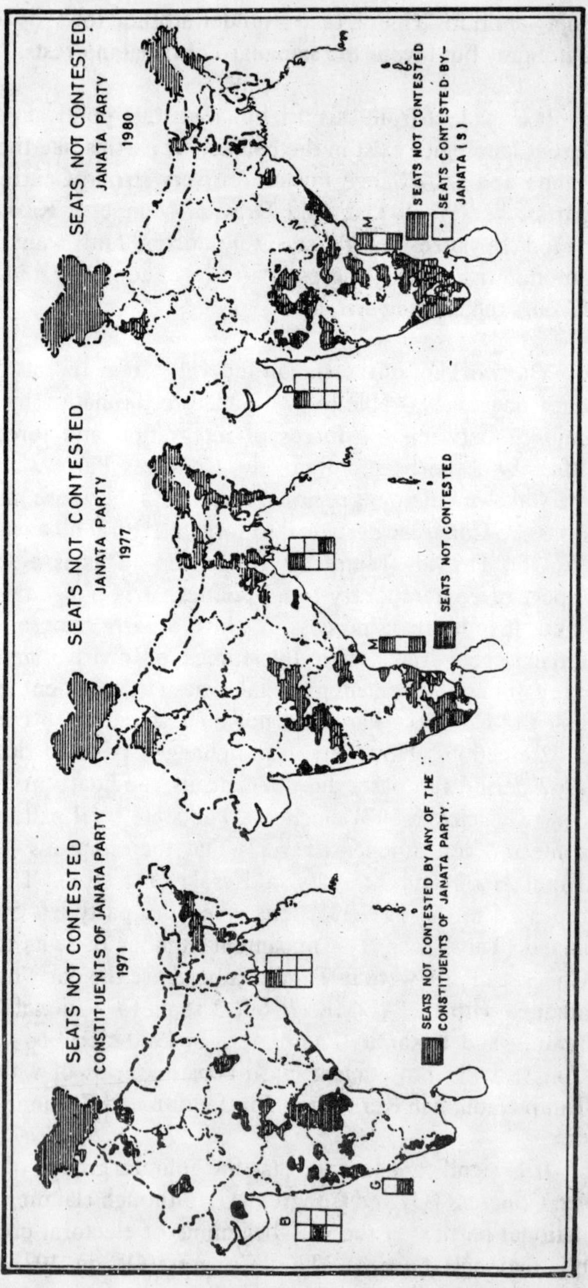

uncontested and Congress (U) did not contest in 330 seats in the 1980 elections. The state level distribution of these constituencies is presented in Table 8.2.

The Janata Party which came into existence on the eve of 1977 elections left 118 seats uncontested. It had to make electoral adjustments with a number of parties in view of the hollowbase of its constituents. It is evident from Table 8.3 that it did not contest 10 seats in Punjab, 17 seats in Kerala, 21 seats in Tamil Nadu and 27 seats in West Bengal. Besides, it did not field its candidates in Arunachal Pradesh, Mizoram, Meghalaya, Nagaland, Sikkim and Indian Islands. The same process was repeated in 1980 elections when it left 110 seats uncontested.

It is significant to note that although the Janata(S) was heading a caretaker government at the time of the 1980 elections, the party did not contest in as many as 248 constituencies. The party left most of the Indian periphery uncontested (Table 8.3).

A more striking feature of this phenomenon emerges if the percentage of electorate is computed in these uncontested constituencies. It is evident from Table 8.1 that the ruling Congress did not seek support of 15.64 per cent of the electorate in 1971 elections. The highest share of electorate was in Tamil Nadu (77.15 per cent) followed by Kerala, Goa, Daman and Diu and West Bengal. Similarly in 1977, the Congress at the very beginning ruled out the support of 9.88 per cent of the electorate. It did not consider 61.70 per cent of electorate in Tamil Nadu, 59.30 per cent of electorate in Jammu and Kashmir and 44.60 per cent of electorate in Kerala. The Janata and Janata(S) excluded 14.37 per cent of electorate at the very beginning. They did not seek support of electorate in Arunachal Pradesh, Meghalaya, Nagaland and Sikkim. This shows that even the ruling parties leave a large portion of the electorate while aspiring for power at the centre.

Although, this may look like a strategy of electoral convenience, it has very significant political implications. It indicates two processes. Firstly,it is a reflection on the weakening of the forces of national integration. Secondly, it signifies a process which not only recognizes the unhealthy centrifugal forces but also legitimizes them by forging alliances with them and by withdrawing from direct contest. This has important implications for the working of the Indian political system because it indicates that the balance between centripetal and centrifugal forces no more exists in the Indian polity.

TABLE 8.2 : SEATS NOT CONTESTED OR LEFT TO ELECTORAL ALLIES BY THE CONGRESS (O) AND CONGRESS (U)

(Figures within brackets indicate seats not contested)

S.No.	State/Union Territory	Number of seats Congress (O) 1971	Congress(U) 1980
1.	Andhra Pradesh	41(29)	42(31)
2.	Assam	14(4)	14(12)*
3.	Bihar	53(29)	54(38)
4.	Gujarat	24(5)	26(14)
5.	Haryana	9(5)	10(8)
6.	Himachal Pradesh	4(1)	4(3)
7.	Jammu & Kashmir	6(6)	6(4)
8.	Karnataka	27(10)	28(1)
9.	Kerala	19(15)	20(14)
10.	Madhya Pradesh	37(32)	40(27)
11.	Maharashtra	45(36)	48(24)
12.	Manipur	2(0)	2(0)
13.	Meghalaya	-	2(2)**
14.	Nagaland	1(1)	1(1)
15.	Orissa	20(14)	21(16)
16.	Punjab	13(9)	13(11)
17.	Rajasthan	23(19)	25(13)
18.	Sikkim	-	1(0)
19.	Tamil Nadu	39(10)	39(29)
20	Tripura	2(2)	2(1)
21.	Uttar Pradesh	85(41)	85(50)
22.	West Bengal	40(6)	42(24)
23.	A.& N. Islands	1(1)	1(1)
24.	Arunachal Pradesh	-	2(0)
25.	Chandigarh	1(0)	1(0)
26.	D & N Haveli	1(1)	1(0)
27.	Delhi	7(2)	7(3)
28.	Goa, Daman & Diu	2(1)	2(1)
29.	Lakshadweep	1(1)	1(0)
30.	Mizoram	-	1(1)
31.	Pondicherry	1(0)	1(1)
	INDIA	518(280)	542(330)

* Excludes 12 Constituencies of Assam

** Excludes one Constituency of Meghalaya

TABLE 8.3 : SEATS NOT CONTESTED OR LEFT TO ELECTORAL ALLIES BY THE JANATA AND JANATA(S) AT RESPECTIVE GENERAL ELECTIONS

(Figures within brackets indicate seats not contested)

S.No.	State/Union Territory	Number of seats			%Electorate Left
		Janata 1977	Janata 1980	Janata(S) 1980	Janata & Janata(S) 1980
1.	Andhra Pradesh	42(5)	42(11)	42(32)	20.98
2.	Assam	14(3)	14(12)*	14(14)*	-
3.	Bihar	54(2)	54(0)	54(18)	-
4.	Gujarat	26(0)	26(0)	26(16)	-
5.	Haryana	10(0)	10(0)	10(0)	-
6.	Himachal Pradesh	4(0)	4(0)	4(1)	-
7.	Jammu & Kashmir	6(4)	6(5)	6(6)	76.08
8.	Karnataka	28(0)	28(0)	28(16)	-
9.	Kerala	20(17)	20(16)	20(20)	80.04
10.	Madhya Pradesh	40(1)	40(0)	40(10)	-
11.	Maharashtra	48(17)	48(17)	48(21)	24.62
12.	Manipur	2(0)	2(0)	2(2)	-
13.	Meghalaya	2(2)	2(2)	2(2)	100.00
14.	Nagaland	1(1)	1(1)	1(1)	100.00
15.	Orissa	21(1)	21(1)	21(3)	-
16.	Punjab	13(10)	13(4)	13(10)	22.85
17.	Rajasthan	25(0)	25(0)	25(9)	-
18.	Sikkim	1(1)	1(1)	1(1)	100.00
19.	Tamil Nadu	29(21)	39(30)	39(26)	56.61
20.	Tripura	2(1)	2(0)	2(2)	-
21.	Uttar Pradesh	85(0)	85(0)	85(6)	-
22.	West Bengal	42(27)	42(7)	42(25)	14.42
23.	A.& N. Islands	2(1)	1(0)	1(0)	-
24.	Arunachal Pradesh	2(2)	2(2)	1(2)	100.00
25.	Chandigarh	1(0)	1(0)	1(0)	-
26.	D & N Haveli	1(0)	1(0)	1(1)	-
27.	Delhi	7(0)	7(0)	7(2)	-
28.	Goa, Daman & Diu	2(0)	2(0)	2(0)	-
29.	Lakshadweep	1(1)	1(0)	1(1)	-
30.	Mizoram	1(1)	1(1)	1(1)	100.00
31.	Pondicherry	1(0)	1(0)	1(0)	-
	INDIA	542(118)	542(110)	542(248)	14.37

* Excludes 12 Constituencies of Assam

** Excludes one Constituency of Meghalaya

METHODOLOGY

It will be pertinent here to describe the methodology involved in the analysis. The methodology adopted in this analysis is based on the assumption that the acceptability of party programmes and policies may be judged through the people's support to political parties in the elections. It also presupposes that the parties may be arranged in a hierarchial order by assigning them the weightages based on their policies pertaining to the issues of (a) state autonomy and constitutional provisions for President's Rule, (b) financial autonomy/centre state relations and (c) language issue. The stand taken by different political parties on these issues has been assessed through their election manifestos. However, besides the election manifestos, the information gathered through personal interviews of some of the leaders of various political parties has also been used to assign weightages.[26]

This analysis is based on electoral data of 41 political parties for the three Parliamentary elections of 1971, 1977 and 1980. Percentage share of votes polled by a party in each elections in a constituency has been multiplied by its weightage. These weighted indices for parties in a constituency have been added together and then divided by the number of parties considered in that constituency. The resultant figure has been termed as centrifugality index. It may be expressed as follows:

$$C_i = \frac{\sum_{t=1}^{3} \sum_{j=1}^{27} \sum W_j \; Xijt}{n}$$

Where, Ci = centrifugality index for ith constituency
Wj = weightage for j th party
Xijt = percentage votes polled by jth party in ith constituency in t election
n = total number of party candidates considered in ith constituency.

The centrifugality indices have been classified into following 5 categories on the basis of their mean and standard deviation by taking the interval of 0.5 standard deviation. The following categories have been recognized:

Above 41.35	Very High
29.80-41.35	High
18.24-29.79	Medium
6.68-18.23	Low
Below 6.68	Very Low

List of political parties and their weightages are presented below:

Weightages	+3	+2	+1	0	-1	-2
Parties	APHLC,ADMK DMK, MRP NNO, PPC PPA, SAD TUJS, UDF, UFN, PHJ, JKD.	CPI, CPI(M) FBL, JKN KEC, KCP, MAG, PWP, RSP, VHP, JKP, SSN, SUCI, TPS.	JNP	CONG. CONG(O) CONG(U) PSP,SSP	JNP(S) Swa-tantra BKD, RPI,RPK	BJS HMS RRP

The weightages for political parties are determined on the basis of the proposed departure from the existing constitutional norms. A high weightage is given to those parties which favour drastic changes in the existing structure. If these changes proposed by a political party will result in weakening the power of the centre and strengthening the political authority of the states then a positive weightage is assigned to the party. However, if the proposed changes are such that they will further enhance the unitary tendencies then a negative weightage has been assigned. The policies of political parties are summarised in Table 8.4.

TABLE 8.4: PARTIES' STAND AND WEIGHTAGES

	Issues	Parties	Weightage
(a)	Greater autonomy to states; transfer of residuary power to states; complete opposition to Hindi	ADMK, DMK	+3

(*Contd. Table 8.4*)

	Issues	Parties	Weightage
(b)	Reorganization of states on the basis of spoken language at the village level; constitutional amendments in order to make it federal; promotion of regional languages.	SAD	+3
(c)	Reorganization of the states on the basis of ethno-lingual reality; autonomy to tribal areas; and promotion of tribal languages.	APHLC, NNO PPA, TUJS, JKD, MRP, UDF PHJ, PPC, UFN.	+3
(d)	Opposition to emergency provisions; review of centre-state relation; regional autonomy to tribal areas.	CPI	+2
(e)	Provision of emergency only in situation of war; constitutional amendments to provide more autonomy to states; equality of all languages; and regional autonomy to tribal areas.	CPI(M)	+2
(f)	More autonomy to states; anti-people and anti-democratic articles to be deleted from the Constitution; Hindi as an optional language.	FBL	+2
(g)	Constitution to be amended in order to provide effective political power to the elected reresentatives; emergency provision and people's Detention Act to be deleted; autonomy to tribal areas.	RSP	+2
(h)	Deletion of anti-people Acts from the Constitution; more power to states.	SUCI	+2
(i)	Review of centre-state relations, deletion of anti-democratic acts from the Constitution.	PWP	+2
(j)	Separate zone of tribal areas in Bihar for administrative purposes.	JKP	+2

(*Contd. Table 8.4*)

	Issues	Parties	Weightage
(k)	Expansion of Haryana by merger of adjoining parts of Rajasthan Delhi and Uttar Pradesh	VHP	+2
(l)	High power commission to settle inter-state disputes including boundary disputes; opposition to machinations of vested interests denying Marathi speaking people their legitimate rights.	SSN	+2
(m)	Defence of Article 370 of the Constitution; review of centre-state relations to provide more financial powers to states.	JKN	+2
(n)	Reorganization of Andhra Pradesh to create separate Telangana	TPS	+2
(o)	More autonomy to states in regard to financial matters	MAG	+2
(p)	More power to states in order to avoid negligence of states	KEC, KCP	+2
(q)	Review of existing constitutional provisions regarding President's rule, decentralization of power, three language formula.	JNP	+1
(r)	Federal system within the existing constitutional framework	CONG.,CONG(U) CONG(O), PSP SSP.	0
(s)	Strong centre; promotion of Hindi as a national link language.	JNP(S), BKD Swatantra	-1
(t)	Opposition to weakening of the centre.	RPI, RPK	-1
(u)	Strong centre; unitary from of government;Hindi as national language.	BJS, HMS, RRP	-2

GEOGRAPHIC PATTERNS

The experience in the post-Independence period reveals that the balance between the centripetal and centrifugal forces has not been maintained. Attempts have been made to nullify the centrifugal forces by generating strong centripetal tendencies. These attempts were noticed on many occasions. For example, it was expressed in the form of strong attitude of central leadership to see Hindi as a national language. They felt that this will bring the various groups under the same national mainstream. Strong centripetal forces have also been noticed in the desire of the Congress Party to crush the regional forces and install own party governments in all the states. This aspect seriously overlooks the existing social diversity in the country. It also ignores the regional sentiments.

These centralized tendencies, which are strengthened by the constitutional provisions, have generated as a reaction, strong centrifugal forces. The slow pace of economic development and the highly uneven nature of regional development have further strengthened the Centrifugal tendencies. The following analysis reveals that the contrifugal forces are well pronounced in the peripheral states (Fig. 8.3). It is noted that the centrifugality index is very high in 57 constituencies. Table 8.5 shows the distribution of constituencies in different categories of centrifugality index.

It is seen from Table 8.5 that the value of the index is above mean in as many as 166 constituencies.

TABLE 8.5: CONSTITUENCIES CLASSIFIED BY CENTRIFUGALITY INDEX, ALL INDIA PATTERN

Centrifugality index	No. of constituencies
Above 41.35	57
29.80-41.35	41
18.24-29.79 (mean 18.24)	68
6.68-18.23	204
Less than 6.68	171
Total	541*

* Excluding Sikkim constituency.

Fig. 8.3
India: Spatial Pattern of Centrifugal Forces

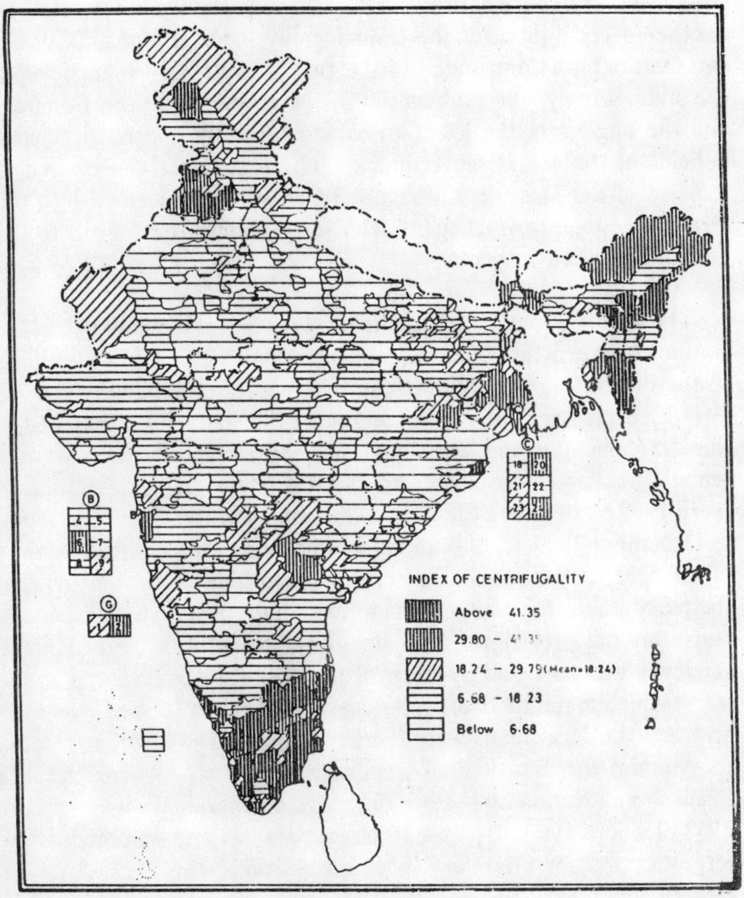

The spatial distribution of constituencies showing high centrifugality index reveals that they lie mainly on the periphery of the nation (Fig. 8.3). The state level distribution of constituencies is presented in Table 8.6.

Areas of Operation of Strong Centrifugal Forces

The operation of centrifugal forces is most pronounced in the state of Tamil Nadu. Out of 39 constituencies in the state, 27 constituencies are characterised by very high centrifugality index. In another 4 constituencies the centrifugality index is high. Basically two factors have contributed to the rise of centrifugal tendencies in the state. Firstly, the domination of the Brahmins in the Congress and the neglect of the lower caste and secondly, the north centric policies of the central government. The first factor contributed to the rise of the Dravida Kazhagam which was transformed into the Dravida Munnetra Kazhagam. The second factor gave birth to the demand for state autonomy.

The origin of the centrifugal tendencies in Tamil Nadu lies in the conflict between the Congress and the DMK. The DMK has been strengthening its mass following since its inception on September 17, 1949 by organizing the non-Brahmins in the state. It participated in the 1957 elections and won 14 assembly seats and 2 Parliamentary seats. The Party was elected to Madras Municipal Corporation in April 1959 by breaking the 22 year monopoly of the Congress. When in December 1959, C. Subramaniam questioned the political motives of the DMK, Annadurai, its President told him in vocal terms that the party stands for a fully autonomous southern state with necessary constitutional provisions. It is significant to mention here that the tendency was nurtured by some of the political organisations in the north which maintain that the Aryans are superior to the Dravidians and that the Dravidians were the late comers. The DMK reiterated its demand for 'Dravidanad' comprising Madras, Mysore, Andhra Pradesh and Kerala on the eve of the third general elections.[27] In the 1962 elections the party won 50 assembly seats and emerged as the largest opposition group in the Madras Assembly.[28]

TABLE 8.6: PATTERN OF CENTRIFUGAL TENDENCIES

S. No.	State/Union Territory	No. of constituencies in different categories of centrifugality index				
		Below 6.68	6.68-18.23	18.24-29.79	29.80-41.35	Above 41.35
1.	Andhra Pradesh	8	20	11	3	-
2.	Assam	2	10	1	-	1
3.	Bihar	17	29	7	1	-
4.	Gujarat	2	24	-	-	-
5.	Haryana	4	5	1	-	-
6.	Himachal Pradesh	1	3	-	-	-
7.	Jammu and Kashmir	-	2	1	1	2
8.	Karnataka	10	18	-	-	-
9.	Kerala	1	1	4	1	13
10.	Madhya Pradesh	27	12	1	-	-
11.	Maharashtra	11	27	8	2	-
12.	Manipur	-	1	1	-	-
13.	Meghalaya	1	1	-	-	-
14.	Nagaland	-	-	-	-	1
15.	Orissa	10	8	-	2	1
16.	Punjab	-	3	2	2	6
17.	Rajasthan	12	11	2	-	-
18.	Sikkim*	-	-	-		
19.	TAmil Nadu	-	1	7	4	27
20.	Tripura	-	-	1	1	-
21.	Uttar Pradesh	58	24	3	-	-
22.	West Bengal	-	2	15	20	5
23.	A. and N. Islands	-	1	-	-	-
24.	Arunachal Pradesh	-	-	-	2	-
25.	Chandigarh	1	-	-	-	-
26.	Dadra and Nagar Haveli	-	1	-	-	-
27.	Delhi	7	-	-	-	-
28.	Goa, Daman and Diu	-	-	1	1	-
29.	Lakshadweep	-	1	-	-	-
30.	Mizoram	-	-	-	-	1
31.	Pondicherry	-	-	-	1	-
	India	172	205	66	41	57

* Excluded from analysis.

This became a serious concern to the Congress Party who masterminded a novel measure to crush the party - 16th Amendment of the Constitution - which made the demand for secession a criminal offence. C.N. Annadurai saw the threat in the amendment and therefore modified his stand. However, on February 13, 1963 he emphasised the need for autonomous states. Besides taking a stand on autonomy, the party is opposed to the introduction of Hindi in any state. Its election manifestos clearly state that there will be no place for Hindi. In fact the party has strengthened its anti-Hindi stand after the 1965 riots. It is in this background that the DMK has been operating in Tamil Nadu. Both the issues - autonomy and imposition of Hindi - have become emotional issues in this polity.

The other party which operates in Tamil Nadu is the Anna Dravida Munnetra Kazhagam. It considers itself a true follower of the policies of C.N. Annadurai. Although, the basic ideology of the ADMK is similar to that of DMK, it has a mild stand on the question of autonomy and favours more autonomy only in fiscal matters.[29] However, during election campaigns the party raises the question of autonomy.[30] It is significant to note that although the masses are emotionally attached to the question of the autonomy, a majority of them are not aware about its real meaning.[31]

These parties have flourished in Tamil Nadu because of the absence of any other political force with sizeable following. The Congress commanded a strong base in Tamil Nadu but much of it was lost in the early seventies. The Congress leadership after the death of Nehru could not project itself on a national plane. The north centric parties could never make any significant dent in the state because of their basic ideology. Even in the contempory situation the Congress and the Janata Party could not do without the support of the Dravida Munnetra Kazhagam and Anna Dravida Munnetra Kazhagam. It is in relation to these multiple factors that the strong centrifugal forces in this state may be understood.

The state of Punjab is also characterized by strong centrifugal tendencies. Out of 13 constituencies, 8 constituencies show high centrifugal index. The high centrifugal tendencies in this state are manifested through the operation of Shiromani Akali Dal. Shiromani Akali Dal since its inception on December 14, 1920 has been a religio-political organization. They believe that "Sikh religion and politics could not be separated" and "anything vitally affecting the Sikhs was a part of their religion."[32] The Akali Dal favoured a separate 'Sikh Homeland.' As early as 1944-45, when they became inimical to the Congress, the Akalis tried to seek support in favour of 'Sikhistan.' After the Independence, their demand for separate linguistic state was not conceded by the State Reorganization Committee on the plea that it will sow seeds of separatism. However, on November 1, 1966, the Punjabi Suba was created. Even this did not satisfy the Akalis who demanded further reorganization of the state on the basis of language at the village level.[33] Some of the leaders have been asking for Khalistan publically. The Akalis probably succeeded in gaining mass support by mixing the issue of language with religion and economic problems and describe the central leadership as exploitative. They base their claim for Khalistan on the premise that Punjab has received a raw deal from the centre despite suffering the most during the partition. They also argue that the state was being exploited, with raw materials being sent out and manufactured goods sent in. There is a feeling that the Sikhs are being discriminated against in the matter of recruitment to defence and other government services. This is not to say that all these misgivings provide sufficient ground to justify their claims. What is significant to note is that there has been no serious attempt to consider these demands by the ruling parties at the centre in searching for an amicable solution.

In the state of Jammu and Kashmir, 3 constituencies out of 6 show a high degree of centrifugality. These three constituencies constitute the Kashmir valley. The social composition of the valley is entirely different from the rest of the state. The origin of centrifugal forces in the valley lies in the political happenings of the past. The constitutional link between the Union Government and Jammu and Kashmir was established on October 26, 1947 by the Instrument of Accession. This agreement provided that the Union Legislature, the Federal Court, the Governor General or any other authority can exercise its control only for the purpose of Dominion and was always to be in agreement with Instrument of Accession. A list of subjects is attached to the Instrument specifying the matters with respect to which the Dominion legislature could make laws for the state. The Instrument provided that the state shall not be bound to accept any further constitution of India. It was on this basis that Article 370 was inserted in the Constitution of India.

Article 370 provides that the Parliament's power to make laws for this state shall be limited to those matters in the Union and Concurrent lists which are so declared by the President in consultation with the Government of the state as corresponding to matters specified in the Instrument of Accession and such other matters in these lists as with the concurrence of the government of the state that the President may specify. With regard to other provisions of the Constitution not relating to matters in the Instrument of Accession, their application to the state would be possible only after obtaining the concurrence of the state government.

It seems that it was only in case of Jammu and Kashmir that the true federal character of the Indian polity was reflected. This helped to maintain the balance between centripetal and centrifugal forces. However, the seeds of centrifugal tendencies were sown by the way in which the Congress Party was installed in the state in 1964 by dissolving the Government of Bakshi Ghulam Mohammad. Usually political parties build their mass base from below but in the case of Kashmir, the Congress Party was imposed from above. This created crisis of identity for the Kashmiris which found an expression in the National Conference. When Sheikh Abdullah was released from detention in 1975, the voice of valley people again enhanced the popularity of the National Conference. The National Conference continues to justify Article 370 of the Constitution. The difference in social composition between the valley and the other parts restrict the operation of National Conference.

The major political parties have contributed to the rise of centrifugal forces in Jammu and Kashmir. A section of the Congress Party was in favour of doing away with the Article 370 of the Constitution. The parties of Hindu revivalism have openly demanded that the Article 370 of the Constitution should be deleted. This policy does not allow these parties to influence the Kashmir valley. The tardy pace of economic development in the state has further added to this situation.

This shows that there are three factors which contributed to the origin of centrifugal tendencies in the Kashmir valley. (1) Provisions of the Article 370 and its stout defence by the National Conference. (2) The crisis of identity in the wake of the detention of Sheikh Abdullah; dissolution of the Bakshi Government and establishment of a Congress Government and (3) the slow pace of socio-economic development.

Centrifugal forces are also discernible in southern Bihar comprising part of Chota-Nagpur plateau. This region is inhabited by tribal people who have experienced age old social as well as economic exploitation.[34] The pace of development in this region has been very slow despite its being one of the richest areas in terms of mineral resources. Political intrigue and lack of sincerity of the higher echelons of the regional society, if is felt, have not allowed this region to progress in economic development. On the state of development of the tribals, Prof. E.J. Rapson Commented:

> We now find, at one extreme of the social scale, communities whose members are contributing to the advancement of the literature, science and art of 20th century, and at the other extreme, tribals still governed by their primitive social Constitution, still using the impliments and weapons and still retaining the religious ideas and customs of their remote ancestors in the stone age.[35]

This stage of development has forced the local tribal groups to demand a Jharkhand State to ensure the development of their region which has an entirely different social mileu. It is this demand for Jharkhand State which has taken the form of centrifugal tendencies.

The demand for a Jharkhand State is not new, [36] but, whenever this demand got momentum, the tribal movement was suppressed. However, the unchecked process of exploitation forced the tribals to organize themselves time and again in order to safeguard their interest. This was done under the banner of the Jharkhand Party. It is significant to note that although, the party does not have any constitution; nor do they publish election manifestos as such, a study of the leaflets broughout by the party from time to time shows that the party has been generating large mass support on the question of Jharkhand State.[37] Despite the activities of major political parties in this region, they do not generate much response among the masses because of the fact that there is a strong feeling that all these parties have betrayed the local people. It is significant to note that at the time of the late Jaipal Singh the Congress Party promised to create separate Jharkhand State but the promise was never fulfilled. Afterwards the Janata Party also assured the local people that the Jharkhand will be created but it also remained an assurance only[38].

Hence, the demand for Jharkhand as a state has an appeal among the masses.

The Telangana region of Andhra Pradesh is also characterized by strong centrifugal tendencies. The behaviour of this region in an otherwise weak zone of centrifugal tendencies finds its origin in the general backwardness of the region and the exploitative behaviour of the two dominant communities - the Kammas and Reddys.[39] It was in this background that the Communist Party of India became active in this region.[40] The movement for a separate Telangana was spearheaded by the then Telangana Praja Samiti which merged with the Congress(N) on September 18, 1971. However, the region has taken a leftist mould as could be seen in the activities of the Communist Parties. In fact, groups of extreme Communists were so active in this region that a large part was declared as a 'disturbed area.'

The centrifugal forces in the polities of West Bengal, Kerala and Tripura are also expressed in a leftist mould. In West Bengal, 25 out of 42 constituencies show a high centrifugal index. In 15 other constituencies the centrifugal forces are comparatively weak. It is significant to note that the highest centrifugality in the state is observed in and around the Calcutta urban agglomeration. The degree of centrifugal tendency decreases towards the boundary of the state. This indicates that the leftist mould is very strong in those areas where there is a high concentration of industrial workers. The leftist mould has nurtured the centrifugal tendencies because of the organized attempts of the Union Government to bypass regional autonomy by exerting strong centripetal forces. In West Bengal the Congress leaders are "accused of complacency, negligence, disregard for social, and in many cases, of moral values and for unresponsiveness to the people's wishes and demands.[41] The centrifugal tendencies have been more pronounced after the fourth general elections when the United Front Government was installed in the state.The Communist Parties, particularly the CPI(M) has been more vocal in maintaining state autonomy. After learning some lessons from the policies of the Union Government, the CPI(M) has been demanding a number of measures to realise and ensure the state autonomy. Some of the incidents when the Union Government bypassed state autonomy may be indicated. The Kerala Government headed by E.M.S. Namboodiripad was dismissed in 1959 on the ground that "the normal constitutional machinery has ceased to function"[42] In West Bengal the United Front Government headed by Ajoy Mukherjee was dismissed on November 21, 1967 and a minority government was installed. There is a long list of occasions when the Union Government interfered in the matter of state autonomy which has forced the leftist mould to express itself in centrifugal tendencies.

In Kerala 18 out of 20 constituencies are characterized by strong contrifugal tendencies. Two constituencies which have weaker expression of centrifugal tendencies are Mangeri and Badgara where the Muslim League has a strong base among the population.

The centrifugal forces are most strong in some parts of the northeast. They are expressed in separatist tendencies in Nagaland and Mizoram and are less pronounced in Manipur, and Arunachal Pradesh. Assam is characterized by weak centrifugal tendencies.

The origin of separatism in the hill states of Nagaland and Mizoram lies in the fact that the Nagas and the Mizos are ethnically closer to the Burmese and the Thais. The British in view of their policy of keeping the northeast away from the mainstream of nationalism began to work very secretly with a view to carrying out the separatist policy.[43]

After Independence the Naga leaders demanded a separate state for Nagaland and their demand was partially conceded by Nehru in 1956 when he detatched the Tuensang area from the NEFA and amalgamated it with the Naga hill district in the name of Naga Hill Tuensang Area (N.H.T.A.). A little later he agreed to place NHTA under the charge of the External Affairs Ministry.[44]

However, this did not satisfy the Naga leaders who insisted on a separate state and therefore in 1961 the Government of India took the decision of forming a Naga Advisory Board of 45 members - the Territorial Council - to advise the Governor of Assam. Even this failed to satisfy a hostile section of Nagas. Ultimately in 1963 Nagaland was created as a separate 16th state of the Indian Union comprising three districts of Kohima, Mokukchung and Tuensang.[45] Even this did not bring satisfaction to a section of the Naga leaders who after getting a separate state demanded inclusion of more areas of Tirap, Mao and Ukhrul region of Manipur in Nagaland.[46]

The question is why is it that the Naga territory exhibits such tendencies despite the fulfilment of their demands time and again? The answer to the problem probably lies in the working of Indian political system. The basic factor, it seems, has been that the national leadership has failed to make any impact on the Naga territory. Even the pace of economic development has been so slow that the tribals still practice the traditional *Jhum* cultivation. The situation has worsened after the death of Nehru who had a different vision of National integration. The present leadership is so short sighted that it does not even recognize the basic factor of diversity and thus further legitimizes the centrifugal tendencies. The centrifugal tendencies in other northeastern states except Tripura and Assam have their roots in this basic factor. However, this tendency in Manipur and Meghalaya is less strong because of the fact that their polities look for a strong Centre in order to get protection against the threat of domination by the strong nationalities of the neighbourhood.

Areas of Operation of Weak Centrifugal Forces

Centrifugal forces are absent in those areas where parties believing in a strong Centre have flourished without any opposition. This region incorporates the whole of the Hindi speaking north, Gujarat, Maharashtra, Coastal Andhra and Rayalaseema, Karnataka, Orissa and Assam. The distribution of constituencies in different categories of centrifugality index is presented in Table 8.6.

The pattern of distribution of the constituencies (Fig. 8.3) reveals that the centrifugal forces are very weak in Uttar Pradesh, Madhya Pradesh and Rajasthan. This tendency in Rajasthan and Madhya Pradesh occurs due to the operation of the parties of Hindu revivalism which believe in a strong Centre. The north centric ideology of these parties did not provoke any centrifugal tendencies in these states. The state of Uttar Pradesh has seen the rise and fall of agrarian parties which were pursuing policies which favoured the local agricultural population. The fact that the Congress Party has been ruling in these states for most of time explains the absence of centrifugal forces in these states. Gujarat, Maharashtra, Karnataka,

Coastal Andhra and Rayalseema have experienced the hegemony of the Congress Party which explains the existence of weak centrifugal forces. It is significant to mention here that although seeds of centrifugal tendencies were sown in urban areas of Maharashtra by the Shiv Sena, the party was soon exposed among the masses.

It is significant to note that in Orissa and Assam centrifugal forces are very weak. This may be explained by the fact that people in both these states have lived under the constant threat of domination by the strong nationalities of the neighbourhood. It is in response to this threat of domination that their polities align with the strong centric parties.

CONCLUSION

The results of this analysis illustrate the operation of centrifugal and centripetal forces in India. It upholds the operation of centrifugal forces on the periphery of the Indian Union. It is seen that centrifugal forces have their roots in social as well as economic discontent among the masses. This can be attributed to the growing centrism in the ruling party at the centre as well as the lack of leadership commanding a national status.

The result of the analysis belies the growing view that the regional forces are of no more significance in their polities. In a situation in which no party is able to provide a leadership which has a national perspective, the states are bound to demand more and more autonomy and larger financial powers. It is noted that the centrifugal tendencies are more pronounced in the areas which have received a raw deal at the hands of the ruling party at the centre. The process of curbing centrifugal tendencies through the liquidation of the regional parties and the wish to capture power in every state without any respect to democratic norms may further lead to divisive tedencies which may act against the process of national integration. Therefore, it is necessary for the ruling party at the centre to recognize the basic characteristics of unity in diversity. It is through the recognition of this fundamental principle that the balance between the centripetal and centrifugal forces may be maintained. This, however, may be achieved only through a true federal system.

NOTES AND REFERENCES

1. C.P. Bhambhri, "Political Parties and Centre-State Relations in India," in S.C. Kashyap (ed.), *Union State Relations in India* (New Delhi : The Institute of Constitutional and Parliamentary Studies, 1969), p.46.
2. K. Santhanam, "Political Parties in India,"cited in S.P. Aiyar, "The Structure of Power in the Indian Federal System," in S.C. Kashyap (ed.), *op.cit.*, p. 58.
3. C.P. Bhambhri, *op.cit.*, p. 46.
4. K.N. Haksar and K.M. Panikkar, *Federal Indian* (London: Martin Hopkinson Ltd., 1930), p.5.
5. K.C. Wheare, *Federal Government* (London : Oxford University Press, 1963), p. 11.
6. A.V. Dicey, *Introduction to the Study of Law of the Constitution* (London : MacMillan Co., 1939), p. 151.
7. Carl J. Friedrich, *Trends of Federalism in Theory and Practice* (London : Oxford University Press, 1968), p.7.
8. Quoted by J.A. Corry, "Constitutional Trends in Federalism," in A.R.M. Lower, et.al., (ed), *Evolving Canadian Federalism*, 1958,p.96
9. W.S. Livingston, *Federalism and Constitutional Change* (London : Oxford University Press, 1956), pp.1-2
10. O.H.K. Spate, "Geography and Federalism", *Indian Geographical Journal,* Vol. 14 1944,pp. 24-36. K.W. Robinson, "Sixty Years of Federation in Australia," *Geographical Review*, Vol. 51, p.2.
11. *Statesman* (New Delhi), July 12, 1977
12. *Ibid.*
13. *Deccan Chronicle*, July 12, 1977.
14. K. Santhanam *Union State Relations in India* (Bombay : Asia Publishing House, 1966), p. 56.
15. S.G. Barve,"Why Congress?" in Ramdas G. Bhatkal (ed.) *Political Alternatives in India* (Bombay : Popular Prakashan, 1966), p. 26.
16. *Ibid.*, p. 61.
17. Balraj Madhok, Presidential Address at the 13th Annual Session at Jullundur on April 3, 1966, *Hindustan Times*, May 1, 1966.
18. L.K. Advani, "The problem of Centre-State Relations," *Jana Deep*, December 1971.
19. Communist Party of India, *Election Manifesto*, 1979.
    Communist Party of India (Marxist), *Election Manifesto,* 1979.
20. Hindu Maha Sabha, *Election Manifesto*, 1951
21. Praja Socialist Party, *Election Manifesto*, 1971.
    Samyukta Socialist Party, *Election Manifesto,* 1971.
22. Shiromani Akali Dal, *Election Manifesto*, 1979.
23. Dravida Munnetra Kazhagam, *Election Manifesto*, 1979.
24. Anna Dravida Munnetra Kazhagam, *Election Manifesto*, 1979.
25. *Jharkhand Warta*, An organ of Jharkhand Movement, No.1, February 1978.
26. These interviews were conducted in December 1979 in Calcutta, Singhbhum, Bombay and Madras.
27. Dravida Munnetra Kazhagam, *Election Manifesto*, 1961.
28. *Report on the Third General Elections to the Legislative Assemblies* (New Delhi : Election Commission of India, 1963).
29. Anna Dravida Munnetra Kazhagam,*Election Manifesto*, 1979.
30. This was noticed in one of the election meeting of ADMK in Madras in December 1979.

31. Personal conversation with a number of people in Madras revealed that they are closely linked with these parties on the issue of Hindi and state autonomy. However, it was noticed that they are not aware about the real meaning of state autonomy.
32. *The Times of India* (Bombay), December 6, 1954.
33. Shiromani Akali Dal, *Election Manifesto*, 1971.
34. *Jharkhand Warta*, An Organ of Jharkhand Movement, No. 1, February 1987, pp. 14-20.
35. E.J. Rapson, *Cambridge History of India*, Vol.I, (Delhi; S. Chand & Co., 1968).
36. The local tribal leaders trace the demand of Jharkhand State to as early as 1912 when a group of educated *Momins* formed a League to demand a separate state for the tribals. *Jharkhand Warta, op.cit.*, p. 7.
37. It is significant to mention here that in the beginning the party was demanding a Jharkhand State ecompassing parts of Madhya Pradesh, Bihar, Bengal and Orissa. Since, this demand could not generate much response in states other than Bihar, the present demand for Jharkhand State includes only a part of Chota-Nagpur plateau.
38. This was revealed during personal conversation with the leaders of the Jharkhand movement.
39. P. Sundarayya, *Telangana People's Struggle and its Lessons* (Calcutta : Communist Party of India (Marxist), 1972), pp. 7-27.
40. *Ibid.*, pp. 28-55.
41. *The Statesman*, March 10, 1967.
42. Quoted in E.M.S. Namboodiriped, *Kerala : Yesterday. Today and Tomorrow* (Calcutta : National Book Agency, 1968), p.217.
43. Kirtinath Hazarika, "The Nebula of the North-East Frontier," in Parag Chaliha (ed.), *The Outlook on NEFA* (Calcutta: Assam Sahitya Sabha, 1958), p.53.
44. It is significant to mention here that the State Reorganization Commission had rejected the case for Assam's division on the ground that the integration of the people of this region with the main currents of national life was a matter of primary importance. The commission said: "Separation will add to the cost of administration and the coordination of the policies and programmes between the state of Assam and the hill areas on the one hand and between the hill districts themselves on the other will become more difficult." *Report of The States Reorganization Commission* (New Delhi: Government of India Press, 1955), p.187. However, Nehru viewed the situation differently. He thought that with the passage of time and the polarisation of democratic institutions in the villages, the administration of Nagaland would increasingly become the responsibility of the representatives of the NAGA people themselve.*Lok Sabha Debates*, III Series, Vol. 7, C4505.
45. Dr. S. Radhakrishanan while inaugurauting the new state on December 1, 1963 desired. "Let all past rancour and misunderstanding be forgotten and let a new chapter of progress, prosperity and goodwill be written on the pages which opens today." *The Statesman*, December 2, 1963.
46. Prof. J.H. Hutton deprecated the Naga movement for independence and admired the concession given to Nagas in these words: It seems to be that by the formation of the state of Nagaland, protected as it is by clauses in the Constitution of India, the Nagas have in fact, got more than might have been expected or even desired - complete internal home rule financed by the Indian Government; indeed they have won the war but to make advantage of their victory, the underground must be persuaded to surrender their arms and order in the hills must be restored. *Assam Tribune*, August 18, 1966.

NINE

CONCLUSION

This study aimed at identifying the process of spatial fragmentation in political behaviour as evident in the voting behaviour of the Indian masses in the three parliamentary elections, held in 1971, 1977 and 1980. Taking congnisance of the changing pattern of voting preference of the Indian people, the study attempts to measure the extent of mass following of the different political parties in different constituencies with the help of a number of derived electoral variables. The study analyses the geographic patterning of

(a) seats won by different political parties;
(b) party following as shown by the share of votes polled by each party;
(c) swings in party support;
(d) consistency in party following;
(e) party domains identified on the basis of a composite index; and
(f) manifestation of centrifugal tendencies.

The elections in India constitute the largest exercise of its kind in the world. Scholars from various disciplines have taken keen interest in analysing various aspects of Indian elections. The reasons are not too difficult to understand. The social organization of India based on a complex set of cultural and historical variables has always attracted attention of the scholars in all over the world. However, the election studies in India have been a preserve of political scientists, sociologists and other social scientists. The geographers' interest in these aspects of elections is an incipient phenomenon. In the case of India the voting behaviour is governed by a complex set of socio-economic factors. The polarization of political forces in India takes place within the framework of main social formations. Since social diversity in India has a geographical expression, a geographical analysis of elections acquires added significance. It is within this framework that the present study was attempted. The main findings of this study may be briefly summarised as below:

(i) Although the Congress Party in 1971 and 1980 and the Janata Party in 1977 emerged as majority parties in Parliament, they have drawn their strength from specific areas in the country. This is more true in the case of the Janata Party in 1977. In these elections the party ruling at the centre commanded following over a part of the nation only. It is observed that the people in the peripheral areas of the country aligned themselves with parties other than those ruling at the Centre. This brings out the flaw in the electoral system in India where a large number of candidates get elected despite securing a strikingly low share of the total votes polled.

(ii) An analysis of the voting strength of the different political parties reveals the fragmented character of their mass base. None of the major parties such as the Congress, Janata, CPI and CPI (M) have extensive bases. Their areas of influence are in the form of enclaves. It is noted that although the voting strength of political parties had its ups and downs during these three elections, the emergent patterns are in close conformity with the historical processes which have shaped the Indian polity.

(iii) Swings in party votes between two consecutive elections are not uniform across the country. This indicates that the people in all regions are not influenced uniformly by issues raised by political parties. The magnitude of swings is such that it is difficult to believe that the political parties have any mass following on a national scale. The geographical pattern of swings, therefore, reflects the fragmented character of the Indian electoral behaviour.

(iv) It is noted that unstable party following is a result of a low degree of political institutionalization. The study reveals that the people's allegiance to major political parties is uneven and changing from time to time. However, the regional parties show a comparatively higher consistency in their mass following than the national parties. The nature of consistency patterns observed in this study lead to the conclusion that the process of politicization itself continues to operate at a low key.

(v) The fragmented nature of political behaviour is further attested to by the fragmentation in party domains. The study reveals that the mass base of the political parties has a high degree of fragmentation. None of the major political parties command extensive following on a cohesive basis in contiguous areas. Their domains are in the form of enclaves. It is seen that the Congress Party is dominant only in 219 constituencies. The Janata Party commanded a dominant position only in 173 constituencies. The CPI and CPI (M) emerged dominant in 26 and 41 constituencies respectively. The pattern of dominance of other parties clearly indicates their regional, rather than national, character.

(vi) An attempt was made to study the operation of centrifugal forces in the Indian polity. The study confirms the operation of centrifugal forces which were highly vigorous in certain areas. It is seen that the centrifugal forces have their roots in social as well as economic discontent among the masses. The policies of the ruling party at the centre have further accentuated the inter-regional conflicts, resulting in the augmentation of the centrifugal tendencies.

The results of this study endorse the view that political identities continue to be fluid. The political forces align and realign themselves so often that a consistent party following becomes a far cry. In a politically immature society, decision-making in elections tends to be motivated by factors other than the principles of good democratic governance.

An explanation for this lies in the social organization. The disparate elements in the Indian polity as expressed in ethinic, linguistic, caste, tribal and religious identities heightened by underlying economic inequalities, stresses and conflicting class interests have engendered the process of political fragmentation.

The results of this study are significant both from the academic point of view and their application to the act of good government. Its academic significance lies in the fact that it provides another dimension to research on electoral behaviour. It lays emphasis on spatial location, distribution and spatial interrelationships in the study of voting behaviour. These aspects appear to be untouched by other disciplines concerned with election studies.

Most of the voting behaviour studies in India have focused on the role of socio-economic variables in shaping the voters' preferences. These studies are attempted either at local level or, if attempted at national level, the reality is lost in empiricism. There has been little attempt to describe the process itself in order to facilitate generalizations at the national level. The present study places voting behaviour in the social context because it is felt that the pattern of social diversity constitutes the most important factor shaping voting behaviour.

The results of the analysis contradicts the generally accepted characterization of Indian political system. The majorities commended by the parties in Parliament have led political scientists to describe this as the process of one-party dominance. What emerges from this analysis is contrary to this generalization. It is evident that despite great majorities enjoyed by the parties in Parliament, the Indian political landscape is dominated by a number of parties. It further shows that no political party in India can be characterized as a national party if the nationwide following is the ultimate criterion.

Its academic significance further lies in the fact that it provides a new dimension to academic discussions on whether the federal system of government should be continued or be replaced by a unitary system. The analysis pleads that in view of the emergent political trends only a federal system in the true sense can foster the process of national integration.

The practical implications of the study are equally important. The study makes some suggestions towards formulation of policies of national cohesion. This is all the more necessary in the present context when the Congress leadership has a strong feeling that the days of regional forces are over. Having altered the basic character of Indian federalism and by imposing unitary tendencies, the party is bent upon capturing power in each of the states. This constitutes a disregard for popular sentiments. It is evident from this analysis that not only do the regional forces continue to operate with full vigour but also that the centrifugal tendencies in the regions on the periphery are becoming more pronounced. In this situation a thirst for power may lead to catastrophic results.

What is more significant is that this phenomenon is taking place despite the fact that the Congress does not command a national following In fact its leadership does not have a national following. This is bound to have serious repercussions if social tensions and the process of economic backwardness continue to operate unchecked. These aggravate the demands for greater autonomy. If the insurgency is a phenomenon in the northeast the reasons are complex. It has its genesis in the fact that before Independence, the entire area was never an integral part of India emotionally and culturally. The local tribals are ethnically closer to the Burmese and the Thais. The British left them on their own without any administrative supervision. After Independence, although attempts were made to knit them into the national mainstream, the fear of social exploitation created understandable resentment. Moreover, not only the pace of economic development remained slow, but domination by the stronger and well advanced communities of other nationalities in the neighbourhood continued to grow unchecked.

Similar reasons may be traced for the existence of regional forces in other areas of the country. Basically two factors have contributed to this situation-fear of social exploitation and the slow pace of economic development. Although, slow pace of economic development may sound odd in the case of Punjab where the Shiromani Akali Dal is a strong political force, the popular sentiments support this view. In fact the demand for Khalistan has its genesis in this fact. Since long the Akalis have been agitating for political and financial autonomy. A strong section of the Akalis feel that the Punjab has received a raw deal from the Centre despite their suffering during partition. An another feeling is that Sikhs are being discriminated against in recruitment to defence and government services. The lack of industrialization has added to the economic misgivings. It is significant to note that when the Akalis were exploiting the popular sentiment on these issues, the central leadership instead of giving proper attention to these emerging feelings branded the operating forces as divisive forces.

The basic problem lies in the fact that the present leadership has a shortsighted view of the Indian polity. It does not recognize the fundamental character of Indian federalism, though, it took recognition of the factors responsible for the evolution of Indian federalism. The Indian polity repeating features of federalism evolved through the processes of history. Throughout its history, India has maintained regional entities having their own social identities. It would not do to gloss over the British period. The British rule initially imposed a strong unitary form of government mainly to safeguard their authority; yet they made several concessions: princely India was allowed considerable authority; though it was in their interest 'to ensure' islands of loyalty in possible streem of political upheaval, as Metcalf expressed it, but later the reorganisation of Presidencies and Provinces and devolution of power to them. It was this fabric which independent India inherited and which had to be substantially changed under the State Reorganisation Act. The lingusitic provinces and subsequent administrative creations were in response to regional sentiments and demands. Even, initially our Constitution framers provided federal structure with forethought. However, soon after this basic factor was, by and large, lost sight of and attempts were made to bring them under a tighter orbit. However, despite this and perhaps because of this the regional identities are trying to maintain their existence by supporting the forces which work for safeguarding their cultural milieu. However, it is not too late to recognize the forces operating in the regional polities. Only a 'true federal system' in constitutional structure, but more importantly in its practice or functioing, will foster the process of national integration. Any attempt to foster unity without recognizing the diversity is bound to strengthen centrifugal tendencies promoting the forces of disintegration and disunity.

BIBLIOGRAPHY

Adrian, Charles R., "Some General Characteristic of Non-Partisan Elections" *American Political Science Review*, Vol.46, No.3. September 1952, pp.766-776.

Ahmad Basiruddin, "Managing the System," *Seminar*, 216, August 1977, pp. 41-47.

"The Electorate," *Seminar*, 212, April 1977, pp. 19-24.

Aiyer, S.P., "The Structure of Power in the Indian Federal System," in Kashyap, S.C. (ed.), *Union State Relations in India* (New Delhi: The Institute of Constitutional and Parliamentary Studies, 1969)

Alford, R.R., "The Role of Social Class in American Voting Behaviour," *Western Political Quarterly,* Vol. 16, No. 1, March 1963, pp. 80-86.

Almond, Gabriel A, and G. Bingham Powell Jr., *Comparative Politics* (New Delhi: Amerind,1972)

Almond, Gabriel A. and Sydney Verba, *The Civic Culture* (Princeton : Princeton University Press, 1972)

Amani, K.Z., "Elections in Haryana : A Study in Electoral Geography" *The Geographer*, Vol. 17, 1970, pp. 27-40.

"Questions Raised by a Map of the 1971 Indian Elections," *The Professional Geographer*, Vol. 26, No.2, May 1974, pp. 207-209.

"Voting Patterns in Indian Elections : Uttar Pradesh - A Case Study," *Geographical Review of India*, Vol. 34, No.2, June 1972, pp.123-133.

Appleby, Paul H., *Policy and Administration* (Tusealoosa : University of Albama Press, 1949).

Arora, N.D., *Lok Sabha Elections in India : A Study in Statistics* (Delhi : Pragati, 1977).

Arora, R.S,. "Government and Opposition in India: A Study of Recent Elections," *Pacific Community,* Vol.8, No.4, July 1977, pp.660-676.

"Assam : Janata Tries Short Cuts," *Economic and Political Weekly*, Vol, 12, No. 35, August 27, 1977, p.15-35.

Atal, Yogesh, *Local Communities and National Politics* (Delhi: National Publishing House, 1971).

Azam, Kousar, "Sixth General Elections: A Study of the Election Manifestos of the National Parties," *Indian Journal of Political Science*, Vol. 38, No.3, July-September 1977, pp. 375-394.

Barve, S.G., "Why Congress?" in Bhatkol Ramdas G. (ed.), *Political Alternatives in India* (Bombay :Popular Prakashan, 1966)

Berelson, B.R., P.F. Lazarsfeld and W.N. McPhee, *Voting* (Chicago:University of Chicago Press, 1954.

Bhambhri, C.P., "Political Parties and Centre-State Relations in India," In Kashyap, S.C.(ed.), *Union State Relations in India* (New Delhi: The Institute of Constitutional and Parliamentary Studies, 1969.

The Janata Party (New Delhi :National Publishing, 1980).

Bhardwaj, Narendra, "Anatomy of Anti Congress Votes, *Secular Democracy* Vol. 10, No.5, March 31, 1977, pp. 8-9.

"Assembly Elections and After," *Secular Democracy,* Vol. 10, No. 13, July 15, 1977, pp. 8-12.

Bhattacharjee, Jayabrata, "Peaceful Revolution Reconsidered," *Seminar*, 215, July 1977, pp. 12-14.

Bhattarcharya, Ajit, "Poisioning the Roots: Black Money and the Elections," *The Times of India*, February 15, 1973.

Birch, A.H. and P. Campbell, "Voting Behaviour in a Lancashire Constituency," *British Journal of Sociology* Vol. 1, 1950, pp. 197-208.

Birdsall, S.S, "Preliminary Analysis of the 1968 Wallae Vote in the Southeast," *Southeastern Geographer,* Vol. 9, No. 2, 1969, pp. 55-66.

Blair, Harry W., *Voting, Caste, Community, Society: Explorations in Aggregate Data Analysis in India and Bangladesh* (New Delhi: Young Asia Publications, 1979).

Blondel, J., *Votes, Parties and Leaders* (Harmondsworth: Penguin Books, 1963).

Brass, Paul, R., "An Industrial Labour Constituency: Kanpur," *The Economic Weekly,* Special Number, July 1962.

"Ethnic Cleavages and the Punjab Party System, 1952-1972," in Weiner, Myron and John Osgood Field (eds.), *Electoral Politics in the Indian States,* Vol. 4, (Delhi: Manohar Book Service, 1975).

Factional Politics in an Indian State: The Congress Party in Uttar Pradesh (Berkeley: University of California Press, 1965).

Brunn, S.D. and W.L. Hoffmann, "The Spatial Response of Negroes and Whites Towards Open Housing: The Flint Referendum," *Annals, Association of American Geographers,* Vol. 60, 1970, pp. 18-36.

Burghardt. A.F, "Regions and Political Party Support in Burgeland (Austria)," *Canadian Geographer,* Vol. 7, 1963, pp. 91-98.

"The Bases of Support for Political Parties in Burgeland," *Annals, Association of American Geographers,* Vol. 54, 1964, pp. 372-390.

Burnham, W.D., "Party System and the Political Process," in Chambers W.N. and W.D. Burnham (eds.), *The American Party System* (New York: Oxford University Press, 1967), pp. 277-307.

"The United States: The Politics of Heterogeneity," in Rose, R. (ed.), *Electoral Behaviour* (New York: Free Press, 1974), pp. 653-726

Busteed, M.A., *Geography and Voting Behaviour* (London: Oxford University Press, 1975).

Busteed, M.A. and H.L. Mason, "Irish Labour in the 1969 Election," *Political Studies*, Vol.18, pp. 373-379.

Butler, D.E. and D. Stokes, *Political Change in Britain: Forces Shaping Electoral Choice* (London: Macmillan, 1970).

Campbell, R.V. and D.B. Knight, "Political Territoriality in Canada - A Choropleth and Isopleth Analysis," *Canadian Cartographer,* Vol. 13, 1976. pp. 1-10.

Chakroborty, Satyesh C., "Split-up Modernisation (Its Relevance in the Study of Modern Indian History and Society)," in *Essays in Honour of Prof. S.C. Sarkar* (New Delhi: People's Publishing House, 1976).

Chandidas, R. and Ward Morehouse (eds.), *Indian Votes* (II): *A Source Book on Indian Elections, 1968-1970* (Bombay: Popular Prakashan, 1971).

Cohn, Bernard, "Regions Subjective and Objective: Their Relation to the Study of Modern Indian History and Society," in Crane, Robert I. (ed.), *Regions and Regionalism in South Asian Studies: An Exploratory Study* (Duke University, 1973).

Cope, C.R., "Regionalisation and the Electoral Districting Problem," *Area*, Vol.3, 1971, pp. 190-195.

Cox, K.R., "A Spatial Interaction Model for Political Geography," *East Lake Geographer*, Vol.4, 1968, pp. 58-76.

Conflict, Power and Politics in the City: A Geographical View (New York: McGraw Hill, 1973).

"Gorgraphy, Social Contexts and Welsh Voting Behaviour 1861-1951," in Rokkan, S. and E. Allardt (eds.). *Mass Politics: Studies in Political Sociology* (New York: Free Press, 1970).

"Suburbia and Voting Behaviour in the London Metropolitan Area: 1950-51," *Annals, Association of American Geographers*, Vol. 58, 1948, pp. 111-127.

"The Neighbourhood Effect in Urban Voting Response Surfaces," *Economic Geography*, Vol. 47, 1971, pp. 27-35.

"The Voting Decision in a Spatial Context," in Board, C., R.J. Chorley and P. Haggett (eds.), *Progress in Geography*, Vol.I (London: Arnold, 1969).

Crisler, R.M., "Voting Habits in the United States," *Geographical Review*, Vol. 42, 1952, pp. 300-301.

da Costa, E.P.W., "The Congress Multiplier in 1971," *Monthly Opinion Surveys* of the Indian Institute of Public Opinion, Vol.16, January-February 1971.

Dasgupta, Biplab, *Patterns and Trends in Indian Politics: An Ecological Analysis of Aggregate Data On Society and Election* (New Delhi: Allied, 1977).

Dean, V.K., "Geographical Aspects of Newfoundland Referendum," *Annals, Association of American Geographers*, Vol. 39, 1949, pp. 70-77.

Dicey, A.V., *Introduction to the Study of Law of the Constitution* (London: Macmillan Co. 1929).

Dikshit, R.D., "On the Place of Electoral Studies in Political Geography," *Transactions, Institute of Indian Geographers*, Vol.2, No.2, July 1980, pp. 23-28.

"Retreat from Political Geography," *Area*, Vol.9, pp. 234-239.

The Political Geography of Federalism (Macmillan, 1975).

Duverger, Maurice, *Political Parties* (London: Methuen, 1954).

"The Influences of the Electoral System on Political Life," *International Social Science Bulletin*, Vol.3, Summer 1971.

Eldersveld, Samuel, "The Developing Pattern of Party Preferences," *Monthly Public Opinion Surveys*, Vol. 9,No. 4, January 1964, pp. 10-20.

"Election Results - 1977: States and Union Territories," *Secular Democracy*, Vol.10, No. 7, March 31, 1977, p.10.

"Election Scene - State to State," *Secular Democracy*, Vol. 10, No. 10 and 11, June 15, 1977, p. 17.

Eulav, Heinz, et.al., *Political Behaviour - A Reader in Theory and Research* (Amerind, 1972)

Farquhar, J.N., *Modern Religious Movements in India* (London, 1915).

Foladare, I.S., "The Effect on Neighbourhood on Voting Behaviour," *Political Science Quarterly*, Vol. 83, 1968, pp. 526-529.

Forrest, J. and R.J. Johnston, "Spatial Aspects of Voting in Dunedin City Council Elections of 1971," *New Zealand Geographers*, Vol.29, 1973, pp. 166-181.

Friedrich, Carl J., *Trends of Federalism in Theory and Practice* (London : Oxford University Press, 1968).

Ganguly B. and Mira Ganguly, *Voting Behaviour in a Developing Society - West Bengal : A Case Study* (New Delhi: Sterling, 1975).

Getis, A. and B.N. Boots, "Spatial Behaviour, Rats and Man," *Professional Geographer*, Vol. 23, No.1, January 1971, pp. 11-14.

Golledge R.G., L.A. Brown and F. Williamson, "Behavioural Approaches in Geography: An Overview,"*Australian Geographers*, Vol.12, 1972, pp. 59-79.

Gould, Harrold A., "Traditionalism and Modernism in U.P. - Faizabad Constituency," *The Economic Weekly*, August 18, 1962.

Green, G., "National City and Ward Components of Local Voting," *Policy and Politics*, Vol. 1, 1972, pp. 45-54.

Gudgin, G. and P.J. Taylor, "Electoral Bias and the Distribution of Party Votes," *Transactions, Institute of British Geographers*, Vol. 63, 1974, pp. 53-74.

Gupta, Sisir, "The Political Outlook," *Souvenir: 66th Session of the Indian National Congress* (Bhavnagar: 1961).

Haksar, K.N. and K.M. Panikkar, *Federal India* (London: Martin Hopkinson Ltd., 1930).

Halappa, G.S. (ed.), *Dilemmas of Democratic Politics in India* (Bombay: Manaktalas, 1966).

Harrison, Selig S., "Caste and the Andhra Communists," *The American Political Science Review*, Vol. 50, June 1956, pp. 378-404.

Hart, Henry, "Urban Politics in Bombay: The Meaning of Community," *The Economic Weekly,* Special Number, June 1960.

Hartshorne, Richard, "The Functional Approach in Political Geography," *Annals, Association of American Geographers*, Vol.40, 1950.

Huntington, Samuel P., *Political Order in Changing Societies* (Bombay: Vakil, Fetter and Simons Pvt. Ltd.,1968).

Hussain, Azim, *Fazl-i-Hussain - A Political Biography* (Bombay: Longmans Green, 1946).

Hutton, J.H., *Caste in India*, (Bombay : Orford University, 1977).

India, Govt. of, *Report of the State Reorganisation Commission* (New Delhi: Govt. of India Press, 1955)

Janaki, V.A., *Some Aspects of the Political Geography of India* (Baroda: M.S. University, 1977).

Janata Party, *Statement on Economic Policy* (New Delhi: 1977).

Johnston, R.J., "Local Effects in Voting in a Local Elections," *Annals, Association of American Geographers*, Vol. 64. 1974, pp. 418-429.

Parliamentary Seat Redistribution: More Opinion on the Theme," *Area*, Vol. 8, 1976, pp.30-34.

Political Behaviour and the Residential Mosaic," in Herbert, D.T. and R.J. Johnston (eds.), *Social Areas in Cities: Vol.II, Spatial Perspectives on Problems and Policies* (London: John Willey, 1976).

Johnston, R.J., *Political, Electoral and Spatial System: An Essay in Political Geography* (Oxford: Clarendon Press, 1979).

"Politics and Social Well Being: An Essay on the Political Geography of the Welfare State," in Busteed, M.A. (ed.), *Developments in Political Geography* (London: Academic Press, 1978).

"Spatial Elements in Voting Patterns at the 1968 Christchurch City Council Election," *Political Science*, Vol.24, 1972, pp. 49-61.

"The Electoral Geography of an Election Campaign," *Scottish Geographical Magazine*, Vol. 93, 1977, pp. 98-108.

Karve, Irawati, *Hindu Society - An Interpretation* (Poona, 1961).

Kashyap, S.C., *Indian Political Parties* (New Delhi: The Institute of Constitutional and Parliamentary Studies, 1969).

Kasperson, R., "On Suburbia and Voting Behaviour," Commentary, *Annals, Association of American Geographers*, Vol. 59, 1969, pp.405-411.

Khan, Rasheeduddin, "Territorial Reorganization," *Seminar*, 137, January 1971, pp. 28-32.

"The Regional Dimension," *Seminar* 164, April 1973, pp. 33-45.

Kinnear,M., *The British Votes: An Atlas and Survey Since 1885* (London: Batsford, 1968).

Kochanek, Stanley, *The Congress Party of India: The Dynamics of One Party Democracy* (Princeton: Princeton University Press, 1968).

Kogekar, S.V., "Elections Under Emergency," *Economic and Political Weekly*, Vol.12, No.6,7,8 (Annual Numbers), February 1977, pp. 173-174.

"Restoring Democracy," *Economic and Political Weekly*, Vol. 12, No. 18, April 13, 1977, p. 723.

Kothari, Rajni, "An Alternative Frame," *Seminar* 216, pp.12-20.

Caste in Indian Politics (Orient Longman, 1973).

Politics in India (Boston: Little Brown, 1970).

"Retrospect and Prospect," *Seminar* 212, April 1977, pp. 12-18.

"The Congress System in India," *Asian Survey*, Vol.4, No. 12, December 1964, pp. 1161-1173.

Kothari, Rajni and Tarun Sheth, "Extent and Limits of Community Voting: The Case of Baroda East," *The Economic Weekly*, September 15, 1962, pp. 1473-1486.

Kothari, Rajni, et.al, *Context of Electoral Change in India - General Elections 1967* (Bombay: Academic Book, 1969).

Krehbiel, E., "Geographical Influences in British Elections," *Geographical Review*, Vol. 2, 1916, pp. 419-432.

Lal, Kanwar, *Elections Extraordinary* (New Delhi: Jeet Publications, 1977).

Laux, H.D. and A. Simms, "Parliamentary Elections in West Germany: The Geography of Electoral Choice," *Area*. Vol.5, 1973, pp. 161-71.

Lewis, P.F., "Impact of Negro Migration on the Electoral Geography of Flint, Michigan, 1932-62: A Cartographic Analysis," *Annals, Association of American Geographers*, Vol. 55, 1965, pp. 1-25.

Lipset, S.M., *Political Man* (New Delhi: Arnold - Heinemann India, 1973).

Livingston, W.S., *Federalism and Constitutional Change* (London: Oxford University Press, 1956).

Manekar, D.R., *The Red Riddle of Kerala* (Bombay: Manaktalas and Sons, 1965).

Mackenzie, R.T., *British Political Parties* (London: Heinemann, 1955).

McPhail, I.R., "The Vote for Mayor in Los Angeles in 1969," *Annals, Association of American Geographers*, Vol. 61, 1971, pp. 744-758.

Milnor, A.J., *Elections and Political Stability* (Boston: Little Brown, 1969).

Mirchandrani, G.G., *320 Million Judges: Analysis of 1977 Lok Sabha and State Elections in India* (New Delhi: Abhinava Publications. 1977).

Mohanti, Manoranjan, "Beyond the Congress Systems," *Seminar*, 212, April 1977, pp. 30-34.

Mookerjee, Shyama Prasad, "Why Bhartiya Jana Sangh," *Presidential Address to the Opening Convention of Akhil Bhartiya Jana Sangh* (Delhi: Delhi Bharat Mudranalaya, 1951).

Morril, R.L., *Spatial Organization of Society* (Belmont California: Woodsworth Publishing Co.,1970

Morris-Jones, W.H., "India Discards Dictatorship," *World Today*, Vol.33, No. 5, May 1977, pp. 161-164.

"India's Political Idiom," in Phillips C.H. (ed.), *Politics and Society in India* (London, 1963), pp. 133-154.

"Parliament and Dominant Party," *Parliamentary Affairs*, Vol. 17, No.3, Summer 1964, pp. 296-307.

The Government and Politics of India (London: Hutchinson University Press, 1971).

Muir, Richard, *Modern Political Geography* (Macmillan, 1975).

Namboodiripad, E.M.S., *Kerala: Yesterday, Today and Tomorrow* (Calcutta: National Book Agency, 1968).

The National Question in Kerala (Bombay: People's Publishing House, 1952).

Narain, Iqbal, "Reflections on Sixth Lok Sabha Poll," *Indian Journal of Political Science,* Vol. 1, No.2, July 1977, pp. 181-186.

Nayar, Baldev Raj, "Religion and Caste in Punjab: Sidhwan Pet Constituency," *The Economic Weekly*, August 4, 1962, pp. 1267-1276.

Nehru, Jawaharlal, *The Discovery of India* (New Delhi: Indian Council for Cultural Relations, 1981).

Neumann, S, *Modern Political Parties* (Chicago, 1956).

Palmer, Norman D., *Elections and Political Development - The South Asian Experience* (New Delhi: Vikas, 1976).

Paul Sharda, *1977 General Elections in India* (New Delhi, 1977).

Paullin, C.O., *Atlas of the Historical Geography of the United States* (New York: American Geographical Society, 1932).

Pelling, H., *The Social Geography of British Elections, 1885-1910* (London: Macmillan, 1967).

Pillai, Devdas S., *The Incredible Elections* (Bombay: Popular Prakashan, 1977).

Prescott, J.R.V., "Electoral Studies in Political Geography," in Kasperson, R.E. and J.V. Minghi (eds.)., *The Structure of Political Geography* (Chicago: Aldine Press, 1969), pp. 376-383.

Political Geography (London: Methuen, 1972).

"The Functions and Methods of Electoral Geography," *Annals, Association of American Geographer,* Vol. 49, 1968, pp. 296-304.

Pye, Lucian W., *Aspects of Political Development* (New Delhi: Amerind Publishing Co. Pvt., Ltd., 1972).

Pye, Lucian W. and Sydney Verba (eds.), *Political Culture and Political Development* (Princeton, Princeton University Press, 1965).

Ram, Mohan, "Elections: The Key Issues," *Economic and Political Weekly*, Vol. 12, Annual Number, February 1977, pp. 175-177.

Rapson, E.J., *Cambridge History of India*, Vol. I,(Delhi: S. Chand & Co., 1968).

Ray Chaudhary, N.C.B., "Indian Elections and After," *Political Quarterly*, Vol. 48, No. 3, July-September 1977, pp. 303-313.

Reynolds, D.R. and J.C. Archer, *An Inquiry into the Spatial Basis of Electoral Geography* (Department of Geography, University of Iowa, Discussion Paper No. 11, 1969).

Roberts, Mc. and K.W. Rumage, "Spatial Variations in Urban Left-Wing Voting in the London Metropolitan Area," *Annals, Association of American Geographers*, Vol. 55, No.2, March 1965, pp. 161-178.

Robinson, K.W., "Sixty Years of Federation in Australia," *Geographical Review*, Vol. 51, 1961, p.1.

Rokkan Stein, *Citizens, Elections, Parties* (New York: David Mckay Co., 1970)

Rowley, G., "Electoral Behaviour and Electoral Behaviour: A Note on Certain Recent Developments in Electoral Geography," *Professional Geographer*, Vol. 21, No. 6, November 1969, 398-400

Roy, Ramashray, "Patterns of Political Instability: A Study of the 1969 Mid-Term Elections," *Economic and Political Weekly*, Vol.6, Annual Number, January 1971.

The Uncertain Verdict (Orietn Longman, 1972)

Rudolph Lloyd I. and Sussanne Hoober Rudolph, *The Modernity of Tradition: Political Development in India* (Chicago: University of Chicago Press, 1967)

Sadasivan, S.N., *Party and Democracy in India* (New Delhi: Tata Mcgraw Hill Publishing Co. Ltd,. 1977).

Santhanam, K., *Union State Relations in India* (Bombay: Asia Publishing Co. Ltd., 1960).

Singh, Har Gopal, "Verdict in Regions without the Wave," *Secular Democracy*, Vol. 10, No.5, March 31, 1977, p.11.

Singh, Jitendra, *Communist Rule in Kerala* (New Delhi: Divan Chand Information Centre, 1959).

Singh, N.K., "Wages of Emergency," *Economic and Political Weekly,* Vol. 12, No. 26, June 25, 1970, p. 1013.

Sirsikar, V.M., *Political Behaviour in India: A Case Study of 1962 General Elections*, (Bombay: Manaktala, 1965).

Sitaramayya, B. Pattabhi, *The History of the Indian National Congress (1885-1935)*, Vol.I (New Delhi: The Working Committee of the Congress, 1935).

Sjoblomgunnar, *Party Strategies in a Multiparty System* (Lund: Studentlitteratur, 1968.

Smith, H.R. and J.F. Hart, "The American Tariff Map," *Geographical Review*, Vol. 45, 1952, pp. 300-301.

Smith, T.E., *Elections in Developing Countries* (New York: St. Martin's Press, 1960).

Sneider, Daniel, "The Cowardice of Indira Gandhi," *Secular Democracy*, Vol. 10, No.12, June 30, 1977, pp. 8-11.

Soja, E.W., "A Paradigm for the Geographical Analysis of Political System," in Cox, K.R., D.R. Reynolds and S.Rokkan (eds.),*Locational Approaches to Power and Conflict* (New York: Halsted Press, 1974), pp. 19-42.

Spate, O.H.K., "Geography and Federalism,"*Indian Geographical Journal*, Vol. 14, 1944, pp. 24-36.

Srinivas, M.N., *Caste in Modern India and Other Essays* (Bombay: Asia Publishing House, 1962).

Report of the Seminar on Casteism and Removal of Untouchability (1965).

Stern, Robert W., *The Process of Opposition in India* (Chicago: University of Chicago Press, 1972)

Stokes, D.E., "A Variance Components Model of Political Effects," in Claunch J.M. (ed.), *Mathematical Applications in Political Science* (Dallas: Southern Methodist University Press, 1965).

Stokes, D.E., "Parties and the Nationalization of Electoral Forces," in Chambers W.N. and W.D. Burnham (eds.), *The American Party System* (New York: Oxford University Press, 1967).

Subbarao, B., *Personality of India* (Baroda: M.S. University, 1956).

Sukhawal, B.L., *India - A Political Geography* (New Delhi: Allied, 1971).

Sundarayya, P., *Telangana People's Struggle and Its Lessons* (Calcutta: Communist Party of India (Marxist), 1972).

Suri, Surinder, "Towards a Theory of Indian Politics: Some Implications of the Results of the General Elections," *The Economic Weekly*, Vol.14, December 1962.

"Tamil Nadu: Glamour Politics in Demand," *Economic and Political Weekly*, Vol. 12, No.26 June 25, 1977, p. 1009.

Taylor, Carl C. et.al., *India's Roots of Democracy* (Orient Longman, 1965).

Taylor, P.J., "Some Implication of the Spatial Organization of Elections,"*Transactions, Institute of British Geographers,* Vol. 60, 1973, pp. 121-136.

Taylor, P.J. and R.J. Johnston, *Geography of Elections* (Hammondsworth: Penguin, 1979).

Thapar, Romesh, "Changing Politics of Consensus," *Economic and Political Weekly,* Vol.12, No. 26, June 25, 1977, p.1005.

"For a Democratic Base, "*Seminar* 212, April 1977, pp. 35-37.

Weiner, Myron, *Party Building in a New Nation - The Indian National Congress* (Chicago: University of Chicago Press, 1967).

"Village and Party Factionalism in Andhra: Ponnur Constituency," *The Economic Weekly*, September 22, 1962, pp. 1509-1518.

Weiner Myron and John Osgood Field (eds.), *Electoral Politics in the Indian States*, Vol. I-IV (Delhi: Manohar, 1975).

Weiner Myron and Rajni Kothari(eds.), *Indian Voting Behaviour: Studies of the 1962 General Elections* (Calcutta: Firma K.L. Mukhopadhyay, 1965).

Wheare, K.C., *Federal Government* (London: Oxford University Press, 1963).

Wint, Guy, *India and Democracy* (London: Macmillan and Co., 1941).

Wright, J.K., "Voting Habits in the United States," *Geographical Review*, Vol. 22, No. 3, October 1932, pp. 666-672.

Appendix - I

AN OVERVIEW OF PAST ELECTORAL TRENDS

Elections in Parliamentary democracies offer one of the occasions when the political system enters into active interaction with the masses. They also provide an opportunity for political parties to check the acceptability of their programmes and thus judge their real following in the country. In 1952 when the electoral process began in India about 77 parties and hundreds of independents participated in these elections. The Congress Party emerged as an all embracing political force due to its role in the freedom struggle for the past several decades. The socialists were routed. A number of small parties too fought in their supposed areas of domain by using cultural and religious symbols, but out of 57 parties only 21 were represented in the Parliament. The Communists concentrated their activities only in West Bengal, Madras and Travancore-Cochin, where they had a sizeable emerge as the largest opposition group in the helped them to emerge as the largest opposition group in the Parliament. However, soon after 1952, the Congress Party under the dominating influence of Nehru began to reveal its real class character and implemented policies which suited the bourgeoise interest. There policies were opposed among others by the Communist Party of India particularly in the south and in West Bengal. Although, the poltical landscape of the country remained more or less same in 1957 parliamentary election, the most significant aspect of the 1957 elections was that the CPI emerged as the majority party in Kerala Assembly. After 1957, the political forces opposed to the Congress adopted a line of cooperation. The results were reflected in the pattern of seat adjustments in 1962 elections. However, these adjustments were highly limited and were made only in case of important persons. But even then they could not challenge and Congress strength. However, the major political event which came on the scene was the emergence of the Shiromani Akali Dal in Punjab and the Dravida Munnetra Kazhagam in Tamil Nadu. Their emergence clearly showed the loosening hold of the Congress over the masses. The other point of significance was the emergence of the parties like the Jana Sangh in the North. This revealed that in the coming future the Congress will have to face the growing opposition. The death of Nehru in 1964 caused a great harm to the Congress Party. The loss was significant in view of the inner party conflicts whch did not surface earlier because of the dominating personality of Nehru. The death of Shastri further accentuated the situation within the Congress. The party was left with no organizational man. As the 1967 elections were nearing, the situation became worse and worse. The leadership of the party was so divided that it forced one or other leader to quit. The opposition found a conducive climate for their expansion and thus forged alliance on the basis of Lohia thesis. The 1967 elections were shaped by this political climate in the country. The results were obvious. The Congress Party lost much of its image and therefore, the growing discontent among the masses acted against Congress interests. The party which had dominated the Indian political scene for so long was almost routed at the hustings in this election. The situation in Vidhan Sabhas was even worse. In many state assemblies the party was reduced to a minority position. In many states the opposition parties formed the Samyukta Vidhayak Dal governments. The regional forces emerged on the Indian political scene with a full vigour.

The post-1967 scene in India was characterized by the instability of the state governments which were installed as a result of coalition of different political parties. Defection from one party to another became a norm. One obvious effect of the process of defection and redefection was that the coalition governments could no longer continue in power and Presidential rule was imposed in the state of Haryana, Punjab, Bihar, West Bengal and Uttar Pradesh. Consequently mid-term elections had to be ordered in these states.

The most significant development after the Fourth Genral Elections was the historic Congress split of November 1969 which marked the beginning of a new era in contemporary Indian politics. The Congress split brought the ruling party at the centre to a minority and thus in December 1970 the Lok Sabha was dissolved and mid term poll to the Lok Sabha was ordered for 1971.

The 1971 elections came in the wake of India's concern for liberation in the erstwhile East Pakistan and the consequent defeat and surrender of the Pakistani armed forces. This, along with the discontent of the masses with the opposition parties in the wake of their performance in the state Vidhan Sabhas brought the Congress back to power with an overwhelming majority in parliament. The rout of the grand alliance was complete. The election to the Vidhan Sabha were held in 1972 and the Congress regained its lost glory through the slogan of 'garibi hatao.'

The post-1972 period was marked by a number of political developments. The beginning was made by the Gujarat and Bihar movements of 1974. However, the most significant event which took place was the imposition of 'internal emergency' following the U.P. High Court's verdict which set aside Mrs. Gandhi's election from the Rae-Bareily Parliamentary constituency. The emergency regime was a blow to all democratic institutions. It suspended all democratic rights, and coercive methods were adopted especially in implementing the family planning and slum clearance programmes. This atmosphere, which prevailed for about 19 months came to a halt on January 18, 1977 when Mrs. Gandhi announced elections for March 1977. Within a few days of this announcement the four opposition parties - Jana Sangh, Bhartiya Lok Dal, Congress (O) and Socialist Party - decided to contest the poll from a common platform, and on January 23, the Janata Party was formally launched. The Janata Party focussed its electoral campaign mainly on emergency excesses with special emphasis on the family planning progremme. Its capacity to capitalise this issue brought the Janata Party to Parliament with an overwhelming majority despite the lack of any economic programme as such. However, the Janata Party came to power at the Centre without making any significant mark on the southern states. The Lok Sabha poll of March 1977 thus changed the complexion of the politics in India highlighting the north-south cleavage. While the regional parties got a new lease of life in the wake of a changed political climate, the political parties emerged as regional in their character. As a result the Indian polity came to a stage of the highest fragmentation. The rout of the Congress created a controversy over the issue of leadership and in January 1978 the party was split. The majority of the existing MPs belonging to the United Congress left Mrs. Gandhi's group. The Janata Party during its rule remained as an agglomeration of political groups and could never work as a homogeneous political party. The result of this was clearly reflected in the party performance especially on the economic front. The constituent groups were so divided that it resulted in the fall of one state ministry after other. It is significant to note that at least one constituent group of the Janata Party, the Bhartiya Lok Dal, never saw itself as a part of the Janata Party. The result was that by June 1979 the situation became unmanageable. The party leaders engaged themselves in accusing each other and finally Morarji Desai submitted his resignation on July 15, 1979. Subsequently, Charan Singh formed the government with the help of Congress (S) on July 28, 1979. Charan Singh could not prove his majority on the floor of the House and therefore he recommended the dissolution of the Lok Sabha on August 20. The President dissolved the Lok Sabha on August 21, and ordered fresh elections.

However, in view of the Election Commission's inability to hold the elections immediately, the elections were held only in January 1980. This provided an opportunity to Charan Singh to act as Caretaker Prime Minister during this period. This was more than sufficient to finish the remaining glory of the Janata Party. The implications were clearly seen in the 1980 poll outcome. The Janata and Janata (S) both were routed and the Congress (I) emerged with an overwhelming majority. The leftist parties improved their position signficantly.

Appendix-IA
SEATS CONTESTED AND WON MAJOR POLITICAL PARTIES 1971, 1977 AND 1980

(Figures within parenthesis indicate seats won)

S. No.	State/Union Territory	BJS	CPI			CPI(M)			Congress			Cong. (O)	Cong. (U)	Janata		JNP (S)	PSP	SSP	Swat-antra
		1971	1971	1977	1980	1971	1977	1980	1971	1977	1980	1971	1980	1977	1980	1980	1971	1971	1971
1.	Andhra Pradesh	5	11 (1)	10	6	5 (1)	6	5	37 (28)	42 (41)	42 (41)	12	11 (1)	37 (1)	31	20	-	2	9
2.	Assam	1	5	2	-	2	1	1	13 (13)	14 (10)	2 (2)	10	2	11 (3)	2	-	5	4	1
3.	Bihar	28 (2)	17 (5)	22	14 (4)	4	2	3	47 (39)	54	54 (30)	24 (3)	16 (4)	52 (52)	54 (8)	36 (5)	12	28 (2)	3
4.	Gujarat	5	-	-	1	-	-	-	23 (11)	26 (10)	26 (25)	19 (11)	12	26 (16)	26 (1)	10	1	1	4 (2)
5.	Haryana	3 (1)	-	2	-	1	1	-	9 (7)	9	10 (5)	4	2	10 (10)	10 (1)	10 (4)	2	1	-
6.	Himachal Pd.	2	1	1	1	-	1	-	4 (4)	4	4 (4)	3	1	4 (4)	4	3	-	-	1
7.	Jammu & Kashmir	3	-	-	-	-	-	-	6 (5)	3 (3)	1 (1)	-	2 (1)	2	1	-	1	-	-
8.	Karnataka	2	1	3	1	2	-	1	27 (27)	28 (26)	28 (27)	17	27	28 (2)	28 (1)	12	5	1	5
9.	Kerala	3	3 (3)	4 (4)	3 (2)	11 (2)	9	7 (6)	7 (6)	11 (11)	11 (5)	4	6 (3)	3	4	-	1	2	1
10.	Madhya Pradesh	28 (11)	4	3	3	1	-	1	36 (21)	38 (1)	39 (35)	5	13	39 (37)	40 (4)	30	9	5 (1)	1

(Contd. Appendix-IA)

S. No.	State/Union Territory	BJS	CPI			CPI(M)			Congress			Cong. (O)	Cong. (U)	Janata		JNP (S)	PSP	SSP	Swat-antra
		1971	1971	1977	1980	1971	1977	1980	1971	1977	1980	1971	1980	1977	1980	1980	1971	1971	1971
11.	Maharashtra	13	8	4	2	2	3 (3)	4	44 (42)	47 (20)	48 (39)	9	24 (1)	31 (19)	31 (8)	17	8 (1)	9	-
12.	Manipur	-	1	2	1 (1)	-	-	-	2 (2)	2 (2)	2 (1)	2	2	2	2	-	-	1	-
13.	Meghalaya	NA	NA	-	1	NA	-	-	NA	2 (1)	1 (1)	NA	-	-	-	-	NA	NA	NA
14.	Nagaland	-	-	-	-	-	-	-	-	-	-	-	-	-	-	-	-	-	-
15.	Orissa	1	3 (1)	5	1	1	1 (1)	1	19 (15)	20 (4)	21 (20)	6	5	20 (15)	20	18 (1)	6	2	13 (3)
16.	Punjab	5	2 (2)	3	1	3	1	1	11 (10)	13 (12)	13	4	2	3 (3)	9	3	1	3	-
17.	Rajasthan	7 (4)	1	3	1	3	2	1	23 (14)	25 (1)	25 (18)	4	12 (1)	25 (24)	25 (4)	16 (2)	- -	2	8 (3)
18.	Sikkim	NA	NA	-	-	NA	-	-	NA	1 (1)	-	NA	1	-	-	-	NA	NA	NA
19.	Tamil Nadu	1	4 (4)	3 (3)	3	6	-	3	9 (9)	15 (14)	22 (20)	29	10	18* (3)	9	13	-	1	9
20.	Tripura	1	2	1	-	2 (2)	2	2 (2)	2	2 (1)	2	-	1	1 (1)	2	-	-	-	-
21.	Uttar Pradesh	37 (4)	9 (4)	13	5 (1)	3	2	1	78 (73)	85	85 (51)	44 (1)	35	85 (85)	85 (3)	79 (29)	7	25	3
22.	West Bengal	4	15 (3)	8	3 (3)	38 (20)	20 (17)	31 (28)	31 (13)	34 (3)	41 (4)	34	18	15 (15)	35	17	3 (1)	4	-
23.	Andaman and Nicobar Islands	-	-	-	-	-	-	1	1 (1)	1 (1)	1 (1)	-	-	-	1	1	-	-	-

(Contd. Appendix-IA)

S. No.	State/Union Territory	BJS	CPI			CPI(M)			Congress			Cong. (O)	Cong. (U)	Janata		JNP (S)	PSP	SSP	Swat-antra
		1971	1971	1977	1980	1971	1977	1980	1971	1977	1980	1971	1980	1977	1980	1980	1971	1971	1971
24.	Arunachal Pd.	NA	NA	-	-	NA	-	-	NA	2 (1)	2 (2)	NA	2	-	-	-	NA	NA	NA
25.	Candigarh	1	-	1	-	-	-	-	1 (1)	1	1 (1)	-	1	1 (1)	1	1	-	-	-
26.	Dadra & Nagar Haveli	-	-	-	-	1	-	-	1 (1)	1 (1)	1 (1)	-	1	1	1	-	-	-	-
27.	Delhi	7	-	1	1	-	-	-	7 (7)	7	7 (6)	5	4	7 (7)	7 (1)	5	2	2	1
28.	Goa, Daman & Diu	-	-	-	-	-	-	-	1 (1)	2 (1)	1	1	1 (1)	2	2	2	-	-	-
29.	Lakshadweep	-	-	-	-	-	-	-	1 (1)	1 (1)	1	-	1 (1)	-	1	-	-	-	-
30.	Mizoram	NA	NA	-	-	NA	-	-	NA	1	-	NA	-	-	-	-	NA	NA	NA
31.	Pondicherry	-	-	-	-	-	-	-	1 (1)	-	1 (1)	1	-	1*	1	1	-	-	-
	INDIA	157 (22)	87 (23)	91 (7)	48 (11)	85 (25)	53 (22)	63 (36)	441 (352)	492 (154)	492 (353)	238 (16)	212 (13)	424 (298)	432 (31)	294 (41)	63 (2)	93 (3)	59 (8)

NA-Not applicable in 1971. *Seats contested on Congress (O) symbol.

Sources:
i) *Report on the Fifth General Election to the House of the People in India, 1971* (New Delhi: Election Commission of India, 1974).
ii) *Report on the Sixth General Elections to the House of the People in India, 1977* (New Delhi: Election Commission of India, 1978).
iii) *Seventh General Elections to the House of the People, 1980, State Abstracts*, (Provisional) (New Delhi: Election Commission of India).

Appendix-IB
SEATS CONTESTED AND WON OTHER POLITICAL PARTIES 19717

(Figures within parenthesis indicate seats won)

S. No.	State/Union Territory	State Parties	Registered Parties	Independents	Total contestants
1.	Andhra Pradesh	-	RPK-4, BCM-1, RRP-1, TPS-14 (10), TC-7, MLP-6.	93 (1)	207 (41)
2.	Assam	APHLC-1 (1), RSP-1.	SUCI-2, RCPI-2.	31	78 (14)
3.	Bihar	BKD-14, Janata-4, FBL-3, Mul-2.	RRP-2, SUCI-2, Prout-5, RCPI-1, ISP-1, SP-2, BKD-16(1), RSP (ML)-1, SSD-4, MSP-9 PHJ-6, BRP-2.	183 (1)	421 (53)
4.	Gujarat	BKD-1.	RPK-4, HMS-2.	58	118 (24)
5.	Haryana	BKD-1, SAD-1, FBL-1, VHP-3 (1).	RPK-5, SUCI-2, Prout-1.	29	63 (9)
6.	Himachal Pradesh	-	LRP-2.	7	20 (4)
7.	Jammu & Kashmir	SAD-2.	-	20 (1)	32 (6)
8.	Karnataka	MUL-1.	-	43	104 (27)
9.	Kerala	KEC-3(3), RSP-2(2), MUL-2(2).	ISP-1	27 (1)	67 (9)
10.	Madhya Pradesh	BKD-1, RSP-1, FBL-1.	HMS-5.	73 (4)	170 (37)
11.	Maharashtra	BKD-3, PWP-12, FBL-3(1).	RPK-14, SSN-5, Prout-3, RPI(G)-1(1).	109	235 (45)

(Contd. Appendix-IB

S. No.	State/Union Territory	State Parties	Registered Parties	Independents	Total contestants
12.	Manipur	-	MRP-1.	4	11 (2)
13.	Meghalaya	NA	NA	NA	NA
14.	Nagaland	UFN-1(1), NNO-1.	-	-	1 (1)
15.	Orissa	Jan Congress-2.	UC-20(1), JKD-2.	10	85 (20)
16.	Punjab	SAD-12(1), BKD-1.	RPK-2	39	83 (13)
17.	Rajasthan	BKD-8, VHP-1.	SP-1.	71	129 (33)
18.	Sikkim	NA	NA	NA	NA
19.	Tamil Nadu	DMK-24 (23), FBL-1(1).	-	27	111 (39)
20.	Tripura	-	-	2	9 (2)
21.	Uttar Pradesh	BKD-67 (1), FBL-4, VHP-1, MUL-2.	RPK-6, HMS-2, RRP-3, Prout-4, ISP-1, MMJ-6, SP-2, RSP(M)-2, RPI(A)-3, KMP-3.	231 (2)	543 (85)
22.	West Bengal	BC-14(1), RSP-5(1), FBL-10.	IGL-1, HMS-1, LSS-2, SUCI-3, JKD-2.	28 (1)	195 (40)
23.	A. and N. Island	NA	-	4	5 (1)
24.	Arunachal Pradesh	NA	NA	NA	NA
25.	Chandigarh	VHP-1.	-	8	11 (1)
26.	Dadra and Nagar Haveli	-	-	-	3 (1)

(Contd. Appendix-IB

S. No.	State/Union Territory	State Parties	Registered Parties	Independents	Total contestants
27.	Delhi	BKD-1, FBL-1, VHP-2.	RPK-2, HMS-1	34	64 (7)
28.	Goa, Daman and Diu	MAG-1, UG-1 (1).	-	9	13 (2)
29.	Lakshadweep	-	-	-	1 (1)
30.	Mizoram	NA	NA	NA	NA
31.	Pondicherry	-	-	2	4 (1)
	INDIA	224(40)	203(13)	1134 (14)	2784 (518)

NA = Not applicable.

Source: *Report on the Fifth General Election to the House of the People in India, 1971* (New Delhi: Election Commission of India, 1974).

Appendix-IC

SEATS CONTESTED AND WON OTHER POLITICAL PARTIES 1977

(Figures within brackets indicate seats won)

S. No.	State/Union Territory	State Parties	Registered Parties	Independents	Total contestants
1.	Andhra Pradesh	-	RPK-1, RRP-1, HMS-1.	67	165 (42)
2.	Assam	-	SUCI-2, RCI-1.	9 (1)	40 (14)
3.	Bihar	MUL-2.	JKP-1 (1), JKD-6, SUCI-3 PHJ-3, SSD-6, RPI-1.	188 (1)	340 (54)
4.	Gujarat			60	112 (26)
5.	Haryana	VHP-1, FBL-1.	SUCI-2.	24	50 (10)
6.	Himachal Pradesh			4	114 (4)
7.	Jammu and Kashmir	JKN-3 (2).		21 (1)	29 (6)
8.	Karnataka		RPK-2.	37	98 (28)
9.	Kerala	KEC-2 (2), KCP-3, MUL-2 (2), MLO-2, RSP-1(1)	SUCI-1.	25	63 (20)
10.	Madhya Pradesh		RPK-1 (1).	71 (1)	152 (40)

(Contd. Appendix-IC)

S. No.	State/Union Territory	State Parties	Registered Parties	Independents	Total contestants
11.	Maharashtra	PWP-6 (5)	RPK-5 (1), RPI-1.	114	211 (48)
12.	Manipur	MRP-2.	-	3	11 (2)
13.	Meghalaya		-	5 (1)	7 (2)
14.	Nagaland	UDP-1 (1).	-		2 (1)
15.	Orissa	-	JKD-1, SUCI-2.	12 (1)	61 (21)
16.	Punjab	SAD-9 (9).	JMD-2, ILP-2, RPK-1.	45	79 (13)
17.	Rajasthan	MUL-1.	RRP-1.	45	102 (25)
18.	Sikkim	-	-	-	
19.	Tamil Nadu	DMK-19 (1), ADK-20 (18).	RPI-1.	117	195 (39)
20.	Tripura	-	TUS-2.	-	8 (2)
21.	Uttar Pradesh	MUL-1.	SSD-2, HMS-2, RRP-2, RPK-2, SUCI-1.	248	443 (85)
22.	West Bengal	FBL-3 (3), RSP-3 (3).	SUCI-7, IGL-1, RPI-1.	79 (1)	171 (42)
23.	Andaman and Nicobar Island	-	-	1	2 (1)
24.	Arunachal Pradesh	-	-	2 (1)	3 (1)

(Contd. Appendix-IC)

S. No.	State/Union Territory	State Parties	Registered Parties	Independents	Total contestants
25.	Chandigarh	-	-	7	10 (1)
26.	Dadra and Nagar Haveli	-	-	1	3 (1)
27.	Delhi	RPI-1, RRP-1.	-	24	41 (7)
28.	Goa, Daman and Diu	MAG-2 (1).	-	9	15 (2)
29.	Lakshdweep	-	-	1	2 (1)
30.	Mizoram	-	-	3 (1)	4 (1)
31.	Pondicherry	ADK-1 (1).	-	2	4 (1)
	INDIA	85 (49)	70 (3)	1224 (9)	2439 (542)

Source: *Report on the Sixth General Election to the House of the People in India, 1977* (New Delhi, Election Commission of India)

Appendix-ID

SEATS CONTESTED AND WON OTHER POLITICAL PARTIES 1980

(Figure within brackets indicate seats won

S. No.	State/Union Territory	State Parties	Registered Parties	Independents	Total contestants
1.	Andhra Pradesh	-	BSP-1, RRP-1.	154	271 (42)
2.	Assam*	-	-	-	7
3.	Bihar	FBL-4.	JKD-3 (1), RPI-1, SUCI-1, SSD-5, RRP-1, BSP-1.	391 (2)	594 (54)
4.	Gujarat	-	-	94	169 (26)
5.	Haryana	FBL-1.	RRP-3, RPK-3, SUCI-1.	97	137 (10)
6.	Himachal Pradesh	-	-	16	29 (4)
7.	Jammu and Kashmir	JKN-5 (3).	-	20 (1)	29 (6)
8.	Karnataka	-	SUCI-1.	92	190 (28)
9.	Kerala	MUL-2 (2), AIML-1, KEC-2 (1), RSP-1.	SUCI-1.	55 (1)	93 (20)
10.	Madhya Pradesh	-	RRP-2, RPK-4.	227 (1)	359 (40)
11.	Maharashtra	PWP-5, FBL-1.	RPK-7, RPI-23, SSN-2, BSP-5.	246	415 (48)
12.	Manipur	MRP-1.	-	7	15 (2)

(Contd. Appendix-ID)

S. No.	State/Union Territory	State Parties	Registered Parties	Independents	Total contestants
13.	Meghalaya**	APHIC-1.	-	1	4 (1)
14.	Nagaland	UDF-1.	-	1 (1)	2 (1)
15.	Orissa	FBL-2.	JKD-5, SUCI-2.	35	110 (21)
16.	Punjab	SAD-7 (1)	ILP-4, RPI-1, BSP-1.	105	147 (13)
17.	Rajasthan		RRP-1, BSP-2,	169	252 (25)
18.	Sikkim	SJP-1 (1), SC (R)-1.	SPC-1.	3	7 (1)
19.	Tamil Nadu	ADK-24 (2), DMK-16 (16)	RPI-2	146 (1)	248 (39)
20.	Tripura	TUS-2.	-	2	11 (2)
21.	Uttar Pradesh	RSP-3, FBL-9	RRP-8, BSP-3, MMJ-4, RPK-11, SUCI-1, SSD-3.	673 (1)	1005 (85)
22.	West Bengal	FBL-4 (3), RSP-4 (4), MUL-3.	SUCI-11, RPI-4, RSP-1, JKD-4.	109	285 (42)
23.	Andaman and Nicobar Island	-	-	6	10 (1)
24.	Arunachal Pradesh	PPA-2.	-	2	8 (2)
25.	Chandigarh	-	-	35	39 (1)
26.	Dadra and Nagar Haveli	-	-	1	4 (1)

(Contd. Appendix-ID)

S. No.	State/Union Territory	State Parties	Registered Parties	Independents	Total contestants
27.	Delhi	-	BSP-2, RRP-5, ILP-3, RPI-1.	133	168 (7)
28.	Goa, Daman and Diu	MAG-2 (1).	-	5	13 (2)
29.	Lakshadweep	-	-	-	3 (1)
30.	Mizoram	PPC-1.	-	1 (1)	2 (1)
31.	Pondicherry	-	-	-	3 (1)
	INDIA	106 (34)	156 (1)	282 (9)	4629 (529)

Source: *Seventh General Election to the House of the People. 1980*, State Abstracts (Provisional), (New Delhim Election Commission of India).
* Excludes 12 constituencies of Assam
** Excludes one constituency of Meghalaya

Appendix-II A

MAJORITY AND MINORITY WINS
BHARATIYA JANSANGH, CONGRESS (O), PSP, SSP AND SWATANTRA
1971

S. No.	State/Union Territory	Total Seats Won					Number of Seats Won by Securing 10-30% votes					30-50% votes					50-70% votes					70-90% votes				
		A	B	C	D	E	A	B	C	D	E	A	B	C	D	E	A	B	C	D	E	A	B	C	D	E
1.	Andhra Pradesh	-	-	-	-	-	-	-	-	-	-	-	-	-	-	-	-	-	-	-	-	-	-	-	-	-
2.	Assam	-	-	-	-	-	-	-	-	-	-	-	-	-	-	-	-	-	-	-	-	-	-	-	-	-
3.	Bihar	2	3	-	2	-	-	-	-	-	-	2	2	-	2	-	-	1	-	-	-	-	-	-	-	-
4.	Gujarat	-	11	-	-	2	-	-	-	-	-	-	2	-	-	1	-	9	-	-	1	-	-	-	-	-
5.	Haryana	1	-	-	-	-	-	-	-	-	-	1	-	-	-	-	-	-	-	-	-	-	-	-	-	-
6.	Himachal Pd.	-	-	-	-	-	-	-	-	-	-	-	-	-	-	-	-	-	-	-	-	-	-	-	-	-
7.	Jammu & Kashmir	-	-	-	-	-	-	-	-	-	-	-	-	-	-	-	-	-	-	-	-	-	-	-	-	-
8.	Karnataka	-	-	-	-	-	-	-	-	-	-	-	-	-	-	-	-	-	-	-	-	-	-	-	-	-
9.	Kerala	-	-	-	-	-	-	-	-	-	-	-	-	-	-	-	-	-	-	-	-	-	-	-	-	-
10.	Madhya Pradesh	11	-	-	1	-	-	-	-	-	-	3	-	-	-	-	8	-	-	1	-	-	-	-	-	-
11.	Maharashtra	-	-	1	-	-	-	-	-	-	-	-	-	-	-	-	-	-	1	-	-	-	-	-	-	-
12.	Manipur	-	-	-	-	-	-	-	-	-	-	-	-	-	-	-	-	-	-	-	-	-	-	-	-	-
13.	Meghalaya*	-	-	-	-	-	-	-	-	-	-	-	-	-	-	-	-	-	-	-	-	-	-	-	-	-
14.	Nagaland	-	-	-	-	-	-	-	-	-	-	-	-	-	-	-	-	-	-	-	-	-	-	-	-	-
15.	Orissa	-	-	-	-	3	-	-	-	-	-	-	-	-	-	1	-	-	-	-	2	-	-	-	-	-
16.	Punjab	-	-	-	-	-	-	-	-	-	-	-	-	-	-	-	-	-	-	-	-	-	-	-	-	-
17.	Rajasthan	4	-	-	-	3	-	-	-	-	-	1	-	-	-	1	3	-	-	-	2	-	-	-	-	-
18.	Sikkim*	-	-	-	-	-	-	-	-	-	-	-	-	-	-	-	-	-	-	-	-	-	-	-	-	-
19.	Tamil Nadu	-	1	-	-	-	-	-	-	-	-	-	-	-	-	-	-	1	-	-	-	-	-	-	-	-
20.	Tripura	-	-	-	-	-	-	-	-	-	-	-	-	-	-	-	-	-	-	-	-	-	-	-	-	-
21.	Uttar Pradesh	4	1	-	-	-	-	-	-	-	-	4	-	-	-	-	-	1	-	-	-	-	-	-	-	-
22.	West Bengal	-	-	1	-	-	-	-	-	-	-	-	-	-	-	-	-	-	1	-	-	-	-	-	-	-

(Contd. Appendix-IIA)

S. No.	State/Union Territory	Total Seats Won					Number of Seats Won by Securing 10-30% votes					30-50% votes					50-70% votes					70-90% votes				
		A	B	C	D	E	A	B	C	D	E	A	B	C	D	E	A	B	C	D	E	A	B	C	D	E
23.	A & N Island	-	-	-	-	-	-	-	-	-	-	-	-	-	-	-	-	-	-	-	-	-	-	-	-	-
24.	Arunachal Pd.*	-	-	-	-	-	-	-	-	-	-	-	-	-	-	-	-	-	-	-	-	-	-	-	-	-
25.	Chandigarh	-	-	-	-	-	-	-	-	-	-	-	-	-	-	-	-	-	-	-	-	-	-	-	-	-
26.	Dadra & N. Haveli	-	-	-	-	-	-	-	-	-	-	-	-	-	-	-	-	-	-	-	-	-	-	-	-	-
27.	Delhi	-	-	-	-	-	-	-	-	-	-	-	-	-	-	-	-	-	-	-	-	-	-	-	-	-
28.	Goa, Daman & Diu	-	-	-	-	-	-	-	-	-	-	-	-	-	-	-	-	-	-	-	-	-	-	-	-	-
29.	Lakshadweep	-	-	-	-	-	-	-	-	-	-	-	-	-	-	-	-	-	-	-	-	-	-	-	-	-
30.	Mizoram	-	-	-	-	-	-	-	-	-	-	-	-	-	-	-	-	-	-	-	-	-	-	-	-	-
31.	Pondicherry	-	-	-	-	-	-	-	-	-	-	-	-	-	-	-	-	-	-	-	-	-	-	-	-	-
	INDIA	22	16	2	3	8	-	-	-	-	-	11	4	-	2	3	11	12	2	1	5	-	-	-	-	-

* Not applicable in 1971.

A: Bhartiya Jan Sangh; B: Congress (O); C: PSP; D: SSP; E: Swatantra Party

Appendix-IIB

MAJORITY AND MINORITY WINS
COMMUNIST PARTY OF INDIA
1971, 1977 AND 1980

S. No.	State/Union Territory	Total Seats Won			Number of Seats Won by Securing: 10-30% votes			30-50% votes			50-70% votes			70-90% votes		
		1971	1977	1980	1971	1977	1980	1971	1977	1980	1971	1977	1980	1971	1977	1980
1	2	3	4	5	6	7	8	9	10	11	12	13	14	15	16	17
1.	Andhra Pradesh	1	-	-	-	-	-	-	-	-	-	-	-	-	-	-
2.	Assam	-	-	-	-	-	-	-	-	-	-	-	-	-	-	-
3.	Bihar	5	-	4	-	-	-	3	-	4	2	-	-	-	-	-
4.	Gujarat	-	-	-	-	-	-	-	-	-	-	-	-	-	-	-
5.	Haryana	-	-	-	-	-	-	-	-	-	-	-	-	-	-	-
6.	Himachal Pradesh	-	-	-	-	-	-	-	-	-	-	-	-	-	-	-
7.	Jammu and Kashmir	-	-	-	-	-	-	-	-	-	-	-	-	-	-	-
8.	Karnataka	-	-	-	-	-	-	-	-	-	-	-	-	-	-	-
9.	Kerala	3	4	2	-	-	-	1	-	-	1	4	2	1	-	-
10.	Madhya Pradesh	-	-	-	-	-	-	-	-	-	-	-	-	-	-	-
11.	Maharashtra	-	-	-	-	-	-	-	-	-	-	-	-	-	-	-
12.	Manipur	-	-	1	-	-	1	-	-	-	-	-	-	-	-	-
13.	Meghalaya	NA	-	-	NA	-	-	NA	-	-	NA	-	-	NA	-	-
14.	Nagaland	-	-	-	-	-	-	-	-	-	-	-	-	-	-	-
15.	Orissa	1	-	-	-	-	-	1	-	-	-	-	-	-	-	-
16.	Punjab	2	-	-	-	-	-	1	-	-	1	-	-	-	-	-

(Contd. Appendix-IIB)

S. No.	State/Union Territory	Total Seats Won			Number of Seats Won by Securing: 10-30% votes			30-50% votes			50-70% votes			70-90% votes		
		1971	1977	1980	1971	1977	1980	1971	1977	1980	1971	1977	1980	1971	1977	1980
1	2	3	4	5	6	7	8	9	10	11	12	13	14	15	16	17
17.	Rajashtan	-	-	-	-	-	-	-	-	-	-	-	-	-	-	-
18.	Sikkim	NA	-	-	NA	-	-	NA	-	-	NA	-	-	NA	-	-
19.	Tamil Nadu	4	3	-	-	-	-	1	-	-	3	3	-	-	-	-
20.	Tripura	-	-	-	-	-	-	-	-	-	-	-	-	-	-	-
21.	Uttar Pradesh	4	-	1	-	-	-	2	-	1	2	-	-	-	-	-
22.	West Bengal	3	-	3	-	-	-	3	-	-	-	-	3	-	-	-
23.	Andaman and Nicobar Island	-	-	-	-	-	-	-	-	-	-	-	-	-	-	-
24.	Arunachal Pradesh	NA	-	-	NA	-	-	NA	-	-	NA	-	-	NA	-	-
25.	Chandigarh	-	-	-	-	-	-	-	-	-	-	-	-	-	-	-
26.	Dadra and Nagar Haveli	-	-	-	-	-	-	-	-	-	-	-	-	-	-	-
27.	Delhi	-	-	-	-	-	-	-	-	-	-	-	-	-	-	-
28.	Goa, Daman and Diu	-	-	-	-	-	-	-	-	-	-	-	-	-	-	-
29.	Lakshadweep	-	-	-	-	-	-	-	-	-	-	-	-	-	-	-
30.	Mizoram	-	-	-	-	-	-	-	-	-	-	-	-	-	-	-
31.	Pondicherry	-	-	-	-	-	-	-	-	-	-	-	-	-	-	-
	INDIA	23	7	11	-	-	1	12	-	5	10	7	5	1	-	-

NA = Not Applicable.

Appendix-IIC

MAJORITY AND MINORITY WINS PARTY OF INDIA (MARXIST)

S. No.	State/Union Territory	Total Seats Won			Number of Seats Won by Securing											
					10-30% votes			30-50% votes			50-70% votes			70-90% votes		
		1971	1977	1980	1971	1977	1980	1971	1977	1980	1971	1977	1980	1971	1977	1980
1	2	3	4	5	6	7	8	9	10	11	12	13	14	15	16	17
1.	Andhra Pradesh	1	-	-	-	-	-	1	-	-	-	-	-	-	-	-
2.	Assam	-	-	-	-	-	-	-	-	-	-	-	-	-	-	-
3.	Bihar	-	-	-	-	-	-	-	-	-	-	-	-	-	-	-
4.	Gujarat	-	-	-	-	-	-	-	-	-	-	-	-	-	-	-
5.	Haryana	-	-	-	-	-	-	-	-	-	-	-	-	-	-	-
6.	Himachal Pradesh	-	-	-	-	-	-	-	-	-	-	-	-	-	-	-
7.	Jammu and Kashmir	-	-	-	-	-	-	-	-	-	-	-	-	-	-	-
8.	Karnataka	-	-	-	-	-	-	-	-	-	-	-	-	-	-	-
9.	Kerala	2	-	6	-	-	-	1	-	1	1	-	5	-	-	-
10.	Madhya Pradesh	-	-	-	-	-	-	-	-	-	-	-	-	-	-	-
11.	Maharashtra	-	3	-	-	-	-	-	-	-	-	-	-	-	-	-
12.	Manipur	-	-	-	-	-	-	-	-	-	-	-	-	-	-	-
13.	Meghalaya	NA	-	-	NA	-	-	NA	-	-	NA	-	-	NA	-	-
14.	Nagaland	-	-	-	-	-	-	-	-	-	-	-	-	-	-	-
15.	Orissa	-	1	-	-	-	-	-	1	-	-	-	-	-	-	-
16.	Punjab	-	1	-	-	-	-	-	-	-	-	1	-	-	-	-

(Contd. Appendix-IIC)

S. No.	State/Union Territory	Total Seats Won			Number of Seats Won by Securing 10-30% votes			30-50% votes			50-70% votes			70-90% votes		
		1971	1977	1980	1971	1977	1980	1971	1977	1980	1971	1977	1980	1971	1977	1980
1	2	3	4	5	6	7	8	9	10	11	12	13	14	15	16	17
17.	Rajasthan	-	-	-	-	-	-	-	-		-	-	-	-	-	-
18.	Sikkim	NA	-	-	NA	-	-	NA	-	-	NA	-	-	NA	-	-
19.	Tamil nadu	-	-	-	-	-	-	-	-		-	-	-	-	-	-
20.	Tripura	2	-	2	-	-	-	2	-	2	-	-	-	-	-	-
21.	Uttar Pradesh	-	-	-	-	-	-	-	-		-	-	-	-	-	-
22.	West Bengal	20	17	28	1	-	-	15	4	5	4	12	23	-	1	-
23.	Andaman and Nicobar Islands	-	-	-	-	-	-	-	-		-	-	-	-	-	-
24.	Arunachal Pradesh	NA	-	-	NA	-	-	NA	-	-	NA	-	-	NA	-	-
25.	Chandigarh	-	-	-	-	-	-	-	-		-	-	-	-	-	-
26.	Dadra and Nagar Haveli	-	-	-	-	-	-	-	-		-	-	-	-	-	-
27.	Delhi	-	-	-	-	-	-	-	-		-	-	-	-	-	-
28.	Goa, Daman and Diu	-	-	-	-	-	-	-	-		-	-	-	-	-	-
29.	Lakshadweep	-	-	-	-	-	-	-	-		-	-	-	-	-	-
30.	Mizoram	NA	-	-	NA	-	-	NA	-	-	NA	-	-	NA	-	-
31.	Pondicherry	-	-	-	-	-	-	-	-		-	-	-	-	-	-
	INDIA	25	22	36	1	-	-	19	5	8	5	16	28	-	1	-

NA: Not Applicable.

Appendix-IID

MAJORITY AND MINORITY WINS CONGRESS PARTY 1971, 1977 and 1980.

S. No.	State/Union Territory	Total Seats Won 1971	Total Seats Won 1977	Total Seats Won 1980	10-30% votes 1971	10-30% votes 1977	10-30% votes 1980	30-50% votes 1971	30-50% votes 1977	30-50% votes 1980	50-70% votes 1971	50-70% votes 1977	50-70% votes 1980	70-90% votes 1971	70-90% votes 1977	70-90% votes 1980
1	2	3	4	5	6	7	8	9	10	11	12	13	14	15	16	17
1.	Andhra Pradesh	28	41	41	-	-	-	1	6	10	16	33	27	11	2	4
2.	Assam	13	10	2	-	-	-	2	2	1	9	8	1	2	-	-
3.	Bihar	39	-	30	3	-	9	19	-	19	15		2	2	-	-
4.	Gujarat	11	10	25	-	-	-	3	1	3	8	9	22	-	-	-
5.	Haryana	7	-	5	-	-	-	2	-	4	5	-	1	-	-	-
6.	Himachal Pradesh	4	-	4	-	-	-	-	-	1	1	-	3	3	-	-
7.	Jammu and Kashmir	5	3	1	-	-	-	-	1	-	5	2	1	-	-	-
8.	Karnataka	27	26	27	-	-	-	-	2	3	13	23	24	14	1	-
9.	Kerala	6	11	5	-	-	-	2	3	2	4	8	3	-	-	-
10.	Madhya Pradesh	21	1	35	-	-	-	4	1	18	16	-	17	1	-	-
11.	Maharashtra	42	20	39	-	-	-	5	2	5	21	15	31	16	3	3
12.	Manipur	2	2	1	1	-	-	1	2	1	-	-	-	-	-	-
13.	Meghalaya	NA	1	1	NA	-	-	NA	-	-	NA	-	-	NA	-	1
14.	Nagaland	-	-	-	-	-	-	-	-	-	-	-	-	-	-	-
15.	Orissa	15	4	20	1	-	-	11	1	2	3	3	18	-	-	-
16.	Punjab	10	-	12	-	-	-	1	-	4	9	-	8	-	-	-
17.	Rajasthan	14	1	18	-	-		3	10	12	10	1	6	1	-	-

(Contd. Appendix-IID)

S. No.	State/Union Territory	Total Seats Won 1971	Total Seats Won 1977	Total Seats Won 1980	10-30% votes 1971	10-30% votes 1977	10-30% votes 1980	30-50% votes 1971	30-50% votes 1977	30-50% votes 1980	50-70% votes 1971	50-70% votes 1977	50-70% votes 1980	70-90% votes 1971	70-90% votes 1977	70-90% votes 1980
1	2	3	4	5	6	7	8	9	10	11	12	13	14	15	16	17
18.	Sikkim	NA	1*	-	NA	-	-	NA	-	-	NA	-	-	NA	-	-
19.	Tamil Nadu	9	14	20	-	-	-	-	-	1	9	13	19	-	1	-
20.	Tripura	-	1	-	-	-	-	-	1	-	-	-	-	-	-	-
21.	Uttar Pradesh	73	-	51	-	-	-	19	-	46	50	-	5	4	-	-
22.	West Bengal	13	3	4	-	-	-	10	2	3	3	1	1	-	-	-
23.	Andaman and Nicobar Island	1	1	1	-	-	-	-	-	-	1	1	1	-	-	-
24.	Arunachal Pradesh	NA	1*	2	NA	-	-	NA	-	2	NA	-	-	NA	-	-
25.	Chandigarh	1	-	1	-	-	-	-	-	1	1	-	-	-	-	-
26.	Dadra and Nagar Haveli	1	1	1	-	-	-	1	1	-	-	-	1	-	-	-
27.	Delhi	7	-	6	-	-	-	-	-	3	7	-	3	-	-	-
28.	Goa, Daman and Diu	1	1	-	-	-	-	1	1	-	-	-	-	-	-	-
29.	Lakshadweep	1*	1	-	-	-	-	-	-	-	-	1	-	-	-	-
30.	Mizoram	NA	-	-	NA	-	-	NA	-	-	NA	-	-	NA	-	-
31.	Pondicherry	1	-	1	-	-	-	-	-	-	1	-	1	-	-	-
	INDIA	352	154	353	5	-	9	85	26	140	207	119	194	54	7	8

NA - Not applicable in 1971
*Declared elected unopposed.

Appendix-IIE

MAJORITY AND MINORITY WINS
JANATA PARTY
1977 and 1980

S. No.	State/Union Territory	Total Seats Won		Number of Seats Won by Securing 10-30% votes		30-50% votes		50-70% votes		70-90% votes	
		1977	1980	1977	1980	1977	1980	1977	1980	1977	1980
1.	2	3	4	5	6	7	8	9	10	11	12
1.	Andhra Pradesh	1	-	-	-	-	-	1	-	-	-
2.	Assam	3	-	-	-	-	-	3	-	-	-
3.	Bihar	52	8	-	1	7	6	24	1	21	-
4.	Gujarat	16	1	-		4	1	12			-
5.	Haryana	10	1	-	-	1	1	4	-	5	-
6.	Himachal Pradesh	4	-	-	-	-	-	4	-	-	-
7.	Jammu and Kashmir	-	-	-	-	-	-	-	-	-	-
8.	Karnataka	2	1	-	-	1	1	1	-	-	-
9.	Kerala	-	-	-	-	-	-	-	-	-	-
10.	Madhya Pradesh	37	4	-	-	5	4	24	-	8	-
11.	Maharashtra	19	8	-	-	2	3	17	4	-	1
12.	Manipur	-	-	-	-	-	-	-	-	-	-
13.	Meghalaya	-	-	-	-	-	-	-	-	-	-
14.	Nagaland	-	-	-	-	-	-	-	-	-	-
15.	Orissa	15	-	-	-	3	-	12	-	-	-
16.	Punjab	3	-	-	-	1	-	2	-	-	-
17.	Rajasthan	24	4	-	-	-	4	16	-	8	-
18.	Sikkim	-	-	-	-	-	-	-	-	-	-
19.	Tamil Nadu	3	-	-	-	1	-	2	-	-	-
20.	Tripura	1	-	-	-	1	-	-	-	-	-

(Contd. Appendix-IIE)

S. No.	State/Union Territory	Total Seats Won		Number of Seats Won by Securing							
				10-30% votes		30-50% votes		50-70% votes		70-90% votes	
		1977	1980	1977	1980	1977	1980	1977	1980	1977	1980
1.	2	3	4	5	6	7	8	9	10	11	12
21.	Uttar Pradesh	85	3	-	1	1	2	48	-	36	-
22.	West Bengal	15	-	-	-	3	-	10	-	2	-
23.	Andaman and Nicobar Islands	-	-	-	-	-	-	-	-	-	-
24.	Arunachal Pradesh	-	-	-	-	-	-	-	-	-	-
25.	Chandigarh	1	-	-	-	-	-	1	-	-	-
26.	Dadra and Nagar Haveli	-	-	-	-	-	-	-	-	-	-
27.	Delhi	7	1	-	-	-	1	5	-	2	-
28.	Goa, Daman and Diu	-	-	-	-	-	-	-	-	-	-
29.	Lakshadweep	-	-	-	-	-	-	-	-	-	-
30.	Mizoram	-	-	-	-	-	-	-	-	-	-
31.	Pondicherry	-	-	-	-	-	-	-	-	-	-
	INDIA	298	31	-	2	30	23	186	5	82	1

Appendix-IIF

MAJORITY AND MINORITY WINS
CONGRESS (U) AND JANATA (S)
1977 and 1980

S. No.	State/Union Territory	Total Seats Won		Number of Seats Won by Securing							
				10-30% votes		30-50% votes		50-70% votes		70-90% votes	
		Cong(U)	JNP(S)	Cong(U)	JNP(S)	Cong(U)	JNP(S)	Cong(U)	JNP(S)	Cong(U)	JNP(S)
1	2	3	4	5	6	7	8	9	10	11	12
1.	Andhra Pradesh	1	-	-	-	1	-	-	-	-	-
2.	Assam	-	-	-	-	-	-	-	-	-	-
3.	Bihar	4	5	-	-	4	3	-	2	-	-
4.	Gujarat	-	-	-	-	-	-	-	-	-	-
5.	Haryana	-	4	-	-	-	2	-	2	-	-
6.	Himachal Pradesh	-	-	-	-	-	-	-	-	-	-
7.	Jammu & Kashmir	1	-	-	-	-	-	1	-	-	-
8.	Karnataka	-	-	-	-	-	-	-	-	-	-
9.	Kerala	3	-	-	-	-	-	3	-	-	-
10.	Madhya Pradesh	-	-	-	-	-	-	-	-	-	-
11.	Maharashtra	1	-	-	-	-	-	1	-	-	-
12.	Manipur	-	-	-	-	-	-	-	-	-	-
13.	Meghalaya	-	-	-	-	-	-	-	-	-	-
14.	Nagaland	-	-	-	-	-	-	-	-	-	-
15.	Orissa	-	1	-	-	-	1	-	-	-	-
16.	Punjab	-	-	-	-	-	-	-	-	-	-
17.	Rajasthan	1	2	-	-	1	2	-	-	-	-
18.	Sikkim	-	-	-	-	-	-	-	-	-	-

(Contd. Appendix-IIF)

S. No.	State/Union Territory	Total Seats Won		Number of Seats Won by Securing							
				10-30% votes		30-50% votes		50-70% votes		70-90% votes	
		Cong(U)	JNP(S)	Cong(U)	JNP(S)	Cong(U)	JNP(S)	Cong(U)	JNP(S)	Cong(U)	JNP(S)
1	2	3	4	5	6	7	8	9	10	11	12
19.	Tamil Nadu	-	-	-	-	-	-	-	-	-	-
20.	Tripura	-	-	-	-	-	-	-	-	-	-
21.	Uttar Pradesh	-	29	-	-	-	28	-	1	-	-
22.	West Bengal	-	-	-	-	-	-	-	-	-	-
23.	Andaman and Nicobar Islands	-	-	-	-	-	-	-	-	-	-
24.	Arunachal Pradesh	-	-	-	-	-	-	-	-	-	-
25.	Chandigarh	-	-	-	-	-	-	-	-	-	-
26.	Dadra and Nagar Havleli	-	-	-	-	-	-	-	-	-	-
27.	Delhi	-	-	-	-	-	-	-	-	-	-
28.	Goa, Daman and Diu	1	-	-	-	-	-	1	-	-	-
29.	Lakshadweep	1	-	-	-	-	-	1	-	-	-
30.	Mizoram	-	-	-	-	-	-	-	-	-	-
31.	Pondicherry	-	-	-	-	-	-	-	-	-	-
	INDIA	13	41	-	-	6	36	7	5	-	-

Appendix-IIG

MAJORITY AND MINORITY WINS
OTHER POLITICAL PARTIES
1971, 1977 and 1980

S. No.	State/Union Territory		Total Seats Won			Number of Seats Won by Securing 10-30% votes			30-50% votes			50-70% votes			70-90% votes		
			1971	1977	1980	1971	1977	1980	1971	1977	1980	1971	1977	1980	1971	1977	1980
1	2		3	4	5	6	7	8	9	10	11	12	13	14	15	16	17
1.	Andhra Pradesh																
		TPS	10	-	-	-	-	-	4	-	-	6	-	-	-	-	-
2.	Assam	APHLC	1	-	-		-	-	-	-	-	1	-	-	-	-	-
3.	Bihar	JKP	-	1	-	-	-	-	-	-	-	-	-	-	-	1	-
		JKD	1	-	1	-	-	-	1	-	1	-	-	-	-	-	-
4.	Haryana	VHP	1	-	-	-	-	-	1	-	-	-	-	-	-	-	-
5.	Jammu and Kashmir																
		JKN	-	2	3*	-	-	-	-	-	-	-	2	2	-	-	-
6.	Kerala	KEC	3	2	1	-	-	-	-	-	1	3	2	-	-	-	-
		MUL	2	2	2	-	-	-	-	-	-	2	2	2	-	-	-
		RSP	2	11	-	-	-	-	-	-	-	2	1	-	-	-	-
7.	Madhya Pradesh																
		RPK	-	1	-	-	-	-	-	-	-	-	1	-	-	-	-
8.	Maharashtra																
		RPI(G)	1	-	-	-	-	-	-	-	-	1	-	-	-	-	-
		RPK	-	1	-	-	-	-	-	-	-	-	1	-	-	-	-
		PWP	-	5	-	-	-	-	-	2	-	-	3	-	-	-	-
		FBL	1	-	-	-	-	-	1	-	-	-	-	-	-	-	-

(Contd. Appendix-IIG)

S. No.	State/Union Territory		Total Seats Won			Number of Seats Won by Securing											
						10-30% votes			30-50% votes			50-70% votes			70-90% votes		
			1971	1977	1980	1971	1977	1980	1971	1977	1980	1971	1977	1980	1971	1977	1980
1	2		3	4	5	6	7	8	9	10	11	12	13	14	15	16	17
9.	Nagaland																
		UFN	1	-	-	-	-	-	-	-	-	1	-	-	-	-	-
		UDF	-	1	-	-	-	-	-	-	-	-	1	-	-	-	-
10.	Orissa	UC	1	-	-	-	-	-	1	-	-	-	-	-	-	-	-
11.	Punjab	SAD	1	9	1	-	-	-	1	-	1	-	8	-	-	1	-
12.	Sikkim	SJP	-	-	1	-	-	-	-	-	-	-	-	1	-	-	-
13.	Tamil Nadu																
		ADK	-	18	2	-	-	-	-	-	2	-	17	-	-	1	-
		DMK	23	1	16	-	-	-	1	-	-	22	1	16	-	-	-
		FBL	1	-	-	-	-	-	-	-	-	1	-	-	-	-	-
14.	Uttar Pradesh																
		BKD	1	-	-	-	-	-	1	-	-	-	-	-	-	-	-
15.	West Bengal																
		BC	1	-	-	-	-	-	1	-	-	-	-	-	-	-	-
		FBL	-	3	3	-	-	-	-	-	-	-	3	3	-	-	-
		RSP	1	3	4	1	-	-	-	-	1	-	3	3	-	-	-
16.	Pondicherry																
		ADK	-	1	-	-	-	-	-	-	-	-	1	-	-	-	-
17.	Goa, Daman and Diu	MAG	-	1	1	-	-	-	-	1	1	-	-	-	-	-	-
		UGS	1	-	-	-	-	-	-	-	-	1	-	-	-	-	-
	INDIA		53	52	35	1	-	-	12	3	7	40	46	27	-	3	-

* Includes one candidate declared elected unopposed.

Appendix-IIIA

PERCENTAGE VOTES POLLED MAJOR POLITICAL PARTIES 1971, 1977 and 1980

S.	State/Union	Jan Sangh	CPI			CPI (M)			Congress			Cong (O)	Cong (U)	Janata			JNP (S)	PSP	SSP	SWT
No.	Territory	1971	1971	1977	1980	1971	1977	1980	1971	1977	1980	1971	1980	1971*	1977	1980	1980	1971	1971	1971
1.	Andhra Pd.	1.57	5.94	2.67	3.68	2.82	4.72	3.56	55.73	57.36	56.24	5.55	7.23	12.00	32.33	15.23	0.40	-	0.31	4.57
2.	Assam	2.46	5.65	1.42	-	1.41	2.88	9.17	56.98	50.56	51.01	2.91	31.80	11.52	35.78	8.02	-	4.56	1.36	0.23
3.	Bihar	12.10	9.85	5.63	7.29	0.76	0.20	0.54	40.06	22.90	36.44	11.51	6.75	35.39	64.98	22.55	16.59	1.13	9.47	0.24
4.	Gujarat	2.22	-	-	0.23	-	-	-	44.85	46.92	54.84	39.70	1.72	49.06	49.54	36.89	2.90	1.59	0.04	5.46
5.	Haryana	11.19	-	0.61	-	0.13	0.03	-	52.56	17.95	32.55	11.34	0.07	25.98	70.35	28.14	33.52	0.20	2.89	-
6.	Himachal Pd.	10.64	1.65	1.38	1.94	-	0.79	-	75.79	38.58	52.08	2.98	0.29	14.47	51.19	36.38	5.31	-	-	0.85
7.	J & K	12.23	-	-	-	-	-	-	54.06	16.37	18.68	-	14.52	12.69	8.23	8.63	-	0.46	-	-
8.	Karnataka	1.90	0.09	0.41	0.25	0.59	-	0.22	70.87	56.74	56.25	16.36	16.69	24.22	39.84	22.93	1.22	1.27	1.03	3.66
9.	Kerala	1.40	9.09	10.38	6.52	26.21	20.33	19.09	19.75	29.13	26.32	1.39	15.85	6.01	7.20	6.70	-	2.20	0.79	0.23
10.	Madhya Pradesh	33.56	1.00	0.53	0.55	0.06	-	0.13	45.60	32.47	47.20	2.27	1.26	38.18	57.90	31.30	7.78	1.21	1.57	0.09
11.	Maharashtra	5.23	1.91	0.67	0.50	0.48	3.56	1.36	63.18	47.02	53.30	2.72	11.81	12.74	31.39	20.42	1.06	1.68	2.19	-
12.	Manipur	-	14.98	11.50	9.74	-	-	-	30.02	45.31	22.99	9.01	16.57	14.07	8.58	17.58	-	-	5.06	-
13.	Meghalaya	NA	NA	-	6.28	NA	-	-	NA	35.92	74.31	NA	-	NA	-	-	-	NA	NA	NA
14.	Nagaland	-	-	-	-	-	-	-	-	48.32	-	-	-	-	-	-	-	-	-	-
15.	Orissa	0.25	4.31	3.15	0.79	1.02	1.98	0.89	38.46	38.18	56.07	2.25	2.14	49.75	51.77	14.11	19.60	6.91	1.83	15.91
16.	Punjab	4.45	6.22	1.65	1.27	2.20	4.94	2.53	45.96	34.85	52.45	4.58	2.56	5.83	12.50	9.97	2.21	0.08	0.71	-
17.	Rajasthan	12.38	0.49	0.48	0.54	0.66	0.38	0.23	50.35	30.56	42.64	1.65	5.98	35.06	65.21	31.65	12.04	-	2.52	14.65
18.	Sikkim	NA	NA	-	-	NA	-	-	NA	-	-	NA	1.83	NA	-	-	-	NA	NA	NA
19.	Tamil Nadu	0.02	5.43	4.60	3.59	1.64	1.56	3.21	12.51	22.27	31.62	30.43	0.23	40.62	17.68**	7.96	0.54	-	0.89	9.28
20.	Tripura	0.49	6.76	2.24	-	43.50	34.09	47.50	36.30	39.74	22.61	-	0.56	0.49	17.83	0.79	-	-	-	-
21.	Uttar Pradesh	12.28	3.70	1.10	1.63	0.19	0.10	0.10	48.56	24.99	35.90	8.58	1.50	38.09	68.08	42.57	29.02	0.23	4.10	0.05

(Contd. Alppendix-IIIA)

S. No.	State/Union Territory	Jan Sangh 1971	CPI 1971	CPI 1977	CPI 1980	CPI (M) 1971	CPI (M) 1977	CPI (M) 1980	Congress 1971	Congress 1977	Congress 1980	Cong (O) 1971	Cong (U) 1980	Janata 1971*	Janata 1977	Janata 1980	JNP (S) 1980	PSP 1971	SSP 1971	SWT 1971
22.	West Bengal	0.85	10.56	6.49	4.28	34.30	26.15	39.91	28.23	29.37	36.51	70.00	1.20	10.00	21.46	4.53	0.54	1.29	0.86	-
23.	A & N Island	-	-	-	-	-	-	20.30	61.48	58.45	53.29	-	-	-	-	2.58	0.91	-	-	-
24.	Arunachal Pd.	NA	NA	-	-	NA	-	-	NA	41.25	44.13	NA	10.87	NA	-	-	-	NA	NA	NA
25.	Chandigarh	23.31	-	2.32	-	-	-	-	66.85	28.37	49.65	-	7.22	23.31	66.13	9.30	0.81	-	-	-
26.	D & N Haveli	-	-	-	-	27.37	-	-	39.17	46.93	61.89	32.96	5.72	33.96	31.82	18.29	-	-	-	-
27.	Delhi	29.57	-	0.36	0.27	-	-	-	64.39	30.15	50.40	1.65	0.83	33.46	68.15	37.89	6.85	0.09	0.11	0.16
28.	Goa, D. & Diu	-	-	-	-	-	-	-	24.43	39.98	12.19	0.73	27.64	0.73	14.70	6.91	3.42	-	-	-
29.	Lakshadweep	-	-	-	-	-	-	-	-	58.59	3.85	-	56.37	-	-	39.78	-	-	-	-
30.	Mizoram	NA	NA	-	-	NA	-	-	NA	37.07	-	NA	-	NA	-	-	-	NA	NA	NA
31.	Pondicherry	-	-	-	-	-	-	-	66.27	-	66.45	27.96	-	27.96	44.44**	26.66	6.89	-	-	-
	INDIA	7.36	4.73	2.82	2.59	5.12	4.30	6.14	43.68	34.52	42.69	10.42	5.28	27.23	43.04	18.95	9.41	1.04	2.42	3.07

N.A. = Not applicable in 1971. *Derived by adding the votes secured by the Janata's constituents in 1971.

** Votes Polled by Congress (O).

Sources: i) *Report on the Fifth General Elections to the House of the People in India, 1971* (New Delhi: Election Commission of India, 1974).

ii) *Report on the Sixth General Elections to the House of the People in India, 1977* (New Delhi: Election Commission of India).

iii) Seventh General Elections to the House of the People in India, 1980, State Abstract (Provisional) (New Delhi: Election Commission of India).

Appendix-IIIB

PERCENTAGE VOTES POLLED OTHER POLITICAL PARTIES 1971

S. No.	State/Union Territory	States Parties	State parties total	Registered Parties	Reg. Parties total	Independent
1	2	3	4	5	6	7
1.	Andhra Pradesh	-	-	RPK-0.26, BCM 0.05, RRP 0.00, TPS 14.33, TC 0.33, MLP 0.31.	15.29 8.21	
2.	Assam	APHIC 3.00, RSP 0.94	13.94	SUC 8.44, RCPI 2.13	2.57	17.92
3.	Bihar	BKD 0.94, Janata 0.93, FBL 0.17, MUL 0.27.	2.31	RRP 0.07, SUC 0.09, Prout 0.12 RCPI 0.01, ISP 0.02, JKD 0.91, RSP (ML) 0.01, SSD 1.30, HSP 0.44 PHJ 0.45, BRP 0.03.	3.46	9.11
4.	Gujarat	BKD 0.05	0.05	RPK 0.30, HMS 0.16.	0.47	5.62
5.	Harayana	BKD 0.36, SAD 0.31,	10.06	RPK 1.11 SUCI 0.59, Prout 0.10.	1.80	9.84
6.	Himachal Pradesh	FBL 0.22, VHP 9.16	-	LRP 5.00	5.00	3.10
7.	Jammu & Kashmir	SAD 1.08	1.08	-	-	32.17
8.	Karnataka	MUL 0.02	0.02	-	-	4.20
9.	Kerala	KEC 8.31, RSP 6.43,	20.35	PSP 0.52	0.52	17.97
10.	Madhya Pradesh	BKD 0.06, RSP 0.11, FBL 0.09.	0.26	HMS 0.43	0.43	13.94
11.	Maharashtra	BKD 0.92, PWP 5.33, FBL 2.47	8.72	RPK 2.87, SSN 1.63, Prout 0.04 RPI (G) 1.11.	5.66	8.26
12.	Manipur	-	-	MPP 11.85	11.85	28.99
13.	Meghalaya*	-	-	-	-	-
14.	Nagaland	UFN 60.47, NNO 39.53	100.00	-	-	-
15.	Orissa	Jancong. 1.35.	1.35	UC 23.60, JKD 1.66	25.26	2.47

(Contd. Appendix-IIIB)

S. No.	State/Union Territory	States Parties	State parties total	Registered Parties	Reg. Parties total	Independent
1	2	3	4	5	6	7
16.	Punjab	BKD 0.01, SAD 30.85	30.86	RPK 0.44.	0.44	4.50
17.	Rajasthan	BKD 3.86, VHP 1.06.	4.92	SP 0.05.	0.05	12.34
18.	Sikkim*					
19.	Tamil Nadu	DMK 35.25, FBL 1.31	36.56	-	-	3.24
20.	Tripura -	- -	-			12.94
21.	Uttar Pradesh	BKD 12.70, FBL 0.02 VHP 0.04, MUL 0.02.	12.83	RPK 0.19, HMS 0.07, RRP 0.06, Prout 0.07, ISP 0.01, MMJ 0.24 SP 0.18, RSP (ML) 0.03, RPI (A) 0.11, KMP 0.15	1.12	8.36
22.	West Bengal	Bang, Cong. 3.97, RSP 2.04, FBL 2.70	8.70	IGL 0.55, HMS 0.07, LSS 0.46, SUCI 0.87, JKD 0.48	2.43	5.78
23.	Andaman & Nicobar Islands	- -	-	-		38.52
24.	Arunchal Pradesh*					
25.	Chandigarh	VHP 0.21	0.21	-	-	9.63
26.	Dadra & Nagar Haveli -	- -	-	-		
27.	Delhi	BKD 1.94, FBL 0.11, VHP 0.12	2.17	RPK 0.03, HMS 0.04	0.07	1.85
28.	Goa, Daman & Diu	MAG 23.14, UG 24.76	47.90	-	-	26.95
29.	Lakshadweep	- -	-	-	-	
30.	Mizoram*	- -	-	-	-	
31.	Pondicherry	- -	-	-	5.78	

* Not applicable.

Source: :*Report on the Fifth General Election to the House of the People in India, 1971* (New Delhi, Election Commission of India, 1974).

Appendix-IIIC

PERCENTAGE VOTES POLLED
OTHER POLITICAL PARTIES
1977

S. No.	State/Union Territory	States Parties	State Parties Total	Registered Parties	Reg. Parties total	Independent
1	2	3	4	5	6	7
1.	Andhra Pradesh	-	-	RPK 0.09, RRP 0.12	0.11	2.81
2.	Assam		-	SUCI 0.54, RCI 1.18	1.72	7.64
3.	Bihar	MUL 0.01	0.01	JKP 0.60, JKD 0.46, SUC 0.07, PHJ 0.13, SSD 0.40, RPI 0.02.]	1.68	4.60
4.	Gujarat	-	-	-	-	3.54
5.	Haryana	VHP 4.64, FBL 0.06.	4.70	SUCI 0.13	0.13	6.23
6.	Himachal Pradesh	-	-	-	-	2.06
7.	Jammu and Kashmir	JKN 33.92	33.92	-	-	41.48
8.	Karnataka	-	-	RPK 0.33	0.33	2.58
9.	Kerala	KEG 5.55, KCP 5.95 MUL 6.03, MLO 3.60 RSP 3.08	24.21	SUCI 0.08	0.08	8.67
10.	Madhya Pradesh	-	-	RPK 1.30.	1.30	7.80
11.	Maharashtra	PWP 6.10	6.10	RPK 4.33, RPI 0.83	5.16	6.09
12.	Manipur	MRP 23.45	23.45	-	-	11.16
13.	Meghalaya	-	-	-	-	64.08
14.	Nagaland	UDF 51.68	51.68	-	-	-
15.	Orissa	-	-	JKD 0.43, SUCI 0.42	0.85	4.07
16.	Punjab	SAD 42.30.	42.30	UMD 0.10, ILP 0.37, RPK 0.07	0.48	3.28
17.	Rajasthan	MUL 0.32.	0.32	RRP 0.09	0.09	2.96
18.	Sikkim	-	-	-	-	-
19.	Tamil Nadu	DMK 18.06, ADK-30.59.	48.65	RPI 0.02	0.02	5.22

(Contd. Appendix-IIIC)

S. No.	State/Union Territory	States Parties	State Parties Total	Registered Parties	Reg. Parties total	Independent
1	2	3	4	5	6	7
20.	Tripura	-	-	TUS 6.10	6.10	-
21.	Uttar Pradesh	-	-	SSD 0.04, HMS 0.12, RRP 0.05,	0.28	5.45
22.	West Bengal	FBL 4.30, RSP 3.94	8.24	SUCI 1.41, IGL 0.09, RPI 0.02	1.52	6.77
23.	Andaman and Nicobar Is.	-	-	-	-	41.55
24.	Arunachal Pr.	-	-	-	-	56.34
25.	Chandigarh	-	-	-	-	3.18
26.	Dadra and Nagar Haveli	-	-	-	-	21.25
27.	Delhi	-	-	RPI 0.21, RRP 0.10.	0.31	1.03
28.	Goa, Daman & Diu	MAG 40.52	40.52	-	-	4.80
29.	Lakshadweep	-	-	-	-	41.41
30.	Mizoram	-	-	-	-	52.97
31.	Pondicherry	ADK 53.32	-	-	-	2.24

Source: *Report on the Sixth General Election to the House of the People in India, 1977 (New Delhi, Election Commission of India).*

Appendix-IIID

PERCENTAGE VOTES POLLED
OTHER POLITICAL PARTIES
1980

S. No.	State/Union Territory	States Parties	State Parties Total	Registered Parties	Reg. Parties Total	Independent
1	2	3	4	5	6	7
1.	Andhra Pradesh	-	-	BSP 0.08, RRP 0.01.	0.09	7.57
2.	Assam	-	-	-	-	-
3.	Bihar	FBL 0.16	0.16	JKD 0.70, RPI 0.01, SUCI 0.05, SSD 0.10, RRP 0.01, BSP 0.01	0.08	7.40
4.	Gujarat	-	-	-	-	3.42
5.	Haryana	FBL 0.04	0.04	RRP 0.11, RPK 0.15, SUCI 0.04.	0.3	5.38
6.	Himachal Pradesh	-	-	-	-	4.00
7.	Jammu & Kashmir	JKN 36.88	36.88	-	-	21.29
8.	Karnataka	-	-	SUCI 0.01.	0.01	2.43
9.	Kerala	MUL 5.56, AIML 2.41, KEC 4.37, RSP 2.27	14.61	SUCI 0.12	0.12	10.79
10.	Madhya Pradesh	RRP 0.09, RPK 0.39	0.48	RRP 0.05, RPK 0.39	0.44	11.30
11.	Maharashtra	PWP 2.54, FBL 0.02.	2.56	RPK 1.52, RPI 1.74, SSN 0.70,	4.01	4.98
12.	Manipur	MRP 6.89	6.89	-	-	26.23
13.	Meghalaya	APHIC 11.79	11.79	-	-	7.62
14.	Nagaland	UDF 48.99	48.99	-	-	51.01
15.	Orissa	FBL 0.24.	0.24	JKD 1.01, SUC 0.42	1.43	4.73
16.	Punjab	SAD 23.37	23.37	ILP 0.22, RPI 0.04, BSP 0.07.	0.33	5.31
17.	Rajasthan	-	-	RRP 0.13, BSP 0.03.	0.16	6.76
18.	Sikkim	SJP 61.65, SC (R) 22.59	84.24	SPC 9.95	9.95	3.90

(Contd. Appendix-IIID)

S. No.	State/Union Territory	States Parties	State Parties Total	Registered Parties	Reg. Parties Total	Independent
1	2	3	4	5	6	7
19.	Tamil Nadu	ADK 25.38, DMK 23.01.	48.39	RPI 0.05	0.05	4.41
20.	Tripura	TUS 13.48	13.48	-	-	14.88
21.	Uttar Pradesh	RSP 0.10, FBL 0.07	0.17	RRP 0.10, BSP 0.02, MMJ 0.09, RPK 0.16, SUCI 0.01, SSD 0.07.	0.45	8.66
22.	West Bengal	FBL 4.56, RSP 5.22 MUL 0.10.	9.88	SUCI 1.24, RPI 0.08, BSP 0.00 JKD 0.25.	1.57	1.61
23.	Andaman and Nicobar Is.	-	-	-	-	22.92
24.	Arunachal Pradesh	PPA 40.22	40.22	-	-	4.78
25.	Chandigarh	-	-	-	-	33.02
26.	Dadra and Nagar Haveli	-	-	-	-	14.10
27.	Delhi	-	-	BSP 0.06, RRP 0.14, ILP 0.08,	0.35	3.41
28.	Goa, Daman and Diu.	MAG 36.04	36.04	-	-	13.80
29.	Lakshadweep	-	-	-	-	-
30.	Mizoram	PPO 42.00.	42.00	-	-	58.00
31.	Pondicherry	-	-	-	-	-

Source: Seventh General Election to the House of the People in India, 1980, State Abstract (Provisional) (New Delhi, Election Commission of India).

Appendix-IVA
NUMBER OF CONSTITUENCIES ACCORDING TO PERCENTAGE VOTES POLLED: BHARTIYA JANA SANDH, CONGRESS (O), PSP, SSP AND SWATANTRA 1971

S.	State/Union Territory	No. of seats Contested					Number of constituencies in different categories of voting strength									
							0-10% votes					10-30% votes				
No.	Territory	A	B	C	D	E	A	B	C	D	E	A	B	C	D	E
1.	Andhra Pradesh	5	12	-	2	9	2	4	-	1	1	3	5	-	1	8
2.	Assam	1	10	5	4	1	-	10	1	4	1	1	-	4	-	-
3.	Bihar	28	24	12	28	3	3	6	12	12	3	17	9	-	11	-
4.	Gujarat	5	19	1	1	4	2	-	-	1	-	3	1	-	-	1
5.	Haryana	3	4	2	1	-	-	1	2	-	-	1	1	-	1	-
6.	Himachal Pd.	2	3	-	-	1	-	3	-	-	1	2	-	-	-	-
7.	Jammu & Kashmir	3	-	1	-	-	1	-	1	-	-	2	-	-	-	-
8.	Karnataka	2	17	5	1	5	-	1	4	-	1	2	10	-	1	4
9.	Kerala	3	4	1	2	1	1	4	-	1	1	2	-	-	1	-
10.	Madhya Pradesh	28	5	9	5	1	-	1	7	4	1	5	3	2	-	-
11.	Maharashtra	13	9	8	9	-	5	5	5	4	-	6	3	2	5	-
12.	Manipur	-	2	-	1	-	-	1	-	1	-	-	1	-	-	-
13.	Meghalaya*	-	-	-	-	-	-	-	-	-	-	-	-	-	-	-
14.	Nagaland	-	-	-	-	-	-	-	-	-	-	-	-	-	-	-
15.	Orissa	1	6	6	2	13	1	5	2	-	-	-	4	3	2	9
16.	Punjab	5	4	1	3	-	2	1	1	3	-	3	2	-	-	-
17.	Rajasthan	7	4	-	2	8	-	3	-	-	-	2	-	-	1	-
18.	Sikkim	-	-	-	-	-	-	-	-	-	-	-	-	-	-	-
19.	Tamil Nadu	1	29	-	1	9	1	-	-	-	-	-	-	-	-	-
20.	Tripura	1	-	-	-	-	1	-	-	-	-	-	-	-	-	-
21.	Uttar Pradesh	37	44	6	25	3	1	13	6	12	3	22	26	-	11	-
22.	West Bengal	4	34	3	4	-	2	26	2	3	-	2	8	-	1	-
23.	A & N Islands	-	-	-	-	-	-	-	-	-	-	-	-	-	-	-
24.	Arunachal Pradesh*	-	-	-	-	-	-	-	-	-	-	-	-	-	-	-
25.	Chandigarh	1	-	-	-	-	-	-	-	-	-	1	-	-	-	-
26.	Dadra & Nagar Haveli	-	1	-	-	-	-	-	-	-	-	-	-	-	-	-
27.	Delhi	7	5	2	2	1	-	5	2	2	1	3	-	-	-	-
28.	Goa, Daman & Diu	-	1	-	-	-	-	1	-	-	-	-	-	-	-	-
29.	Lakshadweep	-	-	-	-	-	-	-	-	-	-	-	-	-	-	-
30.	Mizoram	-	-	-	-	-	-	-	-	-	-	-	-	-	-	-
31.	Pondicherry		1		-	-	-	-	-	-	-	-	-	1	-	-
	INDIA	157	238	62	93	59	22	90	45	48	13	77	71	11	35	22

(Contd. Appendix-IVA)

S. No.	State/Union Territory	Number of constituencies in different categories of voting strength														
		30-50% votes					50-70% votes					Above 70% votes				
		A	B	C	D	E	A	B	C	D	E	A	B	C	D	E
1.	Andhra Pradesh	-	3	-	-	-	-	-	-	-	-	-	-	-	-	-
2.	Assam	-	-	-	-	-	-	-	-	-	-	-	-	-	-	-
3.	Bihar	8	8	-	5	-	-	1	-	-	-	-	-	-	-	-
4.	Gujarat	-	9	1	-	2	-	9	-	-	1	-	-	-	-	-
5.	Haryana	2	2	-	-	-	-	-	-	-	-	-	-	-	-	-
6.	Himachal Pradesh	-	-	-	-	-	-	-	-	-	-	-	-	-	-	-
7.	Jammu & Kashmir	-	-	-	-	-	-	-	-	-	-	-	-	-	-	-
8.	Karnataka	-	6	1	-	-	-	-	-	-	-	-	-	-	-	-
9.	Kerala	-	-	1	-	-	-	-	-	-	-	-	-	-	-	-
10.	Madhya Pradesh	15	1	-	-	-	8	-	-	1	-	-	-	-	-	-
11.	Maharashtra	2	1	1	-	-	-	-	-	-	-	-	-	-	-	-
12.	Manipur	-	-	-	-	-	-	-	-	-	-	-	-	-	-	-
14.	Nagaland	-	-	-	-	-	-	-	-	-	-	-	-	-	-	-
15.	Orissa	-	-	1	-	2	-	-	-	-	2	-	-	-	-	-
16.	Punjab	-	1	-	-	-	-	-	-	-	-	-	-	-	-	-
17.	Rajasthan	2	-	-	1	-	3	-	-	-	2	-	-	-	-	-
18.	Sikkim*	-	-	-	-	-	-	-	-	-	-	-	-	-	-	-
19.	Tamil Nadu	-	28	-	1	9	-	1	-	-	-	-	-	-	-	-
20.	Tripura	-	-	-	-	-	-	-	-	-	-	-	-	-	-	-
21.	Uttar Pradesh	14	5	-	2	-	-	-	-	-	-	-	-	-	-	-
22.	West Bengal	-	-	1	-	-	-	-	-	-	-	-	-	-	-	-
23.	A & N Islands	-	-	-	-	-	-	-	-	-	-	-	-	-	-	-
24.	Arunachal Pradesh*	-	-	-	-	-	-	-	-	-	-	-	-	-	-	-
25.	Chandigarh	-	-	-	-	-	-	-	-	-	-	-	-	-	-	-
26.	Dadra & Nagar Haveli	-	1	-	-	-	-	-	-	-	-	-	-	-	-	-
27.	Delhi	4	-	-	-	-	-	-	-	-	-	-	-	-	-	-
28.	Goa, Daman & Diu	-	-	-	-	-	-	-	-	-	-	-	-	-	-	-
29.	Lakshadweep	-	-	-	-	-	-	-	-	-	-	-	-	-	-	-
30.	Mizoram	-	-	-	-	-	-	-	-	-	-	-	-	-	-	-
31.	Pondicherry	-	-	-	-	-	-	-	-	-	-	-	-	-	-	-
	INDIA	47	66	6	9	19	11	11	-	1	5	-	-	-	-	-

* Not applicable in 1971

A= Bhartiya Jan Sangh: B= Congress (O): C= PSP: D= SSP: E= Swatantra Party

Appendix-IV B

NUMBER OF CONSTITUENCIES ACCORDING TO PERCENTAGE OF VOTES POLLED COMMUNIST PARTY OF INDIA 1971, 1977 and 1980

S. No.	State/Union Territory	No. of Seated Contested			Number of Constituencies in different categories of voting strength: 0-10% votes			10-30% votes			30-50% votes			50-70% votes			Above 70% votes		
		71	77	80	71	77	80	71	77	80	71	77	80	71	77	80	71	77	80
1	2	3	4	5	6	7	8	9	10	11	12	13	14	15	16	17	18	19	20
1.	Andhra Pradesh	11	10	6	1	5	-	8	5	5	1	-	1	1	-	-	-	-	-
2.	Assam	5	2	-	-	1	-	5	1	-	-	-	-	-	-	-	-	-	-
3.	Bihar	17	22	14	2	8	1	8	13	7	5	1	6	2	-	-	-	-	-
4.	Gujarat	-	-	1	-	-	1	-	-	-	-	-	-	-	-	-	-	-	-
5.	Haryana	-	2	-	-	2	-	-	-	-	-	-	-	-	-	-	-	-	-
6.	Himachal Pradesh	1	1	1	1	1	1	-	-	-	-	-	-	-	-	-	-	-	-
7.	Jammu & Kashmir	-	-	-	-	-	-	-	-	-	-	-	-	-	-	-	-	-	-
8.	Karnataka	1	3	1	1	3	1	-	-	-	-	-	-	-	-	-	-	-	-
9.	Kerala	3	4	3	-	-	-	-	-	-	1	-	1	2	4	2	-	-	-
10.	Madhya Pradesh	4	3	3	3	3	3	1	-	-	-	-	-	-	-	-	-	-	-
11.	Maharashtra	8	4	2	6	2	1	1	2	1	1	-	-	-	-	-	-	-	-
12.	Manipur	1	2	1	-	1	-	1	1	1	-	-	-	-	-	-	-	-	-
13.	Meghalaya	NA	-	1	NA	-	1	NA	-	-	NA	-	-	NA	-	-	NA	-	-
14.	Nagaland	-	-	-	-	-	-	-	-	-	-	-	-	-	-	-	-	-	-
15.	Orissa	3	5	1	-	2	-	2	3	1	1	-	-	-	-	-	-	-	-
16.	Punjab	2	3	1	-	2	-	-	1	1	1	-	-	1	-	-	-	-	-
17.	Rajasthan	1	3	1	-	3	-	1	-	1	-	-	-	-	-	-	-	-	-
18.	Sikkim	NA	-	-	NA	-	-	NA	-	-	NA	-	-	NA	-	-	NA	-	-
19.	Tamil Nadu	4	3	3	-	-	-	-	-	-	1	-	3	3	3	-	-	-	-
20.	Tripura	2	1	-	2	1	-	-	-	-	-	-	-	-	-	-	-	-	-

(Contd. Appendix-IVB)

S. No.	State/Union Territory	No. of Seated Contested			Number of Constituencies in different categories of voting strength: 0-10% votes			10-30% votes			30-50% votes			50-70% votes			Above 70% votes		
		71	77	80	71	77	80	71	77	80	71	77	80	71	77	80	71	77	80
1	2	3	4	5	6	7	8	9	10	11	12	13	14	15	16	17	18	19	20
21.	Uttar Pradesh	9	13	5	2	9	-	2	4	3	3	-	2	2	-	-	-	-	-
22.	West Bengal	15	8	3	-	-	-	8	3	-	7	5	-	-	-	3	-	-	-
23.	Andaman & Nicobar Isl.	-	-	-	-	-	-	-	-	-	-	-	-	-	-	-	-	-	-
24.	Arunachal Pradesh	NA	-	-	NA	-	-	NA	-	-	NA	-	-	NA	-	-	NA	-	-
25.	Chandigarh	-	-	-	-	-	-	-	-	-	-	-	-	-	-	-	-	-	-
26.	Dadra & Nagar Haveli	-	-	-	-	1	-	-	-	-	-	-	-	-	-	-	-	-	-
27.	Delhi	-	1	1	-	1	1	-	-	-	-	-	-	-	-	-	-	-	-
28.	Goa, Daman & Diu	-	-	-	-	-	-	-	-	-	-	-	-	-	-	-	-	-	-
29.	Lakshadweep	-	-	-	-	-	-	-	-	-	-	-	-	-	-	-	-	-	-
30.	Mizoram	NA	-	-	NA	-	-	NA	-	-	NA	-	-	NA	-	-	NA	-	-
31.	Pondicherry	-	-	-	-	-	-	-	-	-	-	-	-	-	-	-	-	-	-
	INDIA	87	91	48	18	45	10	37	33	20	21	6	13	11	7	5	-	-	-

NA: Not Applicable in 1971

Appendix-IVC

NUMBER OF CONSTITUENCIES ACCORDING TO PERCENTAGE OF VOTES POLLED COMMUNIST PARTY OF INDIA (MARXIST) 1971, 1977 AND 1980

S. No.	State/Union Territory	No. of Seats Contested			Number of Constituencies in different categories of voting strength: 0-10% votes			10-30% votes			30-50% votes			50-70% votes			Above 70% votes		
		71	77	80	71	77	80	71	77	80	71	77	80	71	77	80	71	77	80
1	2	3	4	5	6	7	8	9	10	11	12	13	14	15	16	17	18	19	20
1.	Andhra Pradesh	5	6	5	1	1	-	3	-	3	1	5	2	-	-	-	-	-	-
2.	Assam*	2	1	*	1	-	-	1	-	-	-	1	-	-	-	-	-	-	-
3.	Bihar	4	2	3	2	2	1	2	-	2	-	-	-	-	-	-	-	-	-
4.	Gujarat	-	-	-	-	-	-	-	-	-	-	-	-	-	-	-	-	-	-
5.	Haryana	1	1	-	1	1	-	-	-	-	-	-	-	-	-	-	-	-	-
6.	Himachal Pradesh	-	1	-	-	1	-	-	-	-	-	-	-	-	-	-	-	-	-
7.	Jammu & Kashmir	-	-	-	-	-	-	-	-	-	-	-	-	-	-	-	-	-	-
8.	Karnataka	2	-	1	2	-	1	-	-	-	-	-	-	-	-	-	-	-	-
9.	Kerala	11	9	7	-	-	-	-	-	-	10	9	2	1	-	5	-	-	-
10.	Madhya Pradesh	1	-	1	1	-	1	-	-	-	-	-	-	-	-	-	-	-	-
11.	Maharashtra	2	3	4	-	-	1	2	-	3	-	-	-	-	3	-	-	-	-
12.	Manipur	-	-	-	-	-	-	-	-	-	-	-	-	-	-	-	-	-	-
13.	Meghalaya	NA	-	-	NA	-	-	NA	-	-	NA	-	-	NA	-	-	NA	-	-
14.	Nagaland	-	-	-	-	-	-	-	-	-	-	-	-	-	-	-	-	-	-
15.	Orissa	1	1	1	-	-	-	1	-	1	-	1	-	-	-	-	-	-	-
16.	Punjab	3	1	1	2	-	-	1	-	-	-	-	1	-	1	-	-	-	-
17.	Rajasthan	3	2	1	3	2	1	-	-	-	-	-	-	-	-	-	-	-	-
18.	Sikkim	NA	-	-	NA	-	-	NA	-	-	NA	-	-	NA	-	-	NA	-	-
19.	Tamil Nadu	6	2	3	3	-	-	3	1	-	-	1	3	-	-	-	-	-	-
20.	Tripura	2	2	2	-	-	-	-	1	-	2	1	2	-	-	-	-	-	-

(Contd. Appendix-IVC)

S. No.	State/Union Territory	No. of Seats Contested			Number of Constituencies in different categories of voting strength														
					0-10% votes			10-30% votes			30-50% votes			50-70% votes			Above 70% votes		
		71	77	80	71	77	80	71	77	80	71	77	80	71	77	80	71	77	80
1	2	3	4	5	6	7	8	9	10	11	12	13	14	15	16	17	18	19	20
21.	Uttar Pradesh	3	2	1	2	2	1	1	-	-	-	-	-	-	-	-	-	-	-
22.	West Bengal	38	20	31	-	-	-	15	-	-	19	7	8	4	12	23	-	1	-
23.	Andaman and Nicobar Islands	-	-	1	-	-	-	-	-	1	-	-	-	-	-	-	-	-	-
24.	Arunachal Pradesh	NA	-	-	NA	-	-	NA	-	-	NA	-	-	NA	-	-	NA	-	-
25.	Dadra and Nagar Haveli	1	-	-	-	-	-	1	-	-	-	-	-	-	-	-	-	-	-
26.	Delhi	-	-	-	-	-	-	-	-	-	-	-	-	-	-	-	-	-	-
27.	Goa, Daman and Diu	-	-	-	-	-	-	-	-	-	-	-	-	-	-	-	-	-	-
28.	Lakshadweep	-	-	-	-	-	-	-	-	-	-	-	-	-	-	-	-	-	-
29.	Mizoram	NA	-	-	NA	-	-	NA	-	-	NA	-	-	NA	-	-	NA	-	-
30.	Pondicherry	-	-	-	-	-	-	-	-	-	-	-	-	-	-	-	-	-	-
	INDIA	85	53	62	18	9	6	30	2	10	32	25	18	5	16	28	-	1	-

* Excluded from the analysis of 1980 Elections
NA = Not applicable in 1971.

Appendix-IVD

NUMBER OF CONSTITUENCIES ACCORDING TO PERCENTAGE OF VOTES POLLED CONGRESS PARTY 1971, 1977 and 1980

S. No.	State/Union T	No. of Seats e		r	Number of Constituencies in different categories of voting strength r			i			t			o			r		
		Contested			0-10% votes			10-30% votes			30-50% votes			50-70% votes			Above 70% votes		
		1971	1977	1980	1971	1977	1980	1971	1977	1980	1971	1977	1980	1971	1977	1980	1971	1977	1980
1.	Andhra Pradesh	37	42	42	-	-	-	3	-	-	7	6	11	16	34	27	11	2	4
2.	Assam*	13	14	-	-	-	-	-	-	-	2	6	-	9	8	-	2	-	-
3.	Bihar	47	54	54	-	3	-	7	39	13	23	12	36	15	-	5	2	-	-
4.	Gujarat	23	26	26	-	-	-	1	-	-	14	17	4	8	9	22	-	-	-
5.	Haryana	9	9	10	-	-	-	-	9	4	4	-	5	5	-	1	-	-	-
6.	Himachal Pd.	4	4	4	-	-	-	-	-	-	-	4	1	1	-	3	3	-	-
7.	Jammu & Kashmir	6	3	1	-	-	-	-	-	-	1	1	-	5	2	1	-	-	-
8.	Karnataka	27	28	28	-	-	-	-	-	-	-	4	4	13	23	24	14	1	-
9.	Kerala	7	11	11	-	-	-	-	-	-	3	3	8	4	8	3	-	-	-
10.	Madhya Pradesh	36	38	39	-	-	-	4	12	-	15	26	22	16	-	17	1	-	-
11.	Maharashtra	44	47	48	-	-	-	-	-	1	7	29	13	21	15	31	16	3	3
12.	Manipur	2	2	2	-	-	-	1	-	1	1	2	1	-	-	-	-	-	-
13.	Meghalaya*	NA	2	-	NA	-	-	NA	1	-	NA	-	-	NA	1	-	NA	-	-
14.	Nagaland	-	1	-	-	-	-	-	-	-	-	1	-	-	-	-	-	-	-
15.	Orissa	19	20	21	-	-	-	3	1	-	13	16	3	3	3	18	-	-	-
16.	Punjab	11	13	13	-	1	-	-	3	-	2	9	5	9	-	8	-	-	-
17.	Rajasthan	23	25	25	-	-	-	-	15	4	12	9	15	10	1	6	1	-	-
18.	Sikkim	NA	1**	-	NA	-	-	NA	-	-	NA	-	-	NA	-	-	NA	-	-
19.	Tamil Nadu	9	15	22	-	-	-	-	-	-	-	1	3	9	13	19	-	1	-

(Contd. Appendix-IVD)

S. No.	State/Union Territory	No. of Seats Contested			Number of Constituencies in different categories of voting strength														
		Contested			0-10% votes			10-30% votes			30-50% votes			50-70% votes			Above 70% votes		
		1971	1977	1980	1971	1977	1980	1971	1977	1980	1971	1977	1980	1971	1977	1980	1971	1977	1980
20.	Tripura	2	2	2	-	-	-	1	-	1	1	2	1	-	-	-	-	-	-
21.	Uttar Pradesh	78	85	85	-	-	-	1	70	19	23	15	61	50	-	5	4	-	-
22.	West Bengal	31	34	41	-	-	-	4	7	1	24	26	39	3	1	1	-	-	-
23.	A & N Island	1	1	1	-	-	-	-	-	-	-	-	-	1	1	1	-	-	-
24.	Arunachal Pd.	NA	2***	2	NA	-	-	NA	-	-	NA	1	2	NA	-	-	NA	-	-
25.	Chandigarh	1	1	1	-	-	-	-	1	-	-	-	1	1	-	-	-	-	-
26.	Dadra & N. Haveli	1	1	1	-	-	-	-	-	-	1	1	-	-	-	1	-	-	-
27.	Delhi	7	7	7	-	-	-	-	4	-	-	3	4	7	-	3	-	-	-
28.	Goa, Daman & Diu	1	2	1	-	-	-	-	-	1	1	2	-	-	-	-	-	-	-
29.	Lakshadweep	1**	1	1	-	-	1	-	-	-	-	-	-	-	1	-	-	-	-
30.	Mizoram	NA	1	-	NA	-	-	NA	-	-	NA	1	-	NA	-	-	NA	-	-
31.	Pondicherry	1	-	1	-	-	-	-	-	-	-	-	-	1	-	1	-	-	-
	INDIA	441	492	489	-	4	1	25	162	45	154	197	239	207	120	197	54	7	7

* Excluded from the analysis of 1980 elections. **Unopposed elected. ***Includes one candidate declared elected unopposed. NA-Not applicable in 1971.

Appendix-IVE

NUMBER OF CONSTITUENCIES ACCORDING TO PERCENTAGE OF VOTES POLLED
JANATA PARTY
1971, 1977 and 1980

S. No.	State/Union Territory	No. of Seats Contested			Number of Constituencies in different categories of voting strength: 0-10% votes			10-30% votes			30-50% votes			50-70% votes			Above 70% votes		
		1971	1977	1980	1971	1977	1980	1971	1977	1980	1971	1977	1980	1971	1977	1980	1971	1977	1980
1.	Andhra Pradesh	28	37	31	8	-	4	16	9	21	4	27	6	-	1	-	-	-	-
2.	Assam**	13	11	-	6	-	-	6	1	-	1	7	-	-	3	-	-	-	-
3.	Bihar	53	52	54	3	-	3	18	-	36	27	7	14	5	24	1	-	21	-
4.	Gujarat	23	26	26	-	-	-	2	-	3	10	14	23	10	12	-	1	-	-
5.	Haryana	7	10	10	1	-	-	1	-	4	5	1	6	-	4	-	-	5	-
6.	Himachal Pd.	4	4	4	2	-	-	2	-	-	-	-	4	-	4	-	-	-	-
7.	Jammu & Kashmir	3	2	1	1	-	-	1	1	1	1	1	-	-	-	-	-	-	-
8.	Karnataka	25	28	28	1	-	4	17	2	21	7	25	3	-	1	-	-	8	-
9.	Kerala	11	3	4	7	-	1	3	-	-	1	3	3	-	-	-	-	-	1
10.	Madhya Pradesh	35	39	40	2	-	-	6	-	20	15	7	20	12	24	-	-	-	-
11.	Maharashtra	36	31	31	16	-	-	15	2	17	4	12	9	1	17	4	-	-	-
12.	Manipur	2	2	2	-	1	-	2	1	2	-	-	-	-	-	-	-	-	-
13.	Meghalaya	NA	-	-	NA	-	-	NA	-	-	NA	-	-	NA	-	-	NA	-	-
14.	Nagaland	-	-	-	-	-	-	-	-	-	-	-	-	-	-	-	-	-	-
15.	Orissa	20	20	20	-	-	3	-	-	16	10	8	1	8	12	-	2	-	-
16.	Punjab	9	3	9	3	-	4	5	-	3	1	1	2	-	2	-	-	-	-
17.	Rajasthan	21	25	25	2	-	1	3	-	8	11	1	16	5	16	-	-	8	-
18.	Sikkim	NA	-	-	NA	-	-	NA	-	-	NA	-	-	NA	-	-	NA	-	-
19.	Tamil Nadu	39	10	9	-	-	-	-	3	1	38	13	8	1	2	-	-	-	-
20.	Tripura	1	1	2	1	-	2	-	-	-	-	1	-	-	-	-	-	-	-
21.	Uttar Pradesh	83	85	85	1	-	1	18	-	76	52	1	8	12	38	-	-	36	-

(Contd. Appendix-IVE)

S. No.	State/Union Territory	No. of Seats Contested			Number of Constituencies in different categories of voting strength: 0-10% votes			10-30% votes			30-50% votes			50-70% votes			Above 70% votes		
		1971	1977	1980	1971	1977	1980	1971	1977	1980	1971	1977	1980	1971	1977	1980	1971	1977	1980
22.	West Bengal	37	15	35	23	-	32	13	-	2	-	3	1	1	10	-	-	2	-
23.	A & N Islands	-	-	1	-	-	1		-	-	-	-	-	-	-	-	-	-	-
24.	Arunachal Pd.	NA	-	-	NA	-	-	NA		-	NA	-	-	NA	-	-	NA	-	-
25.	Chandigarh	1	1	1	-	-	1	1	-	-	-	-	-	-	1	-	-	-	-
26.	Dadra & N. Haveli	1	1	1	-	-	1	1	-	-	-	1	-	-	-	-	-	-	-
27.	Delhi	7	7	7	-	-	-	2	-	1	5	-	6	-	5	-	-	2	-
28.	Goa, Daman & Diu	1	2	2	1	-	2	-	2	-	-	-	-	-	-	-	-	-	-
29.	Lakshadweep	-	-	1	-	-	-	-	-	-	-	-	1	-	-	-	-	-	-
30.	Mizoram	NA	-	-	NA	-	-	NA	-	-	NA	-	-	NA	-	-	NA	-	-
31.	Pondicherry	1	1	1	-	-	-	1	-	1	-	1	-	-	-	-	-	-	-
	INDIA	460	424	430	73	1	60	133	21	233	192	134	131	55	186	5	3	82	1

* Figures for 1971 elections are derived by aggragating votes polled by the Janata's constituents.
** Excluded from the analysis of 1980 elections.
NA - Not applicable in 1971.

Appendix-IVF

NUMBER OF CONSTITUENCIES ACCORDING TO PERCENTAGE VOTES POLLED CONGRESS (U) AND JANATA (S) 1980

S. No.	State/Unio Territory	No. of seats contested		Number of constituencies in different categories of voting strength									
				0-10% votes		10-30% votes		30-50% votes		50-70% votes		Above 70% votes	
		Cong(U)	JNP(S)	Cong(U)	JNP(S)	Cong(U)	JNP(S)	Cong(U)	JNP(S)	Cong(U)	JNP(S)	Cong(U)	JNP(S)
1.	Andhra Pd.	11	20	2	8	4	11	5	1	-	-	-	-
2.	Assam*	-	-	-	-	-	-	-	-	-	-	-	-
3.	Bihar	16	36	5	9	7	15	4	10	-	2	-	-
4.	Gujarat	12	10	12	9	-	1	-	-	-	-	-	-
5.	Haryana	2	10	2	-	-	5	-	3	-	2	-	-
6.	Himachal Pd.	1	3	-	2	1	1	-	-	-	-	-	-
7.	Jammu & Kashmir	2	-	1	-	-	-	-	-	1	-	-	-
8.	Karnataka	27	12	3	12	23	-	1	-	-	-	-	-
9.	Kerala	6	-	-	-	-	-	3	-	3	-	-	-
10.	Madhya Pradesh	13	30	13	18	-	12	-	-	-	-	-	-
11.	Maharashtra	24	17	4	17	15	-	4	-	1	-	-	-
12.	Manipur	2	-	1	-	1	-	-	-	-	-	-	-
13.	Meghalaya*	-	-	-	-	-	-	-	-	-	-	-	-
14.	Nagaland	-	-	-	-	-	-	-	-	-	-	-	-
15.	Orissa	5	18	4	-	1	15	-	3	-	-	-	-
16.	Punjab	2	3	1	2	1	1	-	-	-	-	-	-
17.	Rajasthan	12	16	8	6	2	7	2	3	-	-	-	-
18.	Sikkim	1	-	1	-	-	-	-	-	-	-	-	-
19.	Tamil Nadu	10	13	10	13	-	-	-	-	-	-	-	-

(Contd. Appendix-IVF)

S. No.	State/Unio Territory	No. of seats contested		Number of constituencies in different categories of voting strength									
				0-10% votes		10-30% votes		30-50% votes		50-70% votes		Above 70% votes	
		Cong(U)	JNP(S)	Cong(U)	JNP(S)	Cong(U)	JNP(S)	Cong(U)	JNP(S)	Cong(U)	JNP(S)	Cong(U)	JNP(S)
20.	Tripura	1	-	1	-	-	-	-	-	-	-	-	-
21.	Uttar Pradesh	35	79	30	3	5	38	-	37	-	1	-	-
22.	West Bengal	18	17	17	17	1	-	-	-	-	-	-	-
23.	A. & N. Islands	-	1	-	1	-	-	-	-	-	-	-	-
24.	Arunachal Pr.	2	-	-	-	2	-	-	-	-	-	-	-
25.	Chandigarh	1	1	1	1	-	-	-	-	-	-	-	-
26.	D. & N. Haveli	1	-	1	-	-	-	-	-	-	-	-	-
27.	Delhi	4	5	4	4	-	1	-	-	-	-	-	-
28.	Goa, Daman & Diu	1	2	-	2	-	-	-	-	1	-	-	-
29.	Lakshadweep	1	-	-	-	-	-	-	-	1	-	-	-
30.	Mizoram	-	-	-	-	-	-	-	-	-	-	-	-
31.	Pondicherry	-	1	-	1	-	-	-	-	-	-	-	-
	INDIA	210	294	121	125	63	107	19	57	7	5	-	-

* Excluded from the analysis of 1980 elections.

Appendix-IVG

NUMBER OF CONSTITUENCIES ACCORDING TO PERCENTAGE OF VOTES POLLED
OTHER POLITICAL PARTIES
1971, 1977 and 1980

S. No.	State/Union Territory/Party Party	No. of Seats Contested			Number of Constituencies in different categories of voting strength: 0-10% votes			10-30% votes			30-50% votes			50-70% votes			Above 70% votes		
		1971	1977	1980	1971	1977	1980	1971	1977	1980	1971	1977	1980	1971	1977	1980	1971	1977	1980
	Andhra Pradesh																		
	TPS	14	-	-	-	-	-	-	-	-	8	-	-	6	-	-	-	-	-
	BSP	-	-	1	-	-	1	-	-	-	-	-	-	-	-	-	-	-	-
	RPI	-	-	1	-	-	1	-	-	-	-	-	-	-	-	-	-	-	-
	Others	19	3	-	19	3	-	-	-	-	-	-	-	-	-	-	-	-	-
	Assam																		
	Others	6	3	-	2	2	-	3	1	-	-	-	-	1	-	-	-	-	-
	Bihar																		
	BKD	14	-	-	13	-	-	1	-	-	-	-	-	-	-	-	-	-	-
	JKD	16	6	13	13	5	12	2	-	-	1	1	1	-	-	-	-	-	-
	JKP	-	1	-	-	-	-	-	-	-	-	-	-	-	-	-	-	1	-
	Others	45	15	13	38	15	13	5	-	-	2	-	-	-	-	-	-	-	-
	Gujarat																		
	Others	7	-	-	7	-	-	-	-	-	-	-	-	-	-	-	-	-	-
	Haryana																		
	VHP	3	1	-	1	-	-	1	-	-	1	1	-	-	-	-	-	-	-
	RPK	-	-	3	-	-	3	-	-	-	-	-	-	-	-	-	-	-	-
	Others	11	3	5	11	3	5	-	-	-	-	-	-	-	-	-	-	-	-
	Himachal Pradesh																		
	Others	2	-	-	1	-	-	1	-	-	-	-	-	-	-	-	-	-	-
	Jammu & Kashmir																		

(Contd. Appendix-IVG)

S. No.	State/Union Territory/Party Party	No. of Seats Contested			Number of Constituencies in different categories of voting strength: 0-10% votes			10-30% votes			30-50% votes			50-70% votes			Above 70% votes		
		1971	1977	1980	1971	1977	1980	1971	1977	1980	1971	1977	1980	1971	1977	1980	1971	1977	1980
	JKN	-	3	5*	-	-	-	-	-	-	-	1	2	-	2	2	-	-	-
	Others	2	-	-	2	-	-	-	-	-	-	-	-	-	-	-	-	-	-
	Karnataka																		
	Others	1	2	1	1	2	1	-	-	-	-	-	-	-	-	-	-	-	-
	Kerala																		
	IUML	-	-	1	-	-	-	-	-	-	-	-	1	-	-	-	-	-	-
	KEC	3	2	2	-	-	-	-	-	-	-	-	2	3	2	-	-	-	-
	KCP	-	3	-	-	-	-	-	-	-	-	3	-	-	-	-	-	-	-
	MUL	2	2	2	-	-	-	-	-	-	-	-	-	2	2	2	-	-	-
	MLO	-	2	-	-	-	-	-	-	-	-	2	-	-	-	-	-	-	-
	RSP	2	1	1	-	-	-	-	-	-	-	-	1	2	1	-	-	-	-
	ISP	1	-	-	1	-	-	-	-	-	-	-	-	-	-	-	-	-	-
	SUCI	-	1	1	-	1	1	-	-	-	-	-	-	-	-	-	-	-	-
	Madhya Pradesh																		
	Others	8	1	6	8	-	6	-	-	-	-	-	-	-	1	-	-	-	-
	Maharashtra																		
	PWP	12	6	5	4	-	1	4	1	2	4	2	2	-	3	-	-	-	-
	RPI	-	-	23	-	-	21	-	-	2	-	-	-	-	-	-	-	-	-
	RPK	14	5	7	8	-	4	6	-	2	-	4	1	-	1	-	-	-	-
	Others	15	1	8	7	-	7	4	-	1	3	1	-	1	-	-	-	-	-
	Manipur																		
	MRP	1	2	1	-	-	-	1	1	1	-	1	-	-	-	-	-	-	-
	Nagaland																		
	NNO	1	-	-	-	-	-	-	-	-	1	-	-	-	-	-	-	-	-
	UFN	1	-	-	-	-	-	-	-	-	-	-	-	1	-	-	-	-	-
	UDF	-	1	1	-	-	-	-	-	-	-	-	1	-	1	-	-	-	-

(Contd. Appendix-IVG)

S. No.	State/Union Territory/Party Party	No. of Seats Contested			Number of Constituencies in different categories of voting strength 0-10% votes			10-30% votes			30-50% votes			50-70% votes			Above 70% votes		
		1971	1977	1980	1971	1977	1980	1971	1977	1980	1971	1977	1980	1971	1977	1980	1971	1977	1980
	Orissa																		
	Jan Cong.	2	-	-	-	-	-	2	-	-	-	-	-	-	-	-	-	-	-
	Utkal Cong.	20	-	-	2	-	-	13	-	-	5	-	-	-	-	-	-	-	-
	JKD	2	1	5	1	-	4	1	1	1	-	-	-	-	-	-	-	-	-
	Others	-	2	4	-	2	4	-	-	-	-	-	-	-	-	-	-	-	-
	Punjab																		
	BKD	1	-	-	1	-	-	-	-	-	-	-	-	-	-	-	-	-	-
	SAD	12	9	7	-	-	-	4	-	-	8	-	7	-	8	-	-	1	-
	RPK	2	-	-	2	-	-	-	-	-	-	-	-	-	-	-	-	-	-
	Others	-	5	6	-	5	6	-	-	-	-	-	-	-	-	-	-	-	-
	Rajasthan																		
	BKD	8	-	-	6	-	-	1	-	-	1	-	-	-	-	-	-	-	-
	VHP	1	-	-	-	-	-	1	-	-	-	-	-	-	-	-	-	-	-
	Others	1	2	3	1	2	3	-	-	-	-	-	-	-	-	-	-	-	-
	Sikkim																		
	SJP	-	-	1	-	-	-	-	-	-	-	-	-	-	-	1	-	-	-
	SCR	-	-	1	-	-	-	-	-	1	-	-	-	-	-	-	-	-	-
	SPC	-	-	1	-	-	1	-	-	-	-	-	-	-	-	-	-	-	-
	Tamil Nadu																		
	DMK	24	19	16	-	-	-	-	4	-	2	14	-	22	1	16	-	-	-
	ADK	-	20	24	-	-	-	-	-	-	-	2	24	-	17	-	-	1	-
	FBL	1	-	-	-	-	-	-	-	-	-	-	-	1	-	-	-	-	-
	Others	-	1	2	-	1	2	-	-	-	-	-	-	-	-	-	-	-	-
	Tripura																		
	TUS	-	2	2	-	2	-	-	-	2	-	-	-	-	-	-	-	-	-

(Contd. Appendix-IVG)

S. No.	State/Union Territory/Party Party	No. of Seats Contested			Number of Constituencies in different categories of voting strength: 0-10% votes			10-30% votes			30-50% votes			50-70% votes			Above 70% votes		
		1971	1977	1980	1971	1977	1980	1971	1977	1980	1971	1977	1980	1971	1977	1980	1971	1977	1980
	Uttar Pradesh																		
	BKD	67	-	-	31	-	-	29	-	-	7	-	-	-	-	-	-	-	-
	Others	39	10	42	38	10	42	1	-	-	-	-	-	-	-	-	-	-	-
	West Bengal																		
	Bangla Cong.	14	-	-	8	-	-	5	-	-	1	-	-	-	-	-	-	-	-
	FBL	10	3	4	5	-	-	5	-	-	-	-	1	-	3	3	-	-	-
	RSP	5	3	4	-	-	-	5	-	-	-	-	1	-	3	3	-	-	-
	Others	9	9	23	5	7	22	4	2	1	-	-	-	-	-	-	-	-	-
	Arunachal Pradesh																		
	PPA	-	-	2	-	-	-	-	-	-	-	-	2	-	-	-	-	-	-
	Chandigarh																		
	Others	1	-	-	1	-	-	-	-	-	-	-	-	-	-	-	-	-	-
	Delhi																		
	Others	6	2	11	5	2	11	1	-	-	-	-	-	-	-	-	-	-	-
	Goa, Daman and Diu																		
	UGS	1	-	-	-	-	-	-	-	-	-	-	-	1	-	-	-	-	-
	MAG	1	2	2	-	-	-	-	-	-	1	2	2	-	-	-	-	-	-
	Mizoram																		
	PPC	-	-	1	-	-	-	-	-	-	-	-	1	-	-	-	-	-	-
	Pondicherry																		
	ADK	-	1	-	-	-	-	-	-	-	-	-	-	-	1	-	-	-	-
	INDIA	427	155	261*	242	62	171	100	10	13	45	34	49	40	46	27	-	3	-

* Includes one candidate elected unopposed.

Appendix-VA

SWINGS IN PARTY FOLLOWING MAJOR POLITICAL PARTIES

S. No.	State/Union Territory	Swings between 1971 and 1977				Swings between 1977 and 1980			
		CPI	CPI(M)	Cong.	JNP	CPI	CPI(M)	Cong.	JNP
1	2	3	4	5	6	7	8	9	10
1.	Andhra Pradesh	-3.27	1.9	1.63	20.33	1.01	-1.16	-1.12	-17.10
2.	Assam	-4.23	1.47	-6.42	24.26	-	6.29	0.45	-27.76
3.	Bihar	-4.22	-0.56	-17.76	29.59	1.66	0.74	13.54	-41.43
4.	Gujarat	-	-	2.07	0.48	-	-	7.92	-12.65
5.	Haryana	-	-0.10	-34.61	44.37	-	-	14.60	-42.21
6.	Himachal Pradesh	-0.27	-	-37.21	36.72	0.56	-	13.50	-14.81
7.	Jammu & Kashmir	-	-	-37.69	-4.46	-	-	2.31	-0.40
8.	Karnataka	0.32	-	-14.13	15.62	-0.16	-	-0.49	-16.91
9.	Kerala	1.29	-5.88	9.36	1.19	-3.86	1.24	-2.81	-0.50
10.	Madhya Pradesh	-0.47	-	-13.13	19.72	0.02	-	14.73	-26.60
11.	Maharashtra	-1.24	3.08	-16.16	18.65	-0.17	-2.2	6.28	-10.97
12.	Manipur	-3.48	-	15.29	-5.49	-1.76	-	-22.32	8.8
13.	Meghalaya	-	-	-	-	-	-	38.39	-
14.	Nagaland	-	-	-	-	-	-	-	-
15.	Orissa	-1.16	0.96	-0.28	1.52	-2.36	-1.09	17.89	-37.16
16.	Punjab	-4.57	2.74	-17.11	6.67	-0.38	-2.41	17.60	-2.53
17.	Rajasthan	-0.01	-0.28	-19.79	30.15	0.06	-0.12	12.08	-33.56
18.	Sikkim	-	-	-	-	-	-	-	-
19.	Tamil Nadu	-0.83	-0.08	9.79	-22.94	-1.81	1.65	9.35	-9.72
20.	Tripura	-4.52	-9.41	3.44	17.34	-	13.41	-17.13	-16.86
21.	Uttar Pradesh	-2.60	-0.09	-23.57	29.99	0.53	0.00	18.91	-45.51

(Contd. Appendix-VA)

S. No.	State/Union Territory	Swings between 1971 and 1977				Swings between 1977 and 1980			
		CPI	CPI(M)	Cong.	JNP	CPI	CPI(M)	Cong.	JNP
1	2	3	4	5	6	7	8	9	10
22.	West Bengal	-4.87	-8.15	1.14	11.46	-2.21	13.76	7.14	-16.93
23.	Andaman & Nicobar Islands	-	-	-3.03	-	-	-	-5.16	-
24.	Arunachal Pradesh	-	-	-	-	-	-	-2.88	-
25.	Chandigarh	-	-	-38.48	42.82	-	-	21.28	-56.83
26.	Dadra and Nagar Haveli	-	-	7.76	-2.14	-	-	14.96	-13.53
27.	Delhi	-	-	-34.24	34.69	-0.09	-	20.25	-30.26
28.	Goa, Daman and Diu	-	-	15.55	13.97	-	-	-27.79	-7.79
29.	Lakshadweep	-	-	-	-	-	-	-54.74	-
30.	Mizoram	-	-	-	-	-	-	-	-
31.	Pondicherry	-	-	-	16.48	-	-	-	16.09
	INDIA	-1.91	-0.82	-9.16	15.81	-0.23	1.84	8.17	-24.09

*Votes polled by Janata in 1971 are derived by aggregating votes polled by its constituent.

Appendix -VB
SWINGS IN PARTY FOLLOWING SELECTED OTHER POLITICAL PARTIES

S.No.	State/Union Territory/ Party	Swings between 1971 and 1977	Swings between 1977 and 1980
1.	Bihar		
	JKD	-0.45	0.24
2.	Haryana		
	VHP	-4.52	
3.	Jammu & Kashmir		
	JKN		2.96
4.	Kerala		
	MUL	0.41	-0.47
	KEC	-2.75	-1.18
	RSP	-3.25	-0.81
5.	Maharashtra		
	PWP	0.77	-3.56
6.	Manipur		
	MRP	11.60	-16.56
7.	Punjab		
	SAD	11.45	-18.93
8.	Tamil Nadu		
	ADK	-	-5.21
	DMK	-17.19	4.95
9.	Tripura		
	TUS	-	7.38
10.	West Bengal		
	RSP	1.90	1.28
	FBL	1.60	0.26
	SUCI	0.54	-0.17
11.	Goa, Daman & Diu		
	MAG	17.30	-4.48

Appendix -VC
PATTERN OF PARTY SWINGS
OTHER PARTIES

Party	Number of constituencies in different categories of swings															
	Swings between 1971 and 1977								Swings between 1977 and 1980							
	Positive swings				Negative swings				Positive swings				Negative swings			
	A	B	C	D	A	B	C	D	A	B	C	D	A	B	C	D
ADMK	-	-	-	-	-	-	-	-	-	1	-	-	1	7	5	2
DMK	-	-	-	-	1	4	3	1	2	3	5	-	-	-	-	-
FBL	-	-	-	2	-	-	-	-	-	-	-	-	2	1	-	-
KEC	1	-	-	-	-	-	-	-	-	-	-	-	2	-	-	-
MAG	-	-	-	-	1	-	-	-	-	-	-	-	2	-	-	-
MRP	-	1	-	-	-	-	-	-	-	-	-	-	-	1	-	-
MUL	-	-	-	-	1	-	-	-	-	-	-	-	2	-	-	-
PWP	1	1	1	-	-	-	-	-	-	-	-	-	-	-	3	1
RSP	-	-	-	-1	1	-	-	-	-	-	-	-	2	1	-	-
SAD	-	3	4	2	-	-	-	-	-	-	-	-	-	6	1	-
TUS	-	-	-	-	-	-	-	-	1	1	-	-	-	-	-	-
UDF	-	-	-	-	-	-	-	-	-	-	-	-	1	-	-	-
VHP	-	-	-	-	1	-	-	-	-	-	-	-	-	-	-	-
HMS	-	-	-	-	1	-	-	-	-	-	-	-	-	-	-	-
IGL	-	-	1	-	-	-	-	-	-	-	-	-	-	-	-	-
ILP	-	-	-	-	-	-	-	-	-	-	-	-	2	-	-	-
PHJ	2	-	1	-	1	-	1	-	-	-	-	-	-	-	-	-
JKD	1	1	-	-	4	1	-	1	5	-	-	-	3	-	-	1

(Contd. Appendix-VC)

Party	Number of constituencies in different categories of swings															
	Swings between 1971 and 1977								Swings between 1977 and 1980							
	Positive swings				Negative swings				Positive swings				Negative swings			
	A	B	C	D	A	B	C	D	A	B	C	D	A	B	C	D
RPI	-	-	-	-	-	-	-	-	1	-	-	-	1	-	-	1
RPK	2	3	-	-	-	-	-	-	-	-	-	-	1	1	-	2
RCPI	1	-	-	-	-	-	-	-	-	-	-	-	-	-	-	-
SUCI	1	-	-	-	1	-	-	-	2	-	-	-	10	-	-	-
SSD	-	-	-	-	1	-	-	-	-	-	-	-	2	-	-	-

A: 0-10%: change; B:10-20% change; C: 20-30% change; D Above 30% change.

INDEX